Frank Sinatra
on the Big Screen

ALSO BY JAMES L. NEIBAUR

*Clark Gable in the 1930s: The Films
That Made Him King of Hollywood* (2021)

The Jean Harlow Films (2019)

*The Hal Roach Comedy Shorts
of Thelma Todd, ZaSu Pitts and Patsy Kelly* (2019)

The Andy Clyde Columbia Comedies (2018)

The W.C. Fields Films (2017)

*Chaplin at Essanay:
A Film Artist in Transition, 1915–1916* (2008)

*Arbuckle and Keaton:
Their 14 Film Collaborations* (2007)

The Bob Hope Films (2005)

*The RKO Features:
A Complete Filmography of the Feature Films Released
or Produced by RKO Radio Pictures, 1929–1960*
(1994; paperback 2005)

BY JAMES L. NEIBAUR AND TED OKUDA

*The Jerry Lewis Films:
An Analytical Filmography of the Innovative Comic*
(1994; paperback 2013)

BY TED OKUDA AND JAMES L. NEIBAUR

*Stan Without Ollie:
The Stan Laurel Solo Films, 1917–1927* (2012)

ALL FROM McFARLAND

Frank Sinatra on the Big Screen

The Singer as Actor and Filmmaker

JAMES L. NEIBAUR *and*
GARY SCHNEEBERGER

McFarland & Company, Inc., Publishers
Jefferson, North Carolina

LIBRARY OF CONGRESS CATALOGUING-IN-PUBLICATION DATA

Names: Neibaur, James L., 1958– author. | Schneeberger, Gary, 1965– author.
Title: Frank Sinatra on the big screen : the singer as actor and filmmaker / James L. Neibaur and Gary Schneeberger.
Description: Jefferson : McFarland & Company, Inc., Publishers, 2022. | Includes bibliographical references and index.
Identifiers: LCCN 2022013795 | ISBN 9781476684505 (paperback : acid free paper) ∞
 ISBN 9781476644585 (ebook)
Subjects: LCSH: Sinatra, Frank, 1915-1998—Criticism and interpretation. | BISAC: PERFORMING ARTS / Film / History & Criticism
Classification: LCC PN2287.S39 N45 2022 | DDC 791.4302/8092—dc23/eng/20220406
LC record available at https://lccn.loc.gov/2022013795

BRITISH LIBRARY CATALOGUING DATA ARE AVAILABLE

ISBN (print) 978-1-4766-8450-5
ISBN (ebook) 978-1-4766-4458-5

© 2022 James L. Neibaur and Gary Schneeberger. All rights reserved

No part of this book may be reproduced or transmitted in any form or by any means, electronic or mechanical, including photocopying or recording, or by any information storage and retrieval system, without permission in writing from the publisher.

Front cover: Frank Sinatra, circa 1950's (Photofest)

Printed in the United States of America

McFarland & Company, Inc., Publishers
 Box 611, Jefferson, North Carolina 28640
  www.mcfarlandpub.com

To the memory of Gary's dad
Dale F. Schneeberger (1927–2021)
He did it his way ...
and taught his youngest son Dads can do anything.

Acknowledgments

This book began as a project by Gary Schneeberger some 30 years ago; several chapters were completed, but then life got in the way. It was resurrected at James L. Neibaur's suggestion; together we took the existing material and expanded upon it. From the project's early days, we'd like to thank the late Raymond Burr and Celeste Holm for kindly submitting to interviews.

Special thanks to Katie Carter, who has been working as James's assistant for his past dozen books. Katie continues to screen every film, fact-check, proofread and offer her own suggestions and additions for each chapter. She's invaluable.

Special thanks also for assistance and inspiration to Gary's wife Kelly Schneeberger, whose encouragement ranged from screening every movie with him, sharing his enthusiasm over unearthing little-known facts about their production, and editing each of his chapters with a keen eye and supportive spirit.

Thanks to Christopher Riordan who kindly shared his memories of having worked in two movies with Frank Sinatra, and also to Alexis Hunter for information on her personal friend Joi Lansing's experiences working with Frank.

Thanks also to Terri Lynch, Ted Okuda, Phil Hall, Kelly Parmelee, Allison Schulz, Alyssa Flory, Hunter Flory, Warwick Fairfax, Deane Schneeberger, Jill Sprague, Jim Bishop, John Gallagher and Jerry Lewis.

Gary would also like to thank his late mother, Martha Johnson, for buying him his first electric typewriter when he was 12. Gary's contribution to this book was completed on what would have been her 90th birthday.

And James would like to thank his mother for introducing him to Sinatra as a small child via an album of 78 rpm records, which he still owns.

Finally, James would like to salute the memory of his dear son Max Neibaur, who continues to inspire everything he does.

Table of Contents

Acknowledgments   vi
Introduction   1

Sinatra Before the Movies   5

The Films   8

Higher and Higher (1943)   8
Step Lively (1944)   12
Anchors Aweigh (1945)   16
It Happened in Brooklyn (1947)   21
The Miracle of the Bells (1948)   25
The Kissing Bandit (1948)   29
Take Me Out to the Ball Game (1949)   32
On the Town (1949)   37
Double Dynamite (1951)   42
Meet Danny Wilson (1952)   46
From Here to Eternity (1953)   51
Suddenly (1954)   56
Young at Heart (1954)   61
Not as a Stranger (1955)   66
Guys and Dolls (1955)   70
The Tender Trap (1955)   79
The Man with the Golden Arm (1955)   84
High Society (1956)   94
Johnny Concho (1956)   99
The Pride and the Passion (1957)   103
The Joker Is Wild (1957)   107

Table of Contents

Pal Joey (1957) 113
Kings Go Forth (1958) 122
Some Came Running (1958) 127
A Hole in the Head (1959) 134
Never So Few (1959) 141
Can-Can (1960) 148
Ocean's 11 (1960) 153
The Devil at 4 O'Clock (1961) 159
Sergeants 3 (1962) 163
The Manchurian Candidate (1962) 168
Come Blow Your Horn (1963) 172
4 for Texas (1963) 175
Robin and the 7 Hoods (1964) 180
None But the Brave (1965) 185
Von Ryan's Express (1965) 189
Marriage on the Rocks (1965) 194
Assault on a Queen (1966) 200
The Naked Runner (1967) 205
Tony Rome (1967) 207
The Detective (1968) 211
Lady in Cement (1968) 216
Dirty Dingus Magee (1970) 220
Sinatra in the '70s 224
The First Deadly Sin (1980) 227

Sinatra After the Movies 234

Chapter Notes 237
Bibliography 245
Index 251

Introduction

Frank Sinatra was without question one of the most influential singers in the history of recorded music. He was also an enigmatic figure whose personal life generated innumerable headlines during his 50-plus years in the spotlight. Yet he was also a gifted and courageous actor, a fact often overlooked by critics too busy praising him for his vocal prowess or damning him for his alleged ties to organized crime. Although he certainly was not the first, or the last, pop singer to parlay his success into a film career, he was arguably the one who succeeded most evidently. His success was, of course, in the performances he gave, but also in the often daring choices he made in selecting projects and parts. To be sure, he appeared in some misguided projects, and offered some uninspired performances, but when his talents were matched to a worthy script with a good director, the results were frequently sensational.

That is more than anyone expected from him in the early 1940s. Sinatra, then a skinny young balladeer known in the recording industry as "The Voice," was groomed to be a movie "star," not a movie actor, and the distinction is an important one. He was brought to Hollywood because those in the industry believed he could titillate female audiences as easily from a movie screen as he had been doing from a concert stage. For that reason, his first few roles required no real acting at all: He played an extension of himself, a band singer who crooned one or two numbers during an interlude incidental to the narrative.

Even as he tentatively segued into portraying characters, Sinatra could not be accused of stretching his abilities. His initial character work was tentative and a little laconic, something especially evident during a film's musical portions, in which he commanded the notice of the audience, effortlessly rendering some classic Tin Pan Alley standards. Nonetheless, he developed a screen persona during these years, mostly playing naïve, earnest men who would sing a half-dozen songs as they shyly pursued—or tried to avoid for lack of confidence—young, pretty women. Not surprisingly, the public could take just so much of that. Sinatra's only genuine hits during this period were the musicals *Anchors Aweigh* (1945) and *On the Town* (1949), films in which he was just one member of an ensemble of talented performers, and not the star counted on to sell a production on his own merits.

The 1950s proved to be the breakthrough decade for Sinatra as an actor. Although his recording career and his marriage were near dissolution (Columbia Records did not renew his contract and he was having a much-publicized affair with Ava Gardner), he began to select roles that helped redefine his screen image. *Meet Danny Wilson* (1952) was a shrewd choice, in that it provided a balance of musical and dramatic elements. In this film, Sinatra was able to sing and at the same time demonstrate an ability to play drama as a largely unsympathetic character. Although the movie was not a commercial success, it was a fitting bridge to his next project, *From Here to Eternity*, for which he won the Best Supporting Actor Academy Award. In the small but pivotal role of Maggio, a troubled soldier who is beaten to death in an Army stockade, Sinatra proved unequivocally that he was the dramatic equal to co-stars Burt Lancaster and Montgomery Clift.

A series of consequential dramatic roles followed, each taking Sinatra further from his previous screen image (the likable, uncertain waif). He played a calculating drifter out to kill the U.S. president in *Suddenly* (1954), and in 1955 earned another Oscar nomination, this time for Best Actor, for his chilling portrayal of a heroin addict trying to kick the habit in *The Man with the Golden Arm*. Over the next few years, he appeared in other films that graphically explored then-taboo subjects. He effectively played the alcoholic comedian Joe E. Lewis in the biopic *The Joker Is Wild* (1957). He delivered a solid, subdued performance as a brainwashed ex-soldier trying to unravel a complex murder plot in *The Manchurian Candidate* (1962), a psychological thriller that, some say, features his finest work. He even took a shot at directing, with better results than one might have anticipated.

In his musicals during this period, Sinatra was also trying to expand on the characters he played in his '40s ensemble outings. With films like *Young at Heart* (1955) and *High Society* (1956), he layers maturity and wisdom seemingly hard-earned into his portrayals as both actor and singer. By the time he did *Guys and Dolls* (1955) and *Pal Joey* (1957), his evolution seemed complete: He had morphed from the jittery innocent, intimidated by women, into the cocksure hipster who does the intimidating.

Sinatra wore this persona well—so well, in fact, that he rarely shed it in the later years of his screen career. With few exceptions, the roles he assumed starting in the early 1960s mostly underscore that image, especially in his undertakings with the Rat Pack and in his succession of world-weary private investigators and police detectives. Sinatra obviously enjoyed portraying these characters (he produced a number of these projects himself). And although his performances in these movies are uniformly good, the roles require little of the range and emotion he had shown that he possessed. It is ironic that after he had succeeded in breaking free from studio-imposed typecasting, he chose to impose a different but equally limiting typecasting upon himself.

In this book, we will trace Frank Sinatra's evolution as an actor. Each of his films will be examined in detail, offering a critical assessment as well as behind-the-scenes information about its production. What will emerge is a portrait of an actor who became a star in a manner Hollywood did not foresee. Rather than merely trade on his success as a musical performer, Sinatra struggled to establish himself as a serious dramatic actor. There can be no doubt he succeeded in that effort, even though an argument can be made he stopped working diligently at his craft once he had proven his point.

Sinatra Before the Movies

Francis Albert Sinatra was born on December 12, 1915, in Hoboken, New Jersey, to Italian immigrants Natalina "Dolly" Garaventa and Antonino Martino "Marty" Sinatra. An only child, he was raised in a family where the mother figure was more dominant and inspired a great deal of his self-confidence, even though the two were said to frequently be in conflict.

Early on, Sinatra developed an interest in music, idolizing popular singers of the 1920s like Bing Crosby, Rudy Vallée and Russ Columbo. Crosby was a particular favorite, and Frank had a picture of the crooner on his wall for inspiration. Receiving a ukulele for his 15th birthday from his Uncle Dominic, Sinatra taught himself to play and enjoyed playing at family gatherings. In high school, he helped book bands for the school dances. However, Sinatra was expelled from school for his consistently disruptive behavior, and never graduated.

Sinatra toiled at a series of odd jobs over the next several years while developing his amateur talent as a singer. In 1935, when he was just 20, he joined a vocal group called the 3 Flashes—which was renamed the Hoboken Four once he joined and made it a quartet. They got a six-month contract to perform on the road after winning a Major Bowes talent contest on the radio. Frank became the group's lead singer.

He continued to explore his song phrasing and improve his stage presence. Sinatra was a singing waiter and a radio spot singer, and he even cut a low-budget recording. This led to securing a spot as the lead vocalist in the Harry James band in 1939. His recorded work with James, including the beautiful ballad "All or Nothing at All," sold poorly. Frustrated, Sinatra left James to join Tommy Dorsey's band in 1940. By this time, his vocal range was much improved and his stage presence was more polished. Replacing Jack Leonard as Dorsey's lead singer, Sinatra became an instant success upon his first appearance with the band at the Coronado Theater in Rockford, Illinois, on January 26, 1940. Dorsey later recalled:

You could almost feel the excitement coming up out of the crowds when the kid stood up to sing. Remember, he was no matinee idol. He was just a skinny kid with big ears. I used to stand there so amazed I'd almost forget to take my own solos.[1]

Sinatra achieved great success and popularity with Dorsey's band, recording more than 40 songs during his first year. In July, he topped the charts for 12 weeks with the hit "I'll Never Smile Again." He was the top male singer in the magazines *Billboard* and *Downbeat* in 1941.

Sinatra asked Dorsey to let him record some solo songs, resulting in a session for Bluebird; Axel Stordahl was his arranger and conductor. The success of these recordings made Sinatra want a solo career, but he was bound by a contract with Dorsey that gave the bandleader 43 percent of the singer's earnings. It took a legal battle to get Sinatra out of his contract (it was rumored to include intervention by mobster Willie Moretti, Sinatra's godfather). Although they had once been close, Sinatra and Dorsey never patched things up. Dorsey died in 1956.

When Sinatra signed with Columbia Records in June 1943, it was during a musicians' strike. Columbia re-released Sinatra's recordings with Harry James, and this time "All or Nothing at All" reached #2 on the charts and remained a bestseller for 18 weeks. More hits followed and by 1944, Sinatra was a top music star. Even his idol, Bing Crosby, made jokes about the young crooner who was making a dent in Crosby's own popularity.

A promotional shot from Sinatra's Columbia period.

This sort of popularity had resulted in Bing entering films, so it was determined that Sinatra do so as well. Crosby had started out in a few short subjects produced by Mack Sennett in the early sound era and later appeared in features, including *Mississippi* (1935) with W.C. Fields. Sinatra also started out inauspiciously: In the musicals *Las Vegas Nights* (1941) and *Reveille with Beverly* (1943), he made cameo appearances as himself, singing a song or two. In 1943, RKO offered a two-picture deal for Sinatra to star in musical vehicles tailored for his audience. He would not only sing; he would play a role as an actor. His first was *Higher and Higher.*

The Films

Higher and Higher

Produced and Directed by Tim Whelan
Screenplay: Jay Dratler and Ralph Spence, from the play by Gladys Hurlbut and Joshua Logan
Cinematography: Robert De Grasse (Black and White)
Editor: Gene Milford
Songs:
"It's a Most Important Affair," "Today I'm a Debutante," "I Couldn't Sleep a Wink Last Night," "The Music Stopped," "I Saw You First," "You're on Your Own"; Music: Jimmy McHugh; Lyrics: Harold Adamson
"Minuet in Boogie"; Music: Jimmy McHugh; Based on "Minuet in G" by Ignacy Jan Paderewski; Lyrics: Harold Adamson
"Disgustingly Rich"; Music: Richard Rodgers; Lyrics: Lorenz Hart
Cast: Michele Morgan, Jack Haley, Frank Sinatra, Leon Errol, Marcy McGuire, Victor Borge, Mary Wickes, Elisabeth Risdon, Barbara Hale, Mel Torme, Paul and Grace Hartman, Dooley Wilson, Ivy Scott, Ola Lorraine, Rita Gould, King Kennedy, Rex Evans, Stanley Logan, Robert Anderson, Edward Fielding, Paul Bradley, Jack Gargan, Dick Gordon, Larry Steers, Shirley O'Hara, Dorothy Malone, Shirley O'Hara, Perc Launders, Ralph Brooks, Tanis Chandler, Jeffrey Sayre, Cosmo Sardo, Wilbur Mack, Hans Moebus, Russell Wade, Harold Miller, Drake Thornton, Jay Eaton, Jack Chefe, George Ford, Louis Hightower, Daun Kennedy, Elaine Riley, Edmund Mortiner
Released December 10, 1943
RKO
91 minutes

Higher and Higher (1943)

Under ordinary circumstances, *Higher and Higher* would have come and gone with little notice; just another B movie musical comedy with some mildly entertaining moments and a few familiar faces. But with Frank Sinatra making his acting debut, circumstances were anything but ordinary. Its release was hyped by RKO as a monumental event—the birth of another matinee idol—and Sinatra's millions of fans ensured its box office success. In retrospect, all of this is ironic, since Sinatra was infinitely more important to the marketing strategy of *Higher and Higher* than he was to its narrative. Playing a secondary role, literally the boy next door, he is required to do little more than croon sweet ballads and mill about looking charming and boyish.

Higher and Higher started out as a Broadway musical with a score by Rodgers and Hart, but only one song from the play, "Disgustingly Rich," remains in the film. The other songs were written for the movie by Jimmy McHugh and Harold Adamson. Sinatra's importance to the screen version was foreshadowed by his arriving in Hollywood. His train was met by screaming bobbysoxers who scratched and bit their way through the crowd of thousands while a police escort ushered Sinatra to safety in a nearby garage.

It is clear from Sinatra's role in *Higher and Higher* that RKO—which promoted the film as "The Sinatra Show"—wanted him to elicit identical fanaticism in female moviegoers. Not wanting to stretch his undeveloped acting talents, the studio cast him as a crooner named—Frank Sinatra! He lives with his father in an estate next door to piano tycoon Cyrus Drake (Leon Errol). Drake, a drunkard, has frittered away the family fortune and finds himself with just 30 days to make his mortgage payment before the bank forecloses on his home. With the help of his household staff (led by Jack Haley as his valet), Drake concocts a plan whereby the scullery maid, Millie (Michele Morgan), will impersonate his daughter in order to marry a rich bachelor who can provide the money necessary to get Drake back on his feet financially.

What follows is an entertaining enough farce, complete with the requisite mistaken identities and one-liners deftly delivered by Errol and Haley. Some of them poke fun at Sinatra and his real-life recording rivalry with Bing Crosby; there are also some energetic song-and-dance numbers featuring a young Mel Torme. But Sinatra has little to do with any of this, other than to wind up marrying Millie's chief rival (Barbara Hale). His acting is limited to a pair of emotions: politeness and confusion; and there is little discernible difference between them. His non-musical scenes are static, requiring little blocking and minimal dialogue, serving in each instance to deaden the pace of the film, a particularly damaging occurrence in farce.

Sinatra played himself in his first movie, *Higher and Higher*, with Jack Haley (left).

In many cases, director Tim Whelan shoots him in tight closeup, a cinematographic choice obviously made with bobbysoxers in mind. About the only thing that *New York Herald-Review* critic Howard Barnes had to say about *Higher and Higher* was that Sinatra's "ugly, bony face photographs well."[1]

Sinatra's initial appearance is paradigmatic of the aforementioned weaknesses. In his first scene, he stops at the Drake mansion with a gift of flowers for Millie, with whom he has struck up a casual friendship. Although he believes, correctly, that she is a maid, he is confused when he arrives, as the staff is instructing Millie on the finer points of being a debutante. Millie has just failed to master walking elegantly with a book on her head, a sequence of action, but all action stops when Frank Sinatra makes his entrance. To make things worse, Whelan shoots him in lingering, stationary, two- and three-shots with the other actors as he runs tentatively through his lines. The scene drags motionlessly on and Sinatra attempts to contain his bafflement at the odd circumstances by crinkling up his forehead and squinting.

Fortunately, Sinatra is never called on to act for very long before he is allowed to sing, as the majority of his scenes end in a vocal solo, duet or production number. At the conclusion of his initial appearance, for instance, he strolls over to the piano and serenades Millie with "I Couldn't Sleep a Wink Last Night." During scenes like this, Whelan opts for tight shots of Sinatra's "ugly, bony face" and the results are, indeed, pleasing to both the eye and ear (although Axel Stordahl's saccharine arrangements have not held up over time).

Sinatra falters noticeably during the production numbers, when he is required to perform an action while singing. His dancing is ploddingly amateurish in a scene that takes place at a debutante ball, where he, Michele Morgan and Barbara Hale take to the floor while Frank croons "The Music Stops." And he looks silly riding a bicycle with a handlebar basket while smoking a pipe when performing the playful "I Saw You First" with Marcy McGuire (who is cast, essentially, as a swooning bobbysoxer).

Not surprisingly, *Higher and Higher*, and Sinatra's performance in it, were not treated well by critics. The most scathing review came from *The New York Times*' Bosley Crowther, who suggested *Lower and Lower* might have been a more appropriate title: "[T]he simple fact is that Frankie is no Gable or Barrymore."[2] Sinatra was understandably unhappy about such criticism, so much so that a few months later, he brought it up when he first met his idol Bing Crosby, who had himself made a successful transition from singing to acting. Crosby responded: "Pay 'em no mind!"[3]

Now in the 21st century, *Higher and Higher* is little more than a curio, not only for being Sinatra's first acting role, but also for early appearances by Mel Torme and comic pianist Victor Borge. Welcome veterans Leon Errol, Mary Wickes and Elisabeth Risdon display their well-established skills. Errol's specialty was a drunk act that dated back to the Ziegfeld Follies, so it is appropriate that his character was a drinker. Not so accurate was Dooley Wilson as an accompanying pianist. This is probably due to his being so noted for appearing as Sam in the hit film *Casablanca*, which was still in release while *Higher and Higher* was filmed. Wilson was a singer, but could not play the piano. However, because he so famously played a pianist in an Oscar-winning feature, he would often be cast as pianists in other films. And it is fun to see husband-and-wife Broadway performers Paul and Grace Hartman in one of their few films together. After Grace died in 1955, Paul went solo. He is perhaps best remembered as Emmett the fix-it shop man in the later seasons of TV's *The Andy Griffith Show*.

Ultimately, the poor reviews for *Higher and Higher* had no effect on Sinatra's film career. His popularity as a singer ensured a profitable box office return, which pleased RKO, who quickly placed him in his next contracted picture, *Step Lively*.

Step Lively

Directed by Tim Whelan
Screenplay: Warren Duff and Peter Milne, from the play by John Murray and Allen Boretz
Cinematography: Robert De Grasse (Black and White)
Editor: Gene Milford
Songs:
 "Where Does Love Begin?," "Come Out, Come Out Wherever You Are," "As Long as There's Music," "Some Other Time," "Why Must There Be an Opting Song?," "Ask the Madame"; Music: Jule Styne; Lyrics: Sammy Cahn
Cast: Frank Sinatra, Adolphe Menjou, George Murphy, Gloria DeHaven, Walter Slezak, Eugene Pallette, Wally Brown, Alan Carney, Grant Mitchell, Anne Jeffreys, Tom Burton, Elaine Riley, Shirley O'Hara, Rosemary La Planche, Frances King, Harry Noble, Ronn Marvin, Bob Mascagno, Hubert Bland, Robert Anderson, Sherry Hall, Donald Kerr, Sonny Lamont, Buster Brodie, George Chandler, Sammy Blum, Richard Davies, Tom Coleman, Sam Ash, Iris Bocignon, Joan Carey, Maxine Carole, Eloise Farmer, Nancy Hale, Mary Halsey, Harry Clay, Richard Davies, Christian Drake, Adolph Faylauer, Wheaton Chambers, Jack Gargan, Jimmy Jordan, Coulter Irwin, Laura Lane, Wendy Moncure, Eleanore Leaman, Frank Mayo, Margaret Westburg, Linda Scott, Carol Leonard, Steve Winston, Jewell Partin, Fred Rapport, Larry Wheat, Glen Vernon, John Shaw, Alan Ward, Nickolai
Released July 26, 1944
RKO
88 minutes

Step Lively (1944)

When the Marx Brothers did their screen version of the play *Room Service* for RKO in 1938, they came off as more subdued than they had been in previous films for Paramount and MGM. Still under contract at Metro, the Marxes did this film as an independent deal orchestrated by their agent-brother Zeppo, who had left the act in 1933. Since *Room Service* also featured Lucille Ball and Ann Miller, and had enough of the Marx zaniness to sustain it, it has been notable over time and generations.

Sinatra starred in a musical version of the same play six years later, for the same studio. Portraying the playwright that Frank Albertson essayed in the Marxes' film, Sinatra's approach is less bumbling and naïve than Albertson's take on the role. The comedy lines handled by Chico and Groucho are shifted to Wally Brown and Alan Carney. Brown and Carney were RKO's second-rate answer to the popularity of Abbott and Costello; this duo's B movies included the service comedies *Adventures of a Rookie* and its sequel *Rookies in Burma* (both 1943) as well as *Seven Days Ashore* (1944), before they were cast in *Step Lively*. The character Groucho played in the original is portrayed here by George Murphy, who plays the role as originally written, without the comic lines added to the character for the Marx Brothers movie. While not as good as the Marx Brothers movie, *Step Lively* is breezy and pleasant enough on its own.

Step Lively has some importance to Sinatra's film career as it represents a series of firsts for him as an actor. Most importantly, it is the first film in which he receives top billing and portrays a character at the center of the story. He handles the responsibility surprisingly well. Less important in retrospect, but certainly of interest at the time, is that he also receives his first on-screen kiss here. And finally, it is interesting to note that this film marks the introduction of a scenario which would follow Sinatra through several subsequent musicals and become an integral part of his early screen identity. In *Step Lively* we see, for the first time, his naïve, bumbling persona pursued by an aggressive, more experienced woman whose sexual advances play to the secret dreams of every bobbysoxer in the audience.

Sinatra is Glenn Russell, a small-town would-be playwright who comes to New York to learn what has happened to his drama *Godspeed* and the $1500 he sent along with it to sharp Broadway producer Gordon Miller (Murphy). When Glenn arrives at Miller's swank New York hotel, he finds the producer in the middle of staging, not *his* play, but a financially troubled musical. While waiting for some monetary backing from a mysterious benefactor, Miller—who has spent Glenn's money and forgotten all about *Godspeed*—tries to keep Glenn from discovering that he's been duped. At the same time, Miller is attempting to keep a few steps ahead of the hotel manager (Walter Slezak), who hounds him about long-unpaid room service bills.

Although the Glenn Russell character is once again the endearing waif who looks upon much of what happens around him in wide-eyed bewilderment, the part is fundamental to *Step Lively*. This is a departure from *Higher and Higher* where Sinatra's character was an incidental presence. Glenn is a talented singer and therefore becomes the logical choice to star in Miller's production. Interestingly, Miller is the most confident role in the script (and serves the same function as Jack Haley in *Higher and Higher*). Thus, *Step Lively* becomes mostly concerned with depicting Miller's courting of Glenn, as the producer attempts to fool the young man into abandoning his dreams of being a playwright in favor of becoming a performer—which, of course, does indeed occur at the picture's end.

This scenario presents Sinatra with numerous and various scenes in which to demonstrate his acting abilities, such as they are, and he shows a marked improvement from his prior performance. Early on, for instance, it is necessary for him to become angry when Miller and his assistants (Brown and Carney) attempt to brush him off without an explanation as to what happened to his money and his play. Although not entirely convincing, the scene is noteworthy in that it reveals an incipient dramatic flair that Sinatra was to master a few years later.

In another scene, Miller and his assistants get Glenn drunk so he will appear ill and therefore block the hotel's attempt to throw out the producer's entourage. Sinatra plays the scene competently. Later, feigning illness on his own to once again forestall eviction, he is equally convincing. Sinatra overplays, moans and groans in a manner that demonstrates an understanding of broad comedy.

Sinatra's performance looks especially good when compared to what takes place around him, most notably the exchanges between hotel administrator Wagner (Adolphe Menjou) and Murphy. Lacking the witty repartee exhibited by Groucho Marx and Donald MacBride in the original *Room Service* film, Menjou and Murphy spend inordinate amounts of time screaming at each other. Sinatra's relaxed, low-key approach to his character provides a needed respite from the otherwise abrasive goings-on.

Step Lively also provides Sinatra with his first true romantic scenes as an actor, since most of the wooing he attempted in *Higher and Higher* was done in a musical context. The object of his desire is Christine, Miller's girlfriend (Gloria DeHaven). She first helps Miller dupe Glenn, but later falls for him. Not surprisingly, Sinatra does his best work in these scenes, primarily because his childlike persona is ideally suited to the peculiarities of the courting ritual. In the most talked-about scene between him and DeHaven, he shares with her his first screen kiss. Although long-since

Sinatra tries to resist the charms of Gloria DeHaven in *Step Lively*.

forgotten as far as classic screen kisses are concerned, it generated frenzied interest at the time, including a four-page spread in *Life* magazine to promote the movie.

Perhaps the most intriguing romantic scenes Sinatra plays in *Step Lively* are between Glenn and Miss Abbott (Anne Jeffreys), a woman acquainted with the mysterious benefactor financing Miller's play. These scenes inaugurate a theme that would resurface in later films: Sinatra being brazenly pursued by an aggressive woman and trying to ward off her advances. The most suggestive of these occurs during the musical number "Where Does Love Begin?" It starts off with Glenn doing a typically childlike thing: calling his mother from a pay phone. Miss Abbott slips into the booth with him, pressing herself close to his body, as he repeatedly tries to avoid contact. This is similar to a number Frank had done with Marcy McGuire in *Higher and Higher*, but in that film, Marcy was playing a bobbysoxer who was no threat to Sinatra's character. In *Step Lively*, he is a hapless innocent trying to escape sophisticated feminine wiles.

Sinatra's musical contributions to *Step Lively* are once again solid. Fortunately, Tim Whelan refrains from shooting too many closeups of Sinatra, allowing his musical scenes to breathe a bit more. "Some Other Time" is especially enjoyable, providing Sinatra his first chance in the movie to sing as a crooner on stage.

Sinatra's acting has also improved since *Higher and Higher* as well. He expresses a much broader range of emotions that sell the feeling behind the song, rather than just merely having a nice voice. He likely felt a lot freer playing a fictional character as opposed to playing himself.

Critics were generally more impressed with Sinatra's work in *Step Lively* than they had been with *Higher and Higher*. The *Tampa Bay Times* movie critic offered a full-out rave: "[Y]ou don't have to be a bobby-sock wearer to enjoy the new Frank Sinatra picture, *Step Lively*, now showing. It is gay and tuneful entertainment."[4] This sort of success pleased Sinatra, who had been unsettled by the negative reviews given his first acting role.

Perhaps the most interesting aspect of *Step Lively* is that it represents a point in Sinatra's screen career that was never to be duplicated. At the time of its release, the public's fascination with him had reached its zenith, and his star would gradually dim as the 1940s wore on. Never again would audiences react to one of his films quite the way critics described when *Step Lively* was on the screen.

Anchors Aweigh

Directed by George Sidney
Animation sequences directed by William Hanna and Joseph Barbera
Screenplay: Isobel Lennart, from a story suggested by Natalie Marcin
Producer: Joseph Pasternak
Cinematography: Charles Boyle, Robert Planck (Technicolor)

Anchors Aweigh (1945)

Editors: Adrienne Fazan, Thomas Richards
Songs:
 "We Hate to Leave," "I Begged Her," "What Makes the Sunset?," "The Charm of You," "I Fall in Love Too Easily"; Music: Jule Styne; Lyrics: Sammy Cahn
 "If You Knew Susie"; Music: Joseph Meyer; Lyrics: Buddy G. DeSylva
 "Jealousy" ("Jalousie"); Music: Jacob Gade; Lyrics: Vera Bloom
 "(All of a Sudden) My Heart Sings"; Music: Laurent Herpin; French Lyrics: Jamblan; English Lyrics: Harold Rome
 "The King Who Couldn't Dance" ("The Worry Song"); Music: Sammy Fain; Lyrics: Arthur Freed
 Waltz from "Serenade for Strings in C major, Op. 48"; Music: Pyotr Ilyich Tchaikovsky; Adaptation and Lyrics: Earl K. Brent
 "Anchors Aweigh"; Music: Charles A. Zimmerman; Lyrics: Alfred Hart Miles and R. Lovell
Cast: Frank Sinatra, Kathryn Grayson, Gene Kelly, Jose Iturbi, Dean Stockwell, Pamela Britton, Rags Ragland, Billy Gilbert, Henry O'Neill, Carlos Ramirez, Edgar Kennedy, Grady Sutton, Edgar Kennedy, Leon Ames, Sharon McManus, James Flavin, James Burke, Henry Armetta, Chester Clute, Sondra Rogers, Charles Coleman, Steve Brodie, Wally Cassell, Sara Berner, Bobby Barber, Marjorie Wood, Tom Trout, Jerry Warren, Elinor Troy, Claire Whitney, Florence Wix, Milton Parsons, Garry Owen, Renie Riano, Ray Teal, Tom Quinn, Bill Phillips, Netta Packer, Ruth Lee, Lock Martin, Frank Mitchell, Billy Nelson, Robert Emmett O'Connor, Gloria Hope, Ralph Dunn, Eddie Hall, Ben Heidman, Nolan Leary, Virginia Engels, Lester Dorr, Sam Finn, Jane Green, Ralph Dunn
Released July 19, 1945
MGM
140 minutes

While *Higher and Higher* and *Step Lively* made little overall impact, they were enough to impress powerful Metro-Goldwyn-Mayer head Louis B. Mayer. He borrowed Frank Sinatra from RKO for *Anchors Aweigh*, promising him top billing in a musical more suited to his talents. However, once filming commenced, Sinatra realized that despite his top billing, he was not the leading man. That went to Gene Kelly, who was under contract with MGM. Kelly, a stage star in New York, had made his movie debut for MGM in Busby Berkeley's *For Me and My Gal* (1942), co-starring with Judy Garland. It was a hit and Kelly became very popular, very quickly. On loan to Columbia, he starred with Rita Hayworth and Phil Silvers in another hit, *Cover Girl* (1944). By the time he was cast in *Anchors Aweigh*, his status was such that he was allowed to choreograph the entire film.

Sinatra, hoping that top billing in this big MGM Technicolor production would ensure his movie stardom, was disgruntled to discover he was not the lead, and was playing the same type of character as in his previous movies. In fact, when syndicated columnist Nora Paredes visited the set, Frank angrily spouted off about his situation:

> The Voice is through with the movies. No longer will swooning bobbysoxers clutter up the theater aisles as the picture of Frank Sinatra flashes across the screen. From now on, they'll swoon and sigh only in the privacy of their own homes. "Pictures stink," the Voice said today, in no uncertain terms. "Most of the people in them do, too."[5]

Because this columnist was syndicated through United Press International, Sinatra's quotes appeared in newspapers all over the nation.

This angered Hollywood's upper echelon and contradicted the boy-next-door image the industry had been trying to cultivate for Sinatra. Within days, at the urging of his public relations advisor, Sinatra issued a retraction indicating that he fully intended to complete *Anchors Aweigh* and honor the remainder of his RKO contract.

Anchors Aweigh casts Sinatra and Kelly as sailors aboard the USS *Knoxville*, a World War II cruiser. They are granted four days shore leave in Hollywood due to their heroism in a sea battle. The nature of their characters is alluded to in the opening sequence, a ceremony in which they receive Silver Stars for bravery. It is explained that ship's gunner Clarence Doolittle (Sinatra) was blown overboard during an artillery attack. He was rescued by gunner's mate Joe Brady (Kelly) who, "without regard for his own personal safety, dived into the sea and rescued his shipmate." The relationship between the two men continues in this vein for the entire film. The self-assured Joe will repeatedly be forced to scuttle his plans and come to the aid of the waifish Clarence, who stares at the more experienced man with vacant admiration and entreats him to impart his secrets of wooing women. Clarence calls Joe "the best wolf in the whole Navy."

Given *Anchors Aweigh*'s premise, Sinatra is called upon to do little more than affect a star-struck countenance and bumble endearingly through scene after scene in which he is depicted as a veritable child. He makes loud sucking noises when he sips from his chocolate malt, wears his sailor's cap tipped back to reveal his curly hair, and frequently makes such exclamations as "swell" and "keen." Clarence's childlike nature is especially evident in the scene where *Knoxville* crew members line up at a pay phone to make arrangements for their time on leave. When Joe calls to make a date with a woman named Lola, Clarence passively places his head on Joe's shoulder, like a lovesick schoolboy eavesdropping on his older brother in an attempt to glean tips on romantic technique. When Clarence gets his turn at the phone, he sheepishly dials the time-of-day recording, pretending to call a woman, so as not to lose face among his fellow sailors. Later, realizing he can trust Joe, Clarence confesses his shyness and begs his friend to help him become more of a ladies' man: "Every time we get liberty, all I do is go to the library. I thought it'd be fun to try something different, like going out with girls!" While all of this certainly wins Sinatra the audience's empathy, it also makes his character rather unimportant to the plot.

When a police officer goes looking for a sailor to convince a boy (Dean Stockwell) that he is too young to join the Navy, it is Joe he chooses for this task; when the boy meets Joe, it is he, not Clarence, whom he comes to idolize. Even the students at the boy's school instantly rally around Joe when he pays them a surprise visit. The boy's pretty aunt (Kathryn Grayson), with whom Clarence immediately becomes smitten, winds up falling for Joe, while Clarence ends up with a nice waitress from Brooklyn.

Sinatra assumes a much more equal part in the film's musical numbers, although this aspect of the movie is ultimately dominated by Kelly as well. Sinatra's finest moments, not surprisingly, come during his singing solos. He truly shines when he croons "I Fall in Love Too Easily," conveying genuine emotion through facial expressions which pointedly contrast the blank stare of amazement he wears in the picture's non-musical moments. And, dueting with Kelly on "I Begged Her," a rousing number performed for the benefit of fellow servicemen in a hostel, there is no hint of his character's nervousness and naivete: Clarence has little problem conveying the attitude and patter of a "wolf" like Joe.

What really astonished those who saw *Anchors Aweigh*, however, was Sinatra's vigorous dancing alongside a talent the likes of Kelly, especially in the "I Begged Her" number, which involves some difficult maneuvers on and around the hostel's beds. Edwin Schallert wrote in *The Los Angeles Times*, "Surprise revelation of the picture is the team of Frank Sinatra and Gene Kelly, who go through a remarkable variety of paces. This consists of songs, humor and even dancing. For both of them, too."[6] Sinatra's grumbling in the press during the making of the movie was all but forgotten once the reviews came in.

Despite Sinatra's strong showing, Kelly deserves credit for most of the film's best musical numbers. It was on this film that he firmly established his reputation as an actor and choreographer. Kelly also devised one of the film's top highlights: his dance with the cartoon mouse Jerry of Tom and Jerry fame.

The idea was originally to have Mickey Mouse perform the animated

Gene Kelly (right) tutored Frank Sinatra on the dance routines in *Anchors Aweigh*.

steps with live-action Kelly, and Walt Disney was open to the idea. But his brother Roy Disney, the businessman of the partnership, balked at another studio's product being promoted with one of their characters. So the idea was changed to Jerry, as the Tom and Jerry cartoons were made for MGM. Animators William Hanna and Joseph Barbera created this sequence along with Kelly, matching his movements perfectly, in a scene that took two months and $100,000 to produce. Some of this cost was incurred when early rushes indicated that while Gene had a reflection showing on the floor as he danced, Jerry did not. Hanna and Barbera had to go back and add a reflection (an extra 10,000 drawings). This sequence influenced several later, similar sequences including Kelly again mixing animation and live action in a sequence for *Singin' in the Rain* (1952), and Jerry, with Tom, appearing in a swimming sequence with Esther Williams for her movie *Dangerous When Wet* (1953).

Less successful are two later dance sequences which—although technically sound—stall the narrative as the denouement nears. Kelly himself apparently was not delighted with the fantasy sequence in which he portrays a bandit opposite Grayson's young maiden. And the scene that follows almost immediately, in which Joe dances with a little peasant girl, seems a bit indulgent.

Anchors Aweigh was the fifth-highest grossing movie in 1945. Kelly was nominated for an Academy Award as Best Actor, and the film also secured nominations for Best Picture, Best Color Cinematography and Best Song (for "I Fall in Love Too Easily"). But the only Oscar win was for Best Musical Score. *Anchors Aweigh*'s success led Louis B. Mayer to purchase Sinatra's contract from RKO.

During this same year (1945), Sinatra also hit the music charts with the popular singles "I Dream of You (More Than You Dream I Do)," "Saturday Night (Is the Loneliest Night of the Week)," "Dream" and "Nancy (with the Laughing Face)." At this point, between his music career and his movie career, Sinatra was riding high.

It Happened in Brooklyn

Directed by Richard Whorf
Screenplay: Isobel Lennart, from a story by John McGowan
Producer: Jack Cummings
Cinematography: Robert Planck (Black and White)
Editor: Blanche Sewell
Songs:
   "Whose Baby Are You," "The Brooklyn Bridge," "I Believe,"
      "Time After Time," "The Song's Gotta Come from the Heart,"
      "It's the Same Old Dream"; Music: Jule Styne; Lyrics: Sammy Cahn
   "Invention No. 1"; Music: Johann Sebastian Bach
   "La ci darem la mano" from the opera "Don Giovanni"; Music: Wolfgang Amadeus Mozart; Libretto: Lorenzo da Ponte

"The Bell Song" ("Où va la jeune Indoue?") from "Lakmé"; Music: Léo Delibes; Libretto by Edmond Gondinet and Philippe Gille

Cast: Frank Sinatra, Kathryn Grayson, Peter Lawford, Jimmy Durante, Gloria Grahame, Marcy McGuire, Aubrey Mather, Tamara Shayne, William Roy, Bobby Long, William Haade, Raymond Largay, William Tannen, Leon Tyler, Wilson Wood, Jack Baker, Phil Durham, Bruce Cowling, Chet Brandenburg, Boyd Davis, Leonard Bremen, Harry Adams, John Phipps, Al Hill, Bertha Ferducha, Dell Henderson, Frank Marlowe, Bill Hickman, Angi Poulos, Jane Green, Ralph Hodges, William Leicester, Lumsden Hare, William Tannen, Dick Wessel, Bob Stebbins, Leon Tyler, Wilson Wood, Mickey Roth, Arthur Tovey, Constance Weiler, George Travell, The Starlighters

Released April 7, 1947

MGM

104 minutes

In the nearly two years between the summer 1945 release of *Anchors Aweigh* and the spring 1947 release of *It Happened in Brooklyn*, Sinatra remained busy on- and off-screen. His first album "The Voice of Frank Sinatra," released as a set of four 78 rpm records in March 1946, reached the top of the charts. Some of the sessions had been recorded in Hollywood right after the release of *Anchors Aweigh*, with a few more sessions done in New York City in December 1945. He appeared in a two-reel documentary short, *The All Star Bond Rally* (1945), which promoted War Bond sales. Bob Hope hosted, with Sinatra, Betty Grable, Harpo Marx and Harry James among those appearing. He was seen as himself in *Till the Clouds Roll By* (1946), MGM's lavish Technicolor biopic of composer Jerome Kern.

One of his more interesting movies during this period was an RKO one-reeler, *The House I Live In*. A wartime "message picture," it features Sinatra, as himself, taking a break from a recording session and spotting some boys picking on another because his religion is different. Frank straightens them out by telling him that such bigotry is how the Nazis behave. *The House I Live In* has lived on as a cultural artifact from the wartime era.

Sinatra's popularity was high when he returned to MGM for *It Happened in Brooklyn*. He was pleased to be the bona fide star after playing support to Gene Kelly in *Anchors Aweigh*. Sinatra delivers one of the most assured, polished performances of his early screen career in this easygoing musical comedy. He seems far more relaxed before the cameras than before, and his acting exhibits a broadened range of emotion few would have expected from him after his series of one-note performances.

While much of this improvement can be attributed to his getting a little more comfortable, and competent, each time out, perhaps what helped him most in *It Happened in Brooklyn* is that, for the first time in his young film career, he portrays a character who is not one-dimensional. As Danny Miller, an ex-soldier trying to get his life back together after returning to his hometown of Brooklyn after World War II, Sinatra finally assumes a layered screen persona. While Danny appears to others to be a confident, successful man, he is not altogether sure what to do with his life.

Sinatra's improvement as an actor is evident from the moment he first appears on screen. In the opening sequence, Danny stares out the window of his hospital room in England with a bandage on his head, apparently the result of an injury he sustained in battle. He has a faraway, depressed expression—a look that conveys genuine melancholy, an emotion which Sinatra had not been able to muster so convincingly in any of his earlier movies. When a pretty nurse (Gloria Grahame) chastises him for sitting around and sulking, Danny doesn't stutter and stammer, and behave like a lovesick child as per his previous roles. Rather, he maintains his melancholy attitude, reacting to the nurse not as a beautiful woman to be fawned over but as someone who is trying to cheer him up when he wants no part of it.

The two sides of Danny Miller are presented via the character's relationships with his two best friends. When he is with Jamie Shellgrove (Peter Lawford), a shy, awkward English composer, he is calm and confident since the inexperienced Jamie looks up to him in much the same manner that Sinatra's character looked up to Gene Kelly's in *Anchors Aweigh*. But when Danny is around Nick Lombardi (Jimmy Durante), the curmudgeonly janitor at his old Brooklyn high school, he is free to allow his insecurities and uncertainties to surface. To illustrate, first consider this exchange between Danny and Jamie that occurs as Jamie's nobleman grandfather is trying to persuade Danny to take Jamie back to Brooklyn and show him the ways of the world:

> JAMIE: It is difficult for me to talk to people, and that's unfortunate. And if, as you and Grandfather think, there's something missing in my music, it's because there's something missing in me. I'm afraid that I'd be exactly the same in Brooklyn or anywhere.
> DANNY: Look, Jamie, about "anywhere" I don't know. But in Brooklyn, in one week's time you'll be talking to a girl. A girl? Ten girls! You'll have your pick of ten girls. [*To Jamie's grandfather:*] You send him to me; I'll fix him up. You won't know him when I'm through with him.

In contrast, consider the scene between Danny and Nick after Danny has returned to his job at a sheet music company. What he really wants to do is sing the new music as a demonstrator. When he learns he needs to audition for the demonstrator job, Danny tells Nick he's "just a little guy who's not sure of very much," and that, despite his vocal talents, "Whenever I have to sing before strangers, I freeze up."

All of this makes for some interesting moments. When Jamie shows up in Brooklyn, Danny must try to help him gain the confidence to find a girl while at the same time he must look to Nick for support in his own efforts to woo Anne Fielding (Kathryn Grayson), a pretty schoolteacher who, like Danny, has dreams of singing stardom. Sinatra handles each role-within-a-role well. His scenes with Lawford foreshadow the relationship the two would share more than a decade later in the Rat Pack films: He is all easygoing charm, spouting hip language as he saunters around with his hands stuffed casually in his pockets, as Lawford chases after him looking to glean tips on technique. The romantic scenes Sinatra shares with Grayson differ from the same sort of scenes the duo played in *Anchors Aweigh*. Rather than appearing to be anxious simply because he is in the company of a woman, his shyness emanates more from the fact that he is with a woman he genuinely likes and he conveys these momentary lapses of composure with simple techniques like fingering the band of his fedora as his character struggles to find the proper words. Anne ultimately falls for Jamie, so Sinatra once again fails to get Grayson, although in this instance it is more interesting since he winds up, in effect, losing her to himself, since the character of Jamie so closely resembles his character in *Anchors Aweigh*. In the end, Danny winds up with the nurse from this film's first scene.

Sinatra does his best acting in his scenes with Durante. Although Durante makes every attempt to steal their scenes, Sinatra more than adequately holds his own with the talented veteran, trading fast-paced quips, songs and dance steps with verve. This is especially evident in the musical number "The Song's Gotta Come from the Heart," which Nick and Danny sing after Danny finally agrees to audition for the song demonstrator's job. In this funny, charming segment, Sinatra manages not only to sing well, but also to have a good time doing it, smiling widely throughout and even doing some on-target mimicry of Durante's trademark delivery.

It Happened in Brooklyn lost money at the box office, but the improvement of Sinatra as an actor was noticed by critics. John McManus of *PM* magazine wrote that Sinatra "seems to have loosened up and got into the swing of things as a film player and even as a comedian. Things look promising for Frankie-Boy films even if his wooing notes should one day peter out." Sara Hamilton of *The Los Angeles Examiner* was more lavish in her praise: "Frank, of course, thrills the customers with his vocalizing, but it's his naturalness and easygoing charm that begets applause. It seems like all of a sudden it's spring and Frankie is an actor."[7]

Sinatra gets advice from Jimmy Durante (right) in *It Happened in Brooklyn.*

Despite the film's lack of box office success, it remained an important part of Frank Sinatra's evolution as a screen actor.

While Sinatra's performance in front of the cameras improved, his conduct behind the cameras was beginning to irritate studio executives. MGM production memos reveal a series of late arrivals, leaving early, ducking out on rehearsals, and instances of not showing up at all. He sometimes gave excuses (at one time, Durante was not available to rehearse their number together and he felt it would be silly for him to show up alone). Other times he would simply refuse (including at least once when Durante was available). At a time when Sinatra's stardom was riding high, he felt secure enough to be this "difficult."

The Miracle of the Bells

Directed by Irving Pichel
Screenplay: Ben Hecht and Quentin Reynolds, from a novel by Russell Janney
Producer: Jesse L. Lasky and Walter MacEwen

Cinematography: Robert DeGrasse (Black and White)
Editor: Elmo Williams
Cast: Fred MacMurray, Alida Valli, Frank Sinatra, Lee J. Cobb, Harold Vermilyea, Charles Meredith, James Nolan, Veronica Pataky, Philip Ahn, Frank Ferguson, Frank Wilcox, Oliver Blake, George Chandler, Max Hamilton, Frank Pharr, Richard Mickelson, Michael Raffetto, Dorothy Sebastian, Tom Stevenson, Regina Wallace, Billy Wayne, Charles Wagenheim, Ray Teal, Snub Pollard, Robert Bacon, Roger Creed, Ned Davenport, Paul Cristo, Herbert Evans, Charles Miller, Bobby Barber, Kid Chissell, Jimmy Dime, George Cathey, Mabel Colcord, Lillian Clayes, Franklin Farnum, Fred Graham, Paul Kruger, Jimmy Horan, Sam Lufkin, James Pierce, Dorothy Neumann, Patsy O'Byrne, Thayer Roberts, Frank Roehn, Jean Spangler, Ken Terrell, Perry Ivins, Art Dupuis
Released March 27, 1948
RKO
120 minutes

Despite the failure of *It Happened in Brooklyn*, Sinatra was still a very successful recording artist and had appeared in the hit film *Anchors Aweigh*. As a result, he still commanded some attention in Hollywood. He wanted to grow as an actor despite his misgivings about the way the studios did things. So he accepted a role in an RKO drama in which he would play a Catholic priest. This was not a particularly good move for Sinatra, as he had lately incurred negative publicity about alleged ties to organized crime.

Early in 1947, before the cameras rolled on *The Miracle of the Bells*, Sinatra had a series of private meetings with reputed underworld figures Meyer Lansky, Joe Adonis and Lucky Luciano, with whom he even posed for a few photographs while in Cuba. This led to a scathing attack by newspaper columnist Robert Ruark, who commented on Sinatra's "curious desire to cavort among the scum," and chastised him for "setting a most peculiar example for his hordes of pimply shrieking slaves."[8] The effect of the column was immediate and far-reaching. The next day, Cuban police arrested Luciano and threw him into prison, and later sent him back to Italy. The episode became national news, and Sinatra was depicted as being a friend to mobsters. Sinatra responded in the press: "Any report that I fraternize with goons and racketeers is a vicious lie. ... I was brought up to shake a man's hand when I am introduced to him, without first investigating his past."[9]

A few weeks later, in an effort to salvage Sinatra's besmirched image, it was announced that he would donate his $100,000 *Miracle of the Bells* salary to the Catholic Church. He also received approval from the Catholic Church to play a Catholic priest, which was probably important with everything going on in his personal life.

The Miracle of the Bells (1948)

The Father Paul character that Sinatra plays in *The Miracle of the Bells* is a static depthless character. A kindly Catholic priest in a small Pennsylvania mining town, he serves no function in the script other than to listen earnestly to the maudlin recollections of Hollywood press agent Bill Dunnigan, portrayed by Fred MacMurray.

It is difficult to fathom what attracted Sinatra to *The Miracle of the Bells* to the point that he would reject the advice of several close consultants and persuade MGM to loan him back to RKO so he could participate in the project, in which he receives third billing. The film is based on a best-selling novel, but much of its appeal as a book was due to author Russell Janney's introspective narrative. That proved to be a difficult aspect of the story to duplicate for screenwriter Ben Hecht. In fact, Hecht only agreed to write the screenplay if he didn't have to bother reading the book. Quentin Reynolds read it and reported to Hecht, securing screenplay co-billing for doing so. Hecht's approach was to rely on a series of tritely sentimental voice-overs and speeches by MacMurray as Dunnigan. What Dunnigan thinks and talks about most of the time is his relationship with a native of tiny Coaltown, Pennsylvania, Olga Treskovna (Alida Valli), whose dream is to become a Hollywood movie star.

The film opens with Dunnigan returning to Coaltown with Olga's body. She died of tuberculosis after completing her first starring role as Joan of Arc in a big-budget historical movie. There he arranges to have her buried at Father Paul's church, and through flashbacks the story of her life, and their life together, is told. When the film returns to the present, it focuses on the refusal of a Hollywood producer (Lee J. Cobb) to release the film because he doesn't believe moviegoers will pay to see a movie featuring a deceased star. Dunnigan calls on his talents as a press agent to stage an event in order to raise awareness of Olga and thereby force the producer to release the film. He arranges for all five churches in Coaltown to ring their bells continuously for three days and three nights, and the producer is eventually persuaded.

Little if any of this "rings" true. Although the filmmakers want to depict Dunnigan as a sensitive man who genuinely loved Olga, much of the dialogue sounds like it was written for a film noir gumshoe, most notably in his incessant utterance of the word "baby." During his initial voice-over, in which he bemoans that he never told Olga he loved her, he says, "Show business is full of beautiful faces, and I guess I've seen 'em all. But I never saw one like yours, baby. Never like yours."

The movie-within-a-movie scenes depicting the filming of the Joan of Arc project are equally hollow, especially an embarrassingly overwrought segment in which Olga, as Joan being burned at the stake, recites a clichéd speech about how if her legacy lives on, she will never truly die. RKO

Miracle of the Bells stars Fred MacMurray (left), Alida Valli and Sinatra.

actually did release a film entitled *Joan of Arc* this same year, with Ingrid Bergman in the title role. Comparing that to the production depicted in *The Miracle of the Bells* really shows the latter example's shortcomings, even as part of another film's narrative.

Even the aspect of the story about the producer's refusal to release the picture (which, in itself, is cloying, given the popularity of posthumous film releases, even in the 1940s) concludes on a trite note. Cobb's producer character piously announces that he will donate all profits from the film to build a hospital in Coaltown in Olga's honor. This is to spare miners and their families the horrors of a debilitating disease the likes of tuberculosis. His largesse belies what most recognized as the ego-driven nature of Hollywood power brokers of the era, something which is evident in the opening credits of *The Miracle of the Bells*: On the second title card, it is noted that Valli appears "by special arrangement with David O. Selznick."

Perhaps because Olga was virtually unknown at the time of her passing, no one would recognize her name anyway and that's why they didn't want to release the film. Still, it did seem like a strange and unnatural shift for Cobb's character to go from not wanting to release the film as is because he believes it will lose money, to suddenly wanting to release it and donate all the proceeds to a hospital.

Sinatra is not spared his share of responsibility for the failure of the movie. His portrayal of Father Paul is less characterization than caricature. In an attempt to convey earnestness, he speaks softly, in a monotone, and once again summons an affliction of his earlier work: a blank, intermittently blinking stare. With few exceptions, his method of delivering a speech is to speak one line, pause briefly, speak another line, pause again, then speak another line. He even spends inordinate amounts of time walking around with his hands clasped in front of his body in stereotypically priestly fashion. It is a flat, nondescript performance which is all the more disappointing coming, as it does, on the heels of his inspired work in *It Happened in Brooklyn*.

Some moviegoers reacted negatively to this movie, and Sinatra's performance, before the movie was even released. According to Erskine Johnson's syndicated column:

> The trailer for *Miracle of the Bells* with Frank Sinatra in his role as a priest, is playing in Los Angeles to mixed reactions. At one showing, a spy reports, there was a great deal of laughter and one bobbysoxer moaned for all to hear: "Oh, Frankie! What have you done to yourself?"[10]

Sinatra's difficulty in a role which did not afford him the opportunity to sing, dance or do comedy was noted by critics. Most of them dismissed his performance as wooden, while others compared him unfavorably to Bing Crosby's Oscar-winning priest role in *Going My Way* (1944). At least one critic, however, seemed to defend the performances in his review: "MacMurray and Sinatra, both playing earnestly, honestly and with laudable understatement, make their characters convincing and give admirable performances."[11]

Sinatra's failure in this movie comes down to two things: He is cast as a relatively one-dimensional character, as he was in his first two films, and he was cast against type. Not that Sinatra had a fully developed screen persona by this point in his film career, but as we could see from *It Happened in Brooklyn*, he was definitely more adept at playing a sort of swaggering, confident type of character—not a priest. In any case, *The Miracle of the Bells* was a resounding box office failure, and had a negative effect on Sinatra's film career.

The Kissing Bandit

Directed by Laslo Benedek
Screenplay: John Briard Harding and Isobel Lennart
Producer: Joe Pasternak

Cinematography: Robert Surtees (Technicolor)
Editor: Adrienne Fazan
Songs:
   "Tomorrow Means Romance"; Music: Nacio Herb Brown; Lyrics: William Katz
   "What's Wrong with Me?," "Señorita," "Love Is Where You Find It"; Music: Nacio Herb Brown; Lyrics: Earl K. Brent
   "If I Steal a Kiss"; Music: Nacio Herb Brown; Lyrics: Edward Heyman
   "Dance of Fury"; Music: Nacio Herb Brown
Cast: Frank Sinatra, Kathryn Grayson, J. Carrol Naish, Mildred Natwick, Billy Gilbert, Sono Osato, Clinton Sundberg, Carleton G. Young, Ricardo Montalban, Ann Miller, Cyd Charisse, Edna Skinner, Vincente Gomez, Nick Thompson, Henry Mirelez, Pedro Regas, Alberto Morin, Joe Dominguez, Fred Gilman, Mitchell Lewis, Byron Foulger, Gene Coogan, Carlos Albert, Herman Belmonte, Margarita Martin, Nana Bryant, Sally Forrest, Michael Kostrick, Ginny Jackson, Captain Garcia, Alex Montoya, Wilson Wood, Candy Toxton, Leo Mostovoy, Carl Pitti, Clark Ross, Julian Rivero
Released November 18, 1948
MGM
100 minutes

If *Miracle of the Bells* was a wrongheaded movie for Sinatra to do at this point in his film career, *The Kissing Bandit* shows it could have been much worse. MGM rushed him into this Technicolor musical because they needed him to bounce back from the drama he had just done for another studio. Eager to make him a leading man, the studio re-teamed him with Kathryn Grayson in this lavish production. Sinatra balked upon reading the script, believing he was all wrong for the part of a 19th-century city-bred milquetoast whose father is the notorious title character. He was right.

The plot has Boston-bred Ricardo (Sinatra) traveling to Spanish California to claim an inn his late father owned. His father's friend Chico (J. Carrol Naish) reveals that Ricardo's dad was actually the Kissing Bandit, not a humble innkeeper. Told that the government is looking for the Bandit, Ricardo hides his identity, pretending to be a tax collector. When he becomes smitten with the governor's pretty daughter Teresa, he refrains from kissing her, much to her chagrin, so he does not become identified with the Kissing Bandit.

While MGM had been presenting Sinatra as a shy, unassuming character who nervously approaches girls, in *The Kissing Bandit* they push that

Kathryn Grayson and Sinatra were not particularly fond of their work in *The Kissing Bandit*.

even further. Sinatra's character is a bumbling tenderfoot who, when he tries to ride a horse, is unable to stop and flies through a window in slapstick fashion. When Ricardo discovers that his father was in fact the title character, he faints.

Sinatra wasn't originally slated to appear in this film at all. It was originally slated for Tony Martin and Broadway actress Marion Bell. Martin was still attached to the project when Bell was replaced by Kathryn Grayson. Grayson remained when Martin was replaced by Sinatra. And for the rest of their years, Sinatra and Grayson considered *The Kissing Bandit* their worst movie.

There are some positives to *The Kissing Bandit*, but they have nothing to do with the scenario, direction or performances. Producer Joe Pasternak spent money on the movie, offering a colorful, visually arresting production with nice scenery and colorful costumes. But this is just dross. The film has nothing to offer despite a cast that includes veteran favorites Mildred Natwick, Billy Gilbert, Ricardo Montalban, Ann Miller and Cyd Charisse.

Sinatra misbehaved when filming *It Happened in Brooklyn* and was even more disruptive while working on this wrongheaded production. He showed up hours late to the set; mumbled in a lackluster manner through his scenes, forcing retakes; and when he was scheduled for a 9 a.m. call to shoot a new ending late in the production, he remained in Palm Springs. This, of course, angered the MGM brass.

Songwriter Nacio Herb Brown, composer of such songs as "Singin' in the Rain" and "You Are My Lucky Star," came out of retirement to write songs for this movie, but while MGM touted the score as "out of this world" in their advertising, it failed to produce any hit recordings. Critics were also unimpressed, with Kate Cameron of *The New York Daily News* stating:

> The film has some stunning outdoor scenes of California hills and forests, but is based on a feeble story that lacks good comedy material. It is far from adult entertainment and must find its audiences among the very young and the not-too-hard to please.[12]

The Kissing Bandit was one of the biggest flops in MGM history, losing more than two million dollars.

The MGM powers-that-be realized that they needed to return Sinatra to the formula that generated more positive box office results. So he was once again teamed with Gene Kelly for his next two films, returning to the formula that made *Anchors Aweigh* a hit.

Take Me Out to the Ball Game

Directed by Busby Berkeley
Screenplay: Harry Turgend and George Wells, from a story by Gene Kelly and Stanley Donen, with contributions by Harry Crane
Producer: Arthur Freed
Cinematography: George J. Folsey (Technicolor)
Editor: Blanche Sewell

Take Me Out to the Ball Game (1949)

Songs:
"Take Me Out to the Ball Game"; Music: Albert von Tilzer; Lyrics: Jack Norworth
"Yes, Indeedy," "O'Brien to Ryan to Goldberg," "The Right Girl for Me," "It's Fate Baby, It's Fate"; Music: Roger Edens; Lyrics: Betty Comden and Adolph Green
"Strictly U.S.A."; Music: Roger Edens
"The Hat My Dear Old Father Wore Upon St. Patrick's Day"; Music: Jean Schwartz; Lyrics: William Jerome
Cast: Frank Sinatra, Esther Williams, Gene Kelly, Betty Garrett, Edward Arnold, Jules Munshin, Richard Lane, Tom Dugan, Eddie Parks, Mack Gray, Sol Gorss, Douglas Fowley, Gordon Jones, Harry Allen, John Burger, Henry Kulky, Richard Beavers, Eddie Cutler, Hubie Kerns, Richard Landry, Ramon and Royce Blackburn, Jack Bruce, Joseph Roach, Bob Simpson, Eddie David, Ellsworth Blake, James Burke, Ed Cassidy, Sally Forrest, Wilton Graff, Pat Flaherty, Marilyn Kinsley, Richard Landry, Pete Kooy, Aaron Phillips, Isabel O'Madigan, Bob Koetler, Lee Phelps, Dick Wessel, William Tannen, Robert Skelton, Harry Wilson, Almira Sessions, Dorothy Pina, Hank Tobias, Dolly Walker, Jack Rice
Released April 13, 1949
MGM
93 minutes

Take Me Out to the Ball Game was the second, and weakest, of Sinatra's three formulaic screen teamings with Gene Kelly. While it borrows liberally from the concept and structure of *Anchors Aweigh*, it is actually less a retread of that 1945 musical comedy than a practice run for *On the Town*, which would premiere later in 1949 and improve upon *Take Me Out to the Ball Game* in nearly every regard.

All three films are similar in that they cast Sinatra in his by-now familiar role of the innocent who is shy with women, while making Kelly a brash ladies' man whom Sinatra's character admires and seeks to emulate. No film in this trio is much concerned with plot. Instead, each is essentially a series of comic and musical vignettes spotlighting the singing, dancing and mimicry talents of its stars as they search for the women of their dreams.

Yet, *Anchors Aweigh* and *On the Town,* dealing with sailors on leave exploring a big city, have within their structure an inherent pace. The characters have a limited amount of time to complete their activities, and events build to a logical conclusion. Here, with Sinatra and Kelly portraying professional baseball players who moonlight during the off-season as vaudevillians, the imminent denouement comes in the form of a battle for the baseball championship which is largely played off-screen so there is sparse urgency to the plot, and therefore little pace to the film.

Take Me Out to the Ball Game wastes no time in establishing the differences between the characters played by Sinatra and Kelly. After the requisite musical opener (a rousing rendition of the title tune), we see Denny Ryan (Sinatra) and Eddie O'Brien (Kelly) aboard a train, heading to the spring training site of the Wolves, the baseball team for which they play. Eddie begins to complain about having to leave behind the freedom of his show business career for the restrictions of his baseball career:

> DENNY: Gee, it's gonna be great to be back in that ol' ball game again! I can hear the umps now, "Batters for the day, Rube Waddell and Ossee Schreck." Kinda chokes you up, doesn't it?
> EDDIE: Yeah, it chokes me. When I think of all the dames I lost 'cause I had to be in bed by ten o'clock.
> DENNY: Play a lot of checkers by ten o'clock.
> EDDIE: No, sir, brother. Give me vaudeville, any time. And maybe a musical show—50 girls, 50. Maybe even a hundred girls, a hundred.
> DENNY: Gee, I suppose it would be more fun than playin' checkers.

Their relationship is to continue in this vein throughout the film, Denny always shyly referring to women as "girls," Eddie boasting and using such words as "dames," "quail," "mice," "minx" and "chicks."

It quickly becomes embarrassing for the audience to watch Sinatra—past 30 and with a receding hairline—still trying to act too shy to talk to women. This is the last film which relies so heavily on that persona. While he is far from a lady killer in *On the Town*, he nonetheless plays a character who isn't so much afraid of the women as he is uninterested, preferring to use his time on leave to see the sights of New York.

Once the pair make it to Florida, where the Wolves train, *Take Me Out to the Ball Game* mimics two elements of *Anchors Aweigh*. As soon as Eddie and Denny arrive, they sing to their teammates about what their lives were like while they toured the vaudeville circuit. While the song "Yes, Indeedy" is unquestionably entertaining, it poses the same troubling question that the "I Begged Her" number did in *Anchors Aweigh*. Why is Sinatra's character, who is depicted as so inexperienced with women, suddenly able to convey the attitudes and vocabulary of a lech the likes of Kelly's character? Then, almost as soon as the song is over, Sinatra's character quickly falls in love with a beautiful woman whom he has no idea how to approach; he looks to Kelly's character for assistance. In *Anchors Aweigh* it was Kathryn Grayson, here it is Esther Williams, portraying the new owner of the Wolves, K.C. Higgins.[13]

Again, as in *Anchors Aweigh*, Sinatra's character proves too ineffectual to land his first love, losing her to Kelly's wolfish hero. So Danny settles for Shirley (Betty Garrett), a brazen Wolves fan who pursues him in the aggressive manner which by now had become a staple of Sinatra's screen romances. As if it weren't clear enough to the audience that Eddie's childlike manner is meant to appeal to the nurturing instincts of Sinatra fans, Shirley goes so far as to explain her attraction to Eddie as being caused by "the mother in me."

Shirley also appears to represent the fan girls who wildly pursued Sinatra just a few years earlier. Likely it was appealing to the film's female audience to see a woman aggressively going after the man she wants and eventually succeeding, even if he is at first uninterested. There's also a sort of reversal of expected gender roles in the "It's Fate Baby, It's Fate" number, with Sinatra appearing more physically vulnerable against Garrett, who at one point picks him up and slings him across her shoulders.

Perhaps the most significant difference between *Anchors Aweigh* and *Take Me Out to the Ball Game* is the addition of clownish Jules Munshin to the cast, an addition which appears to have been made to compensate for Sinatra's shrinking status as a comedic lead in the wake of *The Kissing Bandit*. As Nat Goldberg, another of the Wolves' stars, Munshin is called upon to perform much of the movie's outlandish comedy, leaving Sinatra

Sinatra, Jules Munshin and Gene Kelly (left to right across top) portray ballplaying vaudevillians opposite Esther Williams (left, front) and Betty Garrett in *Take Me Out to the Ball Game*.

with even less to do within the narrative structure of this film than he had in *Anchors Aweigh*.

In the movie's musical moments, Sinatra's role is diminished with the incorporation of Munshin into the scheme. This is especially evident in the "O'Brien to Ryan to Goldberg" number, in which a mugging Munshin is an equal partner to Sinatra and Kelly. In fact, the only area in which Munshin does not share screen time with Kelly and Sinatra is during ball-playing scenes, and in that regard he is fortunate. For while Sinatra and Kelly are men of many talents, throwing, catching and hitting a baseball are not among them. While it is easy to see how O'Brien and Ryan could have been star vaudevillians, the athletic ineptitude of the men who portray them makes it impossible to imagine them as star baseball players.

As in *Anchors Aweigh*, however, Sinatra continues to do a great job keeping up with Kelly's choreography, and he, Kelly, and Munshin make a great dance trio. They were each able to bring their own thing to the movie: Munshin the comedy, Kelly the dancing, Sinatra the voice.

The production of *Take Me Out to the Ball Game* was fraught with conflict. First, credited director Busby Berkeley actually had little to do with this film. Arthur Freed hired him to help jumpstart his flagging career, but most of the direction was actually done by Stanley Donen and Gene Kelly. Both, however, allowed Berkeley to take solo screen credit. The benevolence did not, however, extend to Esther Williams. When Kathryn Grayson turned the role down, Judy Garland was considered, but she was having substance abuse problems by this time and was considered too unreliable. June Allyson was then considered, but she had recently become pregnant and didn't want to work. When Esther Williams was hired, it was against Gene Kelly's wishes and he was not kind to her. She bonded with Sinatra, and the two remained friends. Berkeley suggested he direct a swimming sequence since Williams was now in the film, but Kelly nixed it. Betty Garrett fondly recalled Sinatra's kindness toward her for Kitty Kelly:

> [W]e were doing a two-shot, then they shot over my shoulder to get a closeup of Frank and started to move the camera away. He yelled, "Hey, wait a minute! How about a closeup of my girl here?" They gave me that closeup because of Frank.[14]

Garrett again worked with this group in their follow-up, *On the Town*.

Critics were generally unimpressed with *Take Me Out to the Ball Game*. But the critics don't buy tickets, and MGM was pleased when it became a hit. This was good for Sinatra's movie career, after a series of flops.

Even more concerning was Sinatra's music career. In 1949, his song

"The Hucklebuck" reached number 10 on the charts, but it turned out to be the last of his Columbia recordings to chart. His album that year, "Frankly Sentimental," was panned by *Downbeat* magazine and sold poorly. The teenage bobbysoxers who made up the bulk of Sinatra's record-buying fans during the war years had grown up and moved on, while Frank did not appear to be generating many new fans.

On the Town

Directed by Stanley Donen and Gene Kelly
Screenplay: Adolph Green and Betty Comden, from their story and an idea by Jerome Robbins
Producer: Arthur Freed
Cinematography: Harold Rosson (Technicolor)
Editor: Ralph E. Winters
Songs:
   "Miss Turnstiles"; Music: Leonard Bernstein
   "New York, New York," "Come Up to My Place," "I Feel Like I'm Not Out of Bed Yet"; Music: Leonard Bernstein; Lyrics: Adolph Green and Betty Comden
   "A Day in New York"; Music: Leonard Bernstein
   "Prehistoric Man," "Main Street," "You're Awful," "On the Town," "Count on Me," "That's All There Is, Folks"; Music: Roger Edens; Lyrics: Adolph Green and Betty Comden
Cast: Gene Kelly, Frank Sinatra, Betty Garrett, Ann Miller, Jules Munshin, Vera-Ellen, Florence Bates, Alice Pearce, George Meader, Murray Alper, Dick Wessel, Bill Phillips, Tom Dugan, Robert B. Dugan, Hans Conried, Judy Holliday, Sid Melton, Bea Benaderet, Gladys Bake, Hank Mann, Milton Kibbee, Carol Haney, Timmy Hawkins, Curtis Jackson, Gloria Marlen, Lee Scott, Helen Eby-Rock, Diane Nance, Frank Hagney, Dorinda Clifton, Bern Hoffman, Peter Chong, Wanda Flippen, Kerry O'Day, Richard Keane, Royal Raymond, Jack Shea, Alex Romero, Tyra Vaughn
Released December 30, 1949
MGM
98 minutes

On the Town was a hit Broadway musical. The film rights were purchased by MGM in 1945 with the intention of having George Abbott, the stage director, also direct the movie. However, when Louis B. Mayer attended a performance of the show, he was unimpressed, regretting he had secured the film rights. The property was assigned to Stanley Donen and Gene Kelly, and arrangements were made for Betty Comden and Adolph Green to rewrite the book into a screenplay; much of Leonard Bernstein's original score was jettisoned. Songs were instead created for the movie. *On the Town* became the first musical to be shot on location.

The movie is similar in theme but superior in execution to *Anchors Aweigh* and *Take Me Out to the Ball Game*, and represents some significant milestones in Sinatra's career. It was the last film he made under his MGM contract, which ended early and badly, with the star being bought out with a year to go on the deal after a falling out with Mayer. It is arguably the best film Sinatra was in up to this point, a fact that nonetheless could not revive his flagging motion picture career. That is because, as competent as his performance is both musically and comedically, he is once again just one part of a large ensemble cast which is led by Kelly, who here not only receives top billing but also co-directs. *On the Town* is very much his show: He portrays the character at the forefront of the narrative in addition to establishing and overseeing the film's frenetic pace. Sinatra, like his lesser-known co-stars Jules Munshin and Betty Garrett, is a secondary presence.

Like Sinatra's two previous screen teamings with Kelly, *On the Town* is less interested in presenting a compelling narrative as it is in spotlighting a series of comedic and musical vignettes. What plot there is involves Kelly, Sinatra and Munshin as sailors on a 24-hour leave in New York City, endeavoring to see as many sights, and women, as possible. What makes the film work where *Take Me Out to the Ball Game* failed is the urgent pacing maintained by directors Donen and Kelly. The movie begins on a high note and continues to build momentum throughout, dragging at only one point.

The dynamic tone is set in the opening sequence. Using several New York landmarks as backdrops, Kelly and Donen employ a series of quick edits to showcase the sailors engaged in myriad activities: riding horses, bikes, buses and carriages as well as simply looking out at the city's skyline, all the while singing "New York, New York."[15] It took days to get the four minutes of footage used in the film, largely due to the difficulties inherent in setting up the equipment needed to play the pre-recorded background music to which the performers lip-synched.

Once this musical number has concluded, *On the Town* maintains its pace by essentially becoming a chase film. At first, the chasing is done by Gabey (Kelly), who falls for subway poster girl Ivy Smith (Vera-Ellen), who is known as Miss Turnstiles. Gabey enlists the aid of Chip (Sinatra) and Ozzie (Munshin) in his search. By the time Gabey finds Ivy, Chip and Ozzie have sung and danced their way into the hearts of their own women. The sextet find themselves chased by police who suspect them of vandalizing a museum exhibit on prehistoric life.

The pace is quickened further by several whirlwind production numbers, from the clownish "Prehistoric Man" (performed mainly by Ann Miller as an anthropology student who falls for Ozzie) to "Come Up to My Place," yet another sequence that finds Sinatra's Chip pursued by an aggressive woman (Garrett). The only scene that noticeably drags is a fantasy dance segment in which Gabey naively imagines the glamorous life led by Miss Turnstiles, who in reality is not a celebrity but just an ordinary woman who represents work-a-day gals throughout the city. Segments of this nature are a trademark of Kelly's although they almost always slow up a movie's narrative momentum.

Perhaps the most intriguing aspect of *On the Town*, as compared to Sinatra's earlier teamings with Kelly, as well as the majority of his prior screen work, is the subtle change in his and Kelly's characters and, therefore, in the relationship those characters have. While there can be no question that Sinatra is once again relegated to the sidekick's role, his Chip is not the same sort of sidekick audiences had grown accustomed to seeing him portray. That's because Kelly's character is a bit more like Sinatra's characters had customarily been, which in turn allows Sinatra's character to be a bit more like Kelly's had customarily been. Gabey is not a swaggering ladies' man like Kelly in *Anchors Aweigh*. Despite his desire to meet a beautiful woman, he is a bit naïve about how to do so, and so unwise to the ways of the world that he believes Ivy to be a true celebrity. This allows Chip, as played by Sinatra, to become more of an equal partner in their friendship, to the point of briefly taking the dominant role and consoling Gabey when it appears he has lost Ivy forever. Indeed, it is hard to imagine Sinatra speaking to Kelly a line like, "I know how tough you're taking this, kid," in either of their previous films. Even though Kelly is undisputedly the lead, splitting up the characters for a bit allowed everyone, Sinatra included, to really develop their characters and have their own moments.

While Sinatra once again finds himself having to fight off the advances of a woman, there is an important difference. Chip is not so much afraid of Garrett's character, Brunhilde Esterhazy, as he is uninterested. He would rather go sightseeing during his leave than chase women, a fact that makes him more mature than Gabey, who has nothing but women on his mind. Once he resigns himself to spending time with Brunhilde, Chip even becomes self-assured in her presence, confident that he has what it takes to be in control of the romantic situation. There is a level

(Left to right): Sinatra, Jules Munshin and Gene Kelly on the Brooklyn Bridge in *On the Town*, the first musical filmed on location.

of panic in Chip during the "Come Up to My Place" number, which ends with Brunhilde chasing Chip around her taxi, but he comes off as more startled by her advances than intimidated.

The good time that the stars had on screen in *On the Town* carried over into the moments when the cameras were off. Betty Garrett recalled that both Sinatra and Kelly were great fun to work with. For all the

Sinatra and Betty Garrett in *On the Town*.

camaraderie, however, Garrett recalled that Sinatra often held up production by failing to cooperate during the rehearsal process. She also remembered him as a man unsure of himself, a star who at the time was worried about the downturn his career had been taking.

In retrospect, Sinatra's behavior was understandable. In addition to the symmetricals, MGM makeup men had fitted him with a hairpiece to cover up his incipient baldness and for many scenes his ears had to be taped back. Frank Sinatra was 34 years old, his career was reaching its lowest ebb, and his looks had begun to wane.

On the Town was MGM's second biggest box office hit up to that time. Along with pleasing moviegoers, the film also pleased critics who cited it as one of the best films of the year. Even up in Canada, the critics were pleased with this colorful, energetic musical comedy: "*On the Town*, a new musical, is one of the most enjoyable pictures I have seen. It is fresh, lively, tuneful, handsome, and high-spirited."[16]

Hollywood seemed as if it couldn't get enough of the Kelly-Sinatra team. The pair was tentatively slated to star in the circus movie *Jumbo*, likely an adaptation of the 1935 Broadway musical that wound up being made into a Doris Day film in 1962. MGM also planned to star them in *Lovely to Look At*, which ultimately toplined Red Skelton and Howard Keel in 1952.

Six years after *On the Town*, when Sinatra was back on the A-list after his Oscar win, Arthur Freed produced the MGM musical *It's Always Fair Weather* (1955), which was directed by Donen and Kelly. It was suggested that the film be a sort of sequel to *On the Town*, reuniting the three sailors from that film. Kelly loved the idea, and Sinatra told the press at the time:

> I hope to do a musical with Gene Kelly. I'd love to work with that man again; he's such a great talent. They're sending me a script this week, and I hope we can do it. Comden and Green did the story, which concerns two wartime pals who reunite years later and find they have nothing in common.[17]

Apparently MGM's studio head at the time, Dore Schary, didn't want to hire Sinatra because of his difficult reputation, or Jules Munshin, because he had zero box office appeal by then. So, *It's Always Fair Weather* ended up being about three soldiers, not sailors, with Dan Dailey and Michael Kidd filling out the trio with Kelly. The film flopped.

Back in 1949, though, despite the good reviews and box office success that *On the Town* enjoyed, it would be nearly two years before Sinatra appeared in another film, and even then it was a movie that had been shot before *Take Me Out to the Ball Game* and *On the Town*. His career was slipping toward its nadir.

Double Dynamite

Directed by Irving Cummings
Screenplay: Meliville Shavelson, from a story by Leo Rosten, based on a character created by Mannie Manheim
Additional Dialogue: Harry Crane
Cinematography: Robert De Grasse (Black and White)
Editor: Harry Marker
Songs:
   "It's Only Money," "Kisses and Tears"; Music: Jule Styne; Lyrics: Sammy Cahn
Cast: Jane Russell, Groucho Marx, Frank Sinatra, Don McGuire, Howard Freeman, Nestor Paiva, Frank Orth, Harry Hayden, William Edmunds, Russell Thorson, Harry Seymour, James Nolan, Lee Phelps, George Chandler, Helen Dickson, Bill Irwin, Joe Devlin, Harry Kingson, Harold Goodwin, Lillian West, Lou Nova, Gil Perkins, Billy Snyder, Dick Rush, Al Murphy, Dick Gordon, Kermit Kegley, Harold Goodwin, Robert Haines, Wilburn Mack, Tom London, Mike Lally, Claire Du Brey, William Bailey, Fred Aldrich, Jean De Briac

Double Dynamite (1951)

Released December 25, 1951
RKO
80 minutes

This labored comedy was filmed between November 22 and mid-December 1948, but shelved by RKO chief Howard Hughes. It illustrates how far Sinatra's star had plummeted. When it was shot, it was titled *It's Only Money*, and Sinatra received top billing over Groucho Marx and Jane Russell. By the time Hughes reconsidered and released it, however, it had been retitled *Double Dynamite*, a cheap reference to Jane Russell's bust. Russell received top billing. Sinatra was considered such a spoiled commodity that he wasn't even shown in the movie's advertisements. Instead those ads featured Groucho leering at Russell's ample chest below the ad line "Everything Goes Double When Jane and Groucho Start Foolin' Around." All this despite the fact that Sinatra portrayed the film's main character, and that Marx and Russell shared only three scenes.

Most of the reason for this is that Sinatra's personal life had been making headlines that turned off postwar America. There were well-publicized affairs with actresses Marilyn Maxwell, Lana Turner and Joi Lansing. But it was his tumultuous affair with Ava Gardner that was serious enough to break up his marriage. Despite the fact that *On the Town* was a big hit, MGM released him from his contract and Sinatra was offscreen for all of 1950. That year opened with the death of his long-time publicist and friend George Evans. In April, Sinatra had to cancel a performance at the Copa in New York due to a throat hemorrhage. By the time *Double Dynamite* hit movie screens, the name "Frank Sinatra" was no longer one that ensured box office success.

Whatever the title and whatever the billing of *Double Dynamite*, the fact remains that this is an uninspired film that Hughes should have left on the shelf. Sinatra is cast as Johnny Dalton, a milquetoast bank teller in love with a fellow teller, Mildred Goodhug (pronounced good-hugh, but obviously someone's idea of a humorous pun), portrayed by Russell. The two would like to marry, but Johnny doesn't think they have enough money, so they wallow about in romantic limbo, occasionally patronizing a restaurant where Emile J. Keck (Marx) works as a waiter.

As fate, and the uneven script, would have it, Johnny comes to the rescue of a bookie who is getting roughed up in an alley. The bookie rewards him by placing bets in Johnny's name on a series of horses; all of them win. When the day is over, Johnny has $60,000 and no more excuses for not marrying Mildred. However, when he returns to the bank, he discovers $75,000 is missing and that his boss (Harry Hayden) thinks it was stolen by a teller. Fearful of being accused of the crime, Johnny keeps his good fortune a secret and spends the rest of the movie trying to find a way to spend his money without implicating himself in a crime he didn't commit. His resulting confusion puts a strain on his relationship with Mildred, and leaves him plenty of opportunity to get into trouble with Emile, to whom he eventually explains his predicament. In an on-the-nose case of *deus ex machina*, everything is resolved tidily when it turns out that Mildred's broken adding machine created the mistaken impression that money was missing from the vault.

While *Double Dynamite* is not without its share of laughs, its only truly funny moments have nothing to do with the narrative. Most of the humor comes from Marx tossing off one-liners and asides during the dialogue exchanges, or via scenarios concocted to spotlight his comic persona. For instance, a scene in which Emile attempts to deposit Johnny's gambling winnings in the bank where Johnny works is a fun excuse for Groucho to display his noted insult humor by making fun of the bank manager. The money never gets deposited, and Johnny later tells Emile not to deposit it there. So, the scene has no organic connection to the narrative. It's just a set-piece to spotlight Groucho. Later, the comedian has a scene in which he impersonates a millionaire. It too has nothing to do with the flow of the story; it's just a scene for Groucho to be funny. And he is. But it is a tangential distraction from the plot.

For her part, Russell is window dressing, smiling demurely as the film shamelessly exploits her physical attributes. Not only does veteran director Irving Cummings (helming his final film) take every opportunity to shoot her in revealing profile, but a scene in her apartment shows her dressed in a low-cut robe. During this same scene, the camera luridly spies as she suggestively removes both of her stockings, her robe hiked up well past mid-thigh. When the police suspect Mildred and Johnny of stealing the $75,000, a dispatcher is heard reading an all-points bulletin that describes her as "five foot seven inches, 135 pounds, *extremely* well distributed." While a case can be made that such a depiction constitutes exploitation, that is not the most troubling aspect of the way in which the film presents Russell. The script treats her character as a naïve, innocent woman, something certainly not borne out in the way she is depicted.

Sinatra's Johnny, although ostensibly the character around which the action revolves, is a diminished presence since the film is more interested in spotlighting Marx's trademark comedy and Russell's curvaceous figure. The picture lacks momentum whenever he is on-screen, yet his scenes are ostensibly those designed to propel the narrative. He looks terminally bored in some scenes, unhealthily thin in most (Johnny is described in his APB as "wearing elevator shoes, anemic looking, sporting an ill-fitting suit and looks like Frank Sinatra"). Most notable is his failure to shine even during the two musical numbers. This is surprising, since while his acting had many times been uninspired, even flat, in prior films, he could always rise to the occasion during the musical sequences. The first number, "It's Only Money," is a brief, joyless duet with Marx, mostly undone by amateurish backdrop matting designed to look like a city street. More telling of the degree to which Sinatra had sunk as a musical presence is his "Kisses and Tears" duet with Russell, which abandons the premise upon which his earlier screen singing had relied. Instead of focusing on Sinatra's face as he croons the ballad, the camera goes tight on Russell and registers her reaction to his singing. This seemed to indicate that Sinatra's days as a sex symbol to be swooned over had passed. That scene is also dully static in the way it is staged, with both characters literally lying in bed, not even in the same room.

Sinatra's scenes with Groucho are a bit better. They have decent chemistry with the more-straight Sinatra countering Groucho's zaniness. But they are not enough to redeem the feature in the end. Critics savaged the movie and Sinatra's performance in it. *The Brooklyn Daily Eagle* called it

Sinatra (left), Jane Russell and Groucho Marx mug for the camera in *Double Dynamite*.

a "dud" and added that Sinatra's performance as a comedian "consists of being bewildered, period."[18] The *Pittsburgh Sun-Telegraph* called the film a "painfully inept comedy" and, while noting that Marx was responsible for any merits it had, dismissed Sinatra (and Russell) as "not even in the running."[19]

Once the ticket window receipts for *Double Dynamite* were tabulated, it appeared that Sinatra was finished. His affair with Ava Gardner and divorce from his wife had badly tarnished his public image. He badly needed a comeback film. He would not find it in his next outing—although he would plant the seeds for his motion picture career resurgence.

Meet Danny Wilson

Directed by Joseph Pevney
Story and Screenplay: Don McGuire
Producers: Leonard Goldstein and Don McGuire
Cinematography: Maury Gertsman (Black and White)
Editor: Virgil Vogel
Songs:
   "You're a Sweetheart"; Music: Jimmy McHugh; Lyrics: Harold Adamson
   "Lonesome Man Blues"; Written by Sy Oliver
   "She's Funny That Way"; Music: Neil Moret; Lyrics: Richard A. Whiting
   "A Good Man Is Hard to Find"; Written by Eddie Green
   "That Old Black Magic"; Music: Harold Arlen; Lyrics: Johnny Mercer
   "When You're Smiling"; Written by Mark Fisher, Joe Goodwin and Larry Shay
   "All of Me"; Music: Gerald Marks; Lyrics: Seymour Simons
   "I've Got a Crush on You"; Music: George Gershwin; Lyrics: Ira Gershwin
   "How Deep Is the Ocean?"; Written by Irving Berlin
Cast: Frank Sinatra, Shelley Winters, Alex Nicol, Raymond Burr, Vaughn Taylor, Tommy Farrell, Donald MacBride, Barbara Knudson, Carl Sklover, George Eldredge, Bob Donnelly, Pat Flaherty, Colin Kenny, Herbert Lytton, Bob Perry, Ezelle Poule, John Albright, Danny Welton, Phil Arnold, Sue Casey, James Casino, Harold Bostwick, Steve Carruthers, Eddie Coontz, Jack Kruschen, Sandra Farrell, Oliver Cross, Paul Ely, Tom Dillon, Jack Chefe, Sayre Dearing, John Dix, Bobby Faye, Bess Flowers, John

Daheim, Helen Dickson, Kenner Kemp, Charles Horvath, George Ford, Cindy Garner, Charmienne Harker, Jimmie Horan, Paul Kellett, Stuart Holmes, John Indrisano, George Garver, Robert Haines, Earl Lee, Gregg Palmer, Jeanne Tatum, Noreen Michaels, Donna Leary, Forbes Murray, Frank McLure, Bert Keyes, Mike Lally, Carlos Molina, Morty Langer, Lee Miller, Hans Moebus, Bruce Sharp, Phil Resnick, Jack Perry, Bob Reeves, Rose Plumer, Bernard Sell, Ken Terrell, George Wallace, Sally Yarnell, Bert Stevens, Ned Roberts, Albin Robeling, Brick Sullivan, Sam Wolfe, Frank Scannell, Louis Yung, Pete Virgo, Charlie Parlota, Leo Sulky; cameos by Tony Curtis and Jeff Chandler
Released April 1, 1952
Universal-International
88 minutes

In 1951, Sinatra's career remained at low ebb. The audiences for his live performances were dwindling, the nadir being a stop at the Chez Paree in Chicago that attracted only around 150 people in a room that held 1200. His long-time record company, Columbia, decided not to renew his contract.

Despite this, Universal-International still felt the singer had some potential. The studio signed him to a three-year non-exclusive contract to make movies. Louella Parsons reported in her syndicated column, "Those crepe-hangers who said Frank was through in pictures may now cheerfully choke on their words."[20]

Sinatra was excited to start a new film project that might rejuvenate his big-screen career, and wanted to get into production quickly in order to collect the $25,000 he was promised for the role. That plan was thwarted when Shelley Winters, signed to play his love interest, went to Europe with beau Farley Granger and refused to report to the set. The studio suspended her, and the film's production was delayed more than a month. Sinatra opened an office in Hollywood, with an apartment in the back where he lived while the movie was being filmed.

Sinatra plays the title character crooner in *Meet Danny Wilson*, with Alex Nicol as his partner, pianist and pal Mike Ryan. Club singer Joy Carroll (Winters) pays their bail when the two get into yet another of their many fights, which are usually due to Danny's hot temper (this time Danny punched a cop). Joy sings for gangster club owner Nick Driscoll (Raymond Burr), who hires Danny after an audition and then, seeing his potential for success, insists on a 50 percent cut. Meanwhile, a love triangle develops among Danny, Mike and Joy. She loves Mike, who does not want to move in on his best friend's girl, while Danny announces their engagement without first telling her. When Danny discovers his buddy is romancing his betrothed, he gets drunk and bombs at a club gig. In a confrontation with Nick, Mike jumps in front of a bullet intended for Danny. Later, Danny has a late-night meeting with Nick at a park, with police lurking nearby. Danny plans to get even with Nick and a gunfight breaks out, but the police step in. All is forgiven between Danny and Mike. The last scene shows Danny successfully entertaining at a club, with Mike and Joy in attendance to cheer him on.

Meet Danny Wilson was a watershed film in Sinatra's screen career, as it afforded him his first opportunity to portray a character whose primary qualities were something other than naivete, shyness and sincerity. Danny is full of complexity and complications—a man who is cocky yet insecure, caring yet temperamental, crude yet charming: in short, everything the static characters Sinatra had portrayed all through the 1940s were not. He conveys the subtle emotional responses required of the role, deftly handling the comedic and musical moments, which came as no surprise to anyone, while at the same time displaying depth as a dramatic actor. It can be argued that Sinatra delivers one of the finest all-around performances of his career here. While he certainly did more distinguished work in other strictly comedic, musical or dramatic roles, his performance in a single film in all three areas was only bested (and, to be fair, clearly so) by his work in *Pal Joey* five years later.

Perhaps this is because Danny Wilson is more like Frank Sinatra than any other character he ever portrayed—including Joey Evans. Danny is a brash, hotheaded crooner who struggles for years, singing for small change in saloons, before he gets his break and becomes a sensation, attracting hordes of female fans who shriek uncontrollably each time he steps up to the microphone. This is, of course, a summary of Sinatra's rise to prominence, and the fact that the script was written by his friend Don McGuire leaves little doubt that it was intended as such. That Danny only gets his shot after Nick agrees to assist him augments the picture's verisimilitude, given the rumors which linked Sinatra to powerful underworld figures since the start of his career.

Sinatra's command of the character is especially evident in a brief café scene with Winters. Although it is devoid of action (the two sit at a table talking), Sinatra conjures an array of emotions—cockiness, sweetness, innocence, admiration—simply through conversation and facial expressions. It is an effortless performance, alternately comic and serious, suffering from none of the tentativeness apparent in much of his earlier work, when he was portraying, at the studios' insistence, characters with whom he had little in common.

Danny and Mike's buddy relationship is more richly developed than

Sinatra's on-screen friendships with Gene Kelly. While in those earlier films Sinatra was called on to be little more than the wide-eyed sidekick, here he is the duo's unquestioned leader, the one who makes decisions for the pair, many of them misguided. Although their dialogue exchanges are often inane (at one point, Mike tells Danny, "You stink!"), Sinatra and Nicol rarely hit a false note in their interplay, capturing the humorous, frivolous, confrontational and poignant moments that comprise all close friendships. One never doubts that the characters care for one another, or wonders why they would, something which can't be said with similar confidence about many of Sinatra's prior screen friendships. The depth of their relationship is clear in the pivotal sequence when Joy confesses her love to Mike, unaware that Danny is listening from the next room. Sinatra directs most of his anger at Nicol, using a simple, pained stare to impart both the resentment and hurt of what Danny views as a betrayal by the one person closest to him. When Mike and Joy leave, Sinatra's expression leaves little doubt as to who Danny will miss more.

Sinatra also fared well in the film's musical moments, primarily because the structure allowed him to capture the essence of what made him such an exciting performer. As Danny is a crooner, Sinatra is free to

Sinatra used his performance as Danny in *Meet Danny Wilson* (pictured) to help secure his role in *From Here to Eternity*.

sing as a performer on stage, not as an actor in a true musical; he is therefore able to run through the same effective mannerisms that enthralled his real-life audiences. No singer before him, and none since, has been able to wring so much emotion from a song simply by the way he maneuvered a microphone stand, at times cradling it gently like a dance partner.

That Sinatra performed so well in *Meet Danny Wilson* is no small feat, considering the turmoil in his personal and professional lives at the time. Not surprisingly, his offscreen problems made for a hectic set. In her 1980 autobiography, Shelley Winters wrote that the film "began shooting in chaos and ended in disaster"—although she conveniently fails to mention her own initial drag on the production:

> Frank was in the process of divorcing Nancy to marry Ava Gardner. His children were quite young and there were always psychiatrists and priests and his kids visiting him on the set or in the commissary. The priest was a very nice man, but the afternoons he visited Frank on the set we all might as well have gone home. Frank was truly impossible and so disturbed that he couldn't hear anything that anybody said to him, including the other actors, the crew, and the director Joe Pevney.[21]

As a result, the artistic chemistry between Winters and Sinatra quickly soured, and the two bickered throughout filming. According to Winters, during one argument Sinatra called her a "bowlegged bitch of a Brooklyn blonde" and that she retaliated by calling him "a skinny, no-talent, stupid Hoboken bastard."

Although Sinatra never publicly gave his side of the story, Raymond Burr said in a 1991 interview with author Gary Schneeberger that many of the film's squabbles were attributable to Winters:

> We had a couple of problem people on that shoot and she was one of them. She had a particular way of working and Frank had a particular way of working, and she didn't appreciate that his way was different. Actually, I was quite shocked that she didn't write about me because I was a problem to her in one scene. But I had worked with her twice before where she had been just exasperating. The worst thing about the whole experience for me is that Frank really needed that picture, needed to have it good, and although he was marvelous in it, it didn't do well when it came out as far as box office.[22]

Indeed, *Meet Danny Wilson* was a failure; even a personal appearance by Sinatra for the film's opening at the Paramount in New York did not ensure a full house.

Still, *Meet Danny Wilson* turned out to be instrumental in resurrecting his acting career, since it helped him land his role in *From Here to Eternity*. As author Tom Santopietro notes, it "represents the first comprehensive and decisive proof that Frank Sinatra had the makings of a dramatic actor. As such, it's an important precursor of what Sinatra was capable of onscreen, capabilities that were to be fully expressed in *From Here to Eternity*."[23]

Sinatra knew it, too. To prove he could handle the role of Maggio in that film, he arranged for the unit publicist to see *Meet Danny Wilson* as an indication of what he was capable of as an actor. Everything was about to turn golden for Frank Sinatra.

From Here to Eternity

Directed by Fred Zinnemann
Screenplay: Daniel Taradash, from a novel by James Jones
Producer: Buddy Adler
Cinematography: Burnett Guffey (Black and White)
Editor: William A. Lyon
Cast: Burt Lancaster, Montgomery Clift, Deborah Kerr, Frank Sinatra, Philip Ober, Mickey Shaughnessy, Harry Bellaver, Ernest Borgnine, Jack Warden, John Dennis, Merle Travis, Tim Ryan, Arthur Keegan, Barbara Morrison, Claude Akins, Jean Willes, George Reeves, Carleton Young, Joan Shawlee, Bea Benaderet, Angela Stevens, John Bryant, Robert Karnes, Don Dubbins, John Cason, Guy Way, Robert J. Wilke, Delia Salvi, Fay Roope, Manny Klein, Robert Karnes, Douglas Henderson, Elaine DuPont, Edward Laguna, Robert Pike, Carey Leverett, Joe Roach, Weaver Levy, Brick Sullivan, June Horne
Released August 28, 1953
Columbia
118 minutes

When James Jones' novel *From Here to Eternity* won the National Book Award for fiction, every Hollywood studio became interested in the film rights. The 1951 novel, set in the military leading up to the Japanese attack on Pearl Harbor, had enough tension, romance and conflict to attract American readers in the postwar era. The only drawback regarding a movie version was the challenge that a scenarist would encounter when attempting to transfer the seamy passages into cinema during a period when the Production Code was still enforced. Columbia president Harry Cohn bought the movie rights to the book for $82,000 and assigned the screenplay to Daniel Taradash. Taradash had scored with his screenplays for *Knock on Any Door* (1949) with Humphrey Bogart and *Don't Bother to Knock* (1952) with Marilyn Monroe.

On October 23, 1952, Bob Thomas' syndicated column reported Columbia's interest in filming the book:

> They said it couldn't be done. But a producer has gotten a movie script out of *From Here to Eternity*, the best-selling book laden with sex, four-letter words and set in the army. Many Hollywood producers had been interested in the James Jones novel. But most despaired of how to combine its elements into a movie that would get the combined blessing of the censors and Pentagon. Columbia took a chance and bought the book. The gamble apparently has paid off, because the studio claims it has an acceptable script which will be before the cameras in January. The man who accomplished this is Buddy Adler, a distinguished-looking producer who is a reserve army officer himself. The producer takes off this week to scout locations with Director Fred Zinnemann. So far, Montgomery Clift is the only casting; he'll play Pruitt [sic]. ... Among the others is Frank Sinatra, who requested a test as the Italian G.I.[24]

Reports in the press regarding Sinatra's interest in the role of Maggio date back to early September 1952. They also indicate that Aldo Ray was originally hired for the Prewitt role before he was replaced by Clift. The role of Sergeant Warden eventually went to Burt Lancaster after being offered to Humphrey Bogart and Marlon Brando.

Deborah Kerr had been noted for playing prim, proper characters so she was pleased to be hired for the layered role of an officer's wife having an affair with the sergeant. Donna Reed was also cast against type as a prostitute. The role was going to be played by Joan Crawford, but her demands, including insisting on her own personal cameraman, were rejected.

Zinnemann had scored big with the recent *High Noon* and *The Member of the Wedding*, but was likely hired mostly on the strength of his 1950 drama *The Men*, which dealt with a paralyzed war veteran attempting to adjust to civilian life, and featured Brando in an early role. Harry Cohn was against hiring Clift for the role of Prewitt, preferring Aldo Ray, because Cohn said Clift was "not a boxer, not a bugler, and he's probably a homosexual." Zinnemann stood his ground and refused to make the film if Clift did not get the role.

Sinatra was not the first one in mind for the role of Maggio. Eli Wallach was offered the part. Frank stated: "When I heard that Eli Wallach was testing for the part, I thought I was dead. He was such a good actor!"[25] However, Wallach could not take the job due to his commitment to appear on Broadway in Elia Kazan's *Camino Real*. Even when Sinatra was doing screen tests for the role, actor Harvey Lembeck was also being considered. When Lembeck instead accepted a role in Billy Wilder's *Stalag 17*, it cleared the way for Sinatra.

Sinatra had been flying to and from Africa where wife Ava Gardner was working on location in the film *Mogambo* with Clark Gable. His marriage was falling apart and it was overwhelming him emotionally. Plus, Cohn refused to pay for Sinatra's screen test, expecting him to fund it himself.

There have long been rumors surrounding how Sinatra landed the role of Maggio. Some claim that Ava Gardner asked Cohn's wife to use her influence to help Frank get the role. The most notorious claim is that Sinatra used his organized crime connections to land the role. This extended to the famous scene in *The Godfather* (1972) in which singer Al Martino plays a Sinatra-type character who begs the crime don to help him get the role. When the producer is adamantly against it, he finds the severed head of his prized horse in his bed. This is one of the most well-known scenes in motion pictures, so there are many who believe that it is indeed how Sinatra was cast.

However, *From Here to Eternity* cast members, director and producer are on record as insisting that Sinatra was cast as a result of his screen test. In fact, during that test, Frank played Maggio drunk in a bar, and ad-libbed grabbing a couple of olives and rolling them like dice. Zinnemann was so impressed, he kept that bit in the movie.

From Here to Eternity is a series of separate subplots that connect in the end. Clift is Private Prewitt, a bugler who has a reputation as a boxer, but after blinding a man in the ring, he refused to fight again. Because of this, Captain Holmes (Philip Ober) allows the other soldiers to make things difficult for Prewitt in order to goad him into joining their company's boxing unit. Prewitt also takes up with Lorene (Donna Reed), whom he first sees at the Officers' Club. She works for the club in an effort to make the soldiers happy, but Prewitt wants to genuinely get to know her, and not merely use her for sex.

Lancaster's Sergeant Warden is having an affair with Karen Holmes, the wife of Captain Holmes, who neglects her. Holmes respects Warden and has no idea he is having a fling with his wife, but he does know that *something* is going on. He believes the Other Man to be a civilian. Karen wants Warden to become an officer so she can marry him and divorce her husband.

Sinatra's role of Angelo Maggio serves several purposes. He is supportive of his friend Prewitt when the other soldiers give him a hard time. And he has a serious conflict with the imposing "Fatso" Judson (Ernest Borgnine), a guard in charge of the stockade.

Maggio is a small, slender man who is a compassionate, supportive friend, but also has a bit of a chip on his shoulder, feeling he needs to prove himself. He first confronts Fatso at an Officers' Club where the bigger man is playing the piano; Maggio tells him he doesn't like his piano playing. Fatso responds violently and Prewitt breaks it up. Later in the film, a drunken Maggio stumbles into the bar and reveals he is skipping guard duty; he ends up in the stockade. When Prewitt inquires about him, he is told by a recently released prisoner that Fatso has been brutally beating Maggio with a club, but Maggio just defiantly spits in his face.

While it is only in a supporting role, Sinatra's performance as Maggio effectively resonates throughout the production. The character is well-drawn, with complex levels to his personality. Sinatra drew upon his own feelings to better inform his performance. He himself was also a volatile man, a small man with something to prove, and a man who could be tough and defiant. Sinatra was not only able to tap into these aspects of his own personality; he could also use the anger and frustration he was feeling as his marriage was collapsing. Sinatra was taking the dissolution of their marriage hard, and was working on reconciling as he tackled this do-or-die movie project. He was able to use these feelings as another aspect of the character.

Broken and battered, Maggio escapes the stockade and finds his way to Prewitt. He tells him how he's been defiant to Fatso, but this latest beating was too much for him. He dies in Prewitt's arms. When Prewitt later confronts Fatso, the guard is cavalier about the entire situation:

> PREWITT: Remember Maggio?
> FATSO: Oh, the wop? Yeah, real tough monkey.
> PREWITT: You killed him.
> FATSO: Did I? Well if I did, he asked for it.

Prewitt confronts Fatso, who pulls a knife. Prewitt figured he would, so he also pulls out a switchblade, the same one used to kill Maggio. Prewitt ends up seriously injured. Fatso ends up dead.

Ernest Borgnine and Sinatra did not know each other before the movie, and became friends on the project. In his autobiography, Borgnine stated that when he heard Sinatra was cast as Maggio, he thought they were going to somehow make the film into a musical. Borgnine needed the role of Fatso to be significant for him, as his career was also stalled. It would be a couple of years before he scored in the Oscar winner *Marty* (1955). Borgnine recalled:

> The way the set was constructed, Sinatra was down in a sort of pit to make me look larger. We did the scene a few times, but let me tell you, I swore allegiance and everything else to Frank Sinatra. Frank was scared too, he told me later. His film and recording career had kind of hit a slump and this was an important comeback for him. Despite the pressure he was feeling, he did everything he could to make sure I was comfortable and that I looked good.[26]

To the end of Sinatra's life, he and Borgnine sent each other birthday and Christmas cards, signing them Fatso and Maggio.

From Here to Eternity (1953)

Not everyone was fond of Sinatra, who was often tense and demanding on the set because so much rode on the results. Actress Nancy Carver, a Broadway actress who was just starting what would be a long film career, recalls her experience with Sinatra as quite a negative one. In an interview with actor Jim Beaver, she stated:

> I was in the dance hall scenes. I hated working with Frank Sinatra, he was really terrible. He was very nasty. Joan Shawlee was the madam. He got nasty with her and she said, "Look here, you son of a bitch, you do that again and I'll pick you up and throw you across the set." People almost applauded. He was good, but he was a bastard.

Frank Sinatra's alleged "nastiness" did not apparently extend to everyone. Frank would recall for the rest of his life how much he picked up from working with Montgomery Clift, an intense Method actor. Clift learned boxing to be more believable in the role, and even mastered the bugle, despite knowing that his playing would be dubbed. A scene where Prewitt is confronted by a Sergeant Galkovich (John Dennis) is emotionally stirring. Galkovich, attempting to goad Prewitt into representing the company's boxing unit, ends up in a fistfight with the private. At first,

Sinatra (right) won an Oscar for his performance in *From Here to Eternity*, giving him confidence as an actor. Pictured: Montgomery Clift, Sinatra.

Prewitt tries to duck and avoid the punches. Eventually his anger allows him to give his opponent several body shots, but he won't go near Galkovich's face. Finally, as he is being soundly beaten, Prewitt fights back with all of his skills and overpowers the other man. The officer in charge does nothing to stop it.

Much of *From Here to Eternity* concerns top-billed Burt Lancaster and Deborah Kerr, including their famous kiss on the sands of the beach as the waves wash over them. They are perhaps the focal point of the episodic narrative, but Clift was second-billed (apparently to the actor's chagrin) and his story is another important part of the story. He turns in an exceptional performance.

Critics were impressed with *From Here to Eternity*, with *Variety*'s critic William Brogdon stating:

> Frank Sinatra scores a decided hit as Angelo Maggio, a violent, likable Italo-American G.I. While some may be amazed at this expression of the Sinatra talent versatility, it will come as no surprise to those who remember the few times he has had a chance to be something other than a crooner in films.[27]

John McCarten of *The New Yorker* concurred, stating that *From Here to Eternity* reveals that Sinatra "is a first-rate actor."[28]

Sinatra won an Academy Award for his performance. He also signed a contract with Capitol Records, working with arranger Nelson Riddle on some new recordings. As 1953 closed, he was a respected movie actor and his music was again back on the charts.

Suddenly

Directed by Lewis Allen
Screenplay: Richard Sale
Producer: Robert Bassler
Cinematography: Charles G. Clarke (Black and White)
Editor: John F. Schreyer
Cast: Frank Sinatra, Sterling Hayden, James Gleason, Nancy Gates, Kim Charney, Willis Bouchey, Paul Frees, Christopher Dark, James O'Hara, Ken Dibbs, Clark Howat, Charles Smith, Paul Wexler, Richard Collier, Dan White, Roy Engel, John Beradino, Charles Wagenheim, Ted Stanhope
Released September 17, 1954
Libra Productions for United Artists
77 minutes

Suddenly (1954)

Sinatra turns in a bravura performance in this slick thriller about a calculating drifter's attempt to assassinate the president of the United States. The film is a morality play that examines the fine line between evil and heroism, and it is more than a decade before its time in at least partially examining the ethics of war, a theme that did not come to full fruition until the post–Vietnam era. In this case, it is the Korean War that comes under scrutiny—and the good-vs.-evil struggle at the core of the story provides for an intense, thought-provoking ride.

The film's title refers to the small California town where the story takes place. Director Lewis Allen's establishing shots project an innocence and tranquility that are typical of small towns in movies—and set the stage for what's to come. Screenwriter Richard Sale's narrative begins with dialogue between Deputy Sheriff Slim Adams (Paul Wexler) and a passing motorist who comments on the town's unusual name. "That's a hangover from the old days," the deputy explains. "That's the way things used to happen around here." He adds that much has changed since those old days, because "things happen so slowly here now, the town council is thinking of changing the name to Gradually."

The narrative next introduces the family at the center of the story. Pidge Benson (Kim Charney), eight-year-old son of Ellen Benson (Nancy Gates), complains to Sheriff Tod Shaw (Sterling Hayden) that his mother won't let him have a toy gun. Ellen's husband, Pidge's father, was killed in the Korean War, which has resulted in her being repulsed at the idea of gunplay. The sheriff scolds Ellen, explaining that guns aren't bad, it's the people handling them. "When a house is on fire, everybody has to help put it out," he tells her. "Because the next time, it might be your house."

These scenes foreshadow the arrival of John Baron (Sinatra), a sadistic criminal who comes to Suddenly with a pair of thugs (Paul Frees and Christopher Dark) to kill the president, whom they discover will be stopping in town by train for a fishing trip. By the time Shaw is alerted by visiting Secret Service agents of the president's arrival, Baron and his men are already executing their plan, for which they will be paid $500,000. That plan involves taking over the house of Ellen's father-in-law, Pop Benson (James Gleason), which provides them the ideal vantage point from which to shoot the president. Once the would-be assassins—who enter the home impersonating FBI agents—kill a Secret Service officer and take the Benson family and the sheriff hostage, the themes foreshadowed in the opening sequence are played out as the arrival of the president's train draws nearer. With Baron in town, events in Suddenly are once again going to occur as in the old days. In fact, the government code name for the president's visit is "Hangover," the same word Deputy Adams used when referring to the town's fast-paced past.

The central issue explored in *Suddenly* is the nature of good and evil, and how those concepts are not as disparate as one might first think. It is played out in the struggle between Baron and Shaw, men of similar experience on quite divergent paths at the moment those paths cross. Although both men are World War II veterans who have killed in combat, Baron has become a criminal, a killer for hire, while Shaw has become a law enforcement officer, a protector of rights. The film posits that at the root of their differences are their contrasting views on the function served by the guns

Sinatra played a cold-blooded assassin in *Suddenly*.

they have grown adept at using. Shaw views a gun as an object which is not good or bad unto itself, but which takes on the characteristics of the person using it. It is only a negative force when the intent of its wielder is negative. Baron, conversely, believes his gun to be a tool of empowerment, an object that makes him strong, and hence "right," regardless of his reason for using it.

This analysis is supported throughout the film by the actions of the two men. Baron repeatedly taunts Shaw, referring to him sarcastically as "brave boy," clearly enjoying being in control of the sort of man who customarily has control in society. Shaw bides his time, accepting the killer's taunts tacitly until he can pinpoint a flaw in Baron's plan and hatch a plan of his own. The subject of their differing view on guns is not addressed directly until the denouement, when Shaw—recognizing that talking might be Baron's weakness—begins badgering him for bullying Pidge and the other hostages:

> SHAW: Don't play God because you've got a gun!
> BARON: But you see, sheriff, that's the way it is. When you've got a gun, you are a sort of god. If you had the gun, I'd be the chump, and you'd be the god. The gun gives you the power of life and death.
> You must have had it during the war. You could miss a man if you had

a mind to. Or you could kill him dead in his tracks. And that makes you a kind of god. And I liked it. Without the gun I'm nothing, and I never had anything before I got one. First time I got one in my hand and killed a man, then I got some self-respect. I was somebody.

In the end, good triumphs over evil, and Baron proves he is indeed nobody without the benefit of a gun. His plan comes apart when Jud Hobson (James Lilburn), a young TV repairman also being held hostage, runs the electricity from the set through the metal table onto which Baron has bolted his rifle. When one of the henchmen touches the gun, he is electrocuted. In the ensuing commotion, Baron is shot, and just before he dies, no longer in possession of his gun, he loses his self-confidence and begs Shaw not to kill him. He has lost the power of life and death and, in his moral economy, he has become the chump.

Screenwriter Sale got the idea for his screenplay when he read newspaper accounts of President Dwight D. Eisenhower traveling to and from Palm Springs, California, by train. The script raises several pertinent issues in examining the possible reasons why Baron has turned evil. In one exchange, it is suggested that his war experience may have been a contributing factor. Baron muses about how the same skills that labeled him a good soldier in wartime—he claims to have killed 23 Germans and earned a Silver Star—now make him a criminal in peacetime. In another scene, Sale hypothesizes that a dysfunctional childhood or failed marriage might be the cause of Baron's ruthlessness. While Baron is alone with Ellen, she asks him whether he has any feelings at all, given the callous, flippant manner he exhibits as he waits to kill the president:

> No, I haven't, lady. They were taken out of me by experts. Feeling's a trap. Show me a guy with feelings and I'll show you a sucker. It's a weakness, makes you think of something besides yourself. If I had any feelings left, they'd all be for myself.

In the end, Sale doesn't allow Baron to pass the buck for his murderous impulses. It is made clear that Baron turned out bad and Shaw turned out good because Baron enjoys killing and Shaw does not; Baron sees it as an action, Shaw as a reaction. The screenwriter deals in much the same manner with the secondary theme of *Suddenly*: the ethical issues of war in general and the Korean conflict in particular. His script raises several questions about the propriety of war, not just in the case of Baron and what he has become, but also via the history of Ellen, who despises guns and violence of any kind, ever since her husband's death in combat. Yet, it is Ellen, ironically, who must pick up a gun and shoot Baron once his plan goes awry. She is forced by a second tragic circumstance to live out the point of Shaw's earlier speech: "When a house is on fire, everybody has to help put it out."

Sinatra holds Kim Charney (left), Nancy Gates and Sterling Hayden hostage in *Suddenly*.

Suddenly is structured simply, yet still expertly conveys complex themes and an intense feeling of fear. It's less than 80 minutes long, almost entirely set in the same place. We never learn exactly why Baron is going to assassinate the president, or for whom. But we don't need to know. Maybe it's that sense of not knowing that contributes to the suspense.

The strength of the script, its layers of conflict and its powerful dialogue are matched by the performances of the actors, especially Sinatra and Hayden, whose acting styles are as polar as their characters' dispositions. Sinatra, short and slight, brings an almost demonic edge to his portrayal of Baron, a tough guy not because of who he is but because of the gun he carries. Hayden, conversely, is a tall, imposing presence whose low-key approach to playing Shaw indicates the character has none of Baron's insecurities. That makes it pretty clear who is going to win in the end—and yet the journey there is taut. One of the most effective mannerisms Sinatra brings to the role is a crooked, half-sneering smile that he wears every time Baron kills or threatens someone. It conveys the character's evil while suggesting there is a deeply rooted problem causing that evil.

Suddenly, coming on the heels of *From Here to Eternity,* solidified Sinatra's reestablished stardom. He'd now racked up back-to-back movies in which he played serious dramatic roles. Back-to-back movies in which he does no singing. Back-to-back movies that obliterated any cinematic misfires of the past.

At the same time, signing with Capitol Records and collaborating with Nelson Riddle reignited his recording career. Songs like "A Foggy Day," "I Get a Kick Out of You," "My Funny Valentine," "Violets for Your Furs" and "They Can't Take That Away from Me" put him back on top on the music charts. Considered a has-been in 1952, Sinatra was more successful than he ever had been in 1954. The film roles would start coming in fast and furious, kicking off his busiest, most critically successful five-year run as an actor.

Young at Heart

Directed by Gordon Douglas
Screenplay: Jules Epstein and Lenore Coffee, from the story "Sister Act" by Fannie Hurst, adapted by Liam O'Brien
Producer: Henry Blanke
Cinematography: Ted McCord (Color)
Editor: William Ziegler
Songs:
"Just One of Those Things"; Written by Cole Porter
"Someone to Watch Over Me"; Music: George Gershwin; Lyrics: Ira Gershwin
"One for My Baby (and One More for the Road)"; Music: Harold Arlen; Lyrics: Johnny Mercer
"Hold Me in Your Arms"; Written by Ray Heindorf, Charles Henderson and Don Pippin
"Ready, Willing and Able"; Written by Floyd Huddleston, Al Rinker and Dick Gleason
"Till My Love Comes Back to Me"; Lyrics: Paul Francis Webster; Music: Felix Mendelssohn-Bartholdy
"There's a Rising Moon for Every Falling Star"; Music: Sammy Fain; Lyrics: Paul Francis Webster
"You, My Love"; Music: Jimmy Van Heusen; Lyrics: Mack Gordon
"Young at Heart"; Music: Johnny Richards; Lyrics: Carolyn Leigh

Cast: Frank Sinatra, Doris Day, Gig Young, Ethel Barrymore, Dorothy Malone, Robert Keith, Elisabeth Fraser, Alan Hale, Jr., Lonny Chapman, Frank Ferguson, Marjorie Bennett, Barbara Pepper, Kathleen Case, Jack Perrin, Kid Chissell, Celeste Bryant, Bill McLean, Michael Cirillo, Wanda Barbour, Jay Lawrence, Joseph Forte, Robin Raymond, Murray Pollack, Forbes Murray, Beulah Christian, Grazia Narciso, Tito Vuolo, Harte Wayne, Steve Wooten, Edward McNally, Ivan Browning, John Maxwell

Released December 29, 1954

Arwin Productions for Warner Bros.

117 minutes

In 1938, Warner Bros. released *Four Daughters,* which featured John Garfield in his movie debut, Claude Rains and Priscilla Lane. It was nominated for several Oscars, including Garfield as Best Supporting Actor. There were several sequels and even a partial reworking, *Daughters Courageous* (1939).

Young at Heart is a musical remake of the original picture intended to complete Doris Day's contract with Warner Bros. For the old Garfield role, director Gordon Douglas wanted Sinatra, who had proven his acting mettle in *From Here to Eternity* and had just wrapped up shooting *Suddenly.* The film could be named *Young at Heart* after Sinatra's latest hit song, which had climbed to the top of the charts and became a million-seller. The tune would figure prominently in the movie.

Jack Warner realized that Sinatra not only could handle the acting side of the role, but his baritone would blend beautifully with star Doris Day's singing voice in the musical numbers. However, Sinatra was not under studio contract, and as a freelancer he had the freedom, and recently the clout, to make some demands before agreeing to a project. In the case of *Young at Heart,* he liked the idea of the movie representing his hit song, and having the opportunity to work with Day, but he recalled that John Garfield's character died at the end of *Four Daughters.* He didn't want to do a death scene so soon after *From Here to Eternity* and *Suddenly,* both of which had him dying at the end. Frank wasn't keen on his character not surviving in a third film, especially a musical, preferring that his character have a happier ending. A substantial amount of negotiating followed, with Sinatra wanting a major portion of the story involving his character rewritten. And since Warners wanted him in the movie, they acquiesced.

Director Douglas had started out with Our Gang comedy short in the late 1930s. His *Bored of Education* won an Oscar. He also helmed the Laurel and Hardy feature *Saps at Sea* (1940). However, by the 1950s, he was helming more dramatic productions, such as the James Cagney features

Kiss Tomorrow Goodbye (1950) and *Come Fill the Cup* (1951). In the latter, he directed Gig Young to an Oscar nomination, so Douglas asked that Young also appear in *Young at Heart*. When he started work on this project, Douglas had just finished filming *Them!* (1954), which has lived on as a science fiction classic.

Young at Heart was Sinatra's first musical since *Meet Danny Wilson*. The dramas *From Here to Eternity* and *Suddenly* are better films, but *Young at Heart* is a more pivotal one in his on-screen arc. It is fascinating to watch him inhabit a role so far removed from his previous roles, in a film which, in many ways, is similar to those earlier films. *Young at Heart* clearly illustrates, in ways those two more celebrated pictures did not, the seasoning of Sinatra's screen persona—from naïve man-child to world-weary adult. What serves Sinatra best in this regard here is not so much his newly minted status as a serious actor, but that he was nearly 40. With his facial wrinkles and noticeably receding hairline, he looks nothing like the wide-eyed kid with curly hair who was balancing a sailor's cap on his head and performing dance duets with Gene Kelly.

The physical changes, coupled with his emerging acting talent, make him a good fit for Barney Sloan, a self-loathing, cynical musical arranger who wanders into a small California town inhabited by those he can't help but see as luckier than himself: the Tuttle sisters, Laurie (Doris Day), Fran (Dorothy Malone) and Amy (Elisabeth Fraser). They live with their widower father (Robert Keith) and matronly Aunt Jessie (Ethel Barrymore) and spend most of their time discussing how desperately they want to get married. This somewhat alters the gist of Fannie Hurst's original 1937 story "Sister Act" on which *Four Daughters* was based. The sisters are now of the 1950s postwar culture, which supported the societal notion that most women wanted little else out of life than to get married and raise children.

Early on, Fran is ecstatic to become engaged to a dull real estate developer (Alan Hale, Jr.), even though she isn't sure she loves him. Laurie and Amy—who the script apparently depicts in their mid- to late 20s—behave like schoolgirls, lying in their beds late at night giggling and agreeing that neither of them will get married until the other does, so that neither one is left behind as "the old maid." Laurie says that the most important characteristic of a potential husband is a sense of humor: "There is one thing I have got to have: lots of laughs. You know, that's the trouble with most marriages I've seen, Amy, not enough laughs."

Laurie's laughs appear to come in the person of Alex Burke (Young), a charming composer who wins over every member of the Tuttle household and is quickly invited to live with them as he works on the score for a musical comedy. Alex is the sort of character Gene Kelly portrayed in

Anchors Aweigh and *Take Me Out to the Ball Game*: a confident, capable man who has never had a problem attracting the opposite sex, or with anything else. Before long, each of the Tuttle sisters is in love with him. Laurie, laughing all the while, runs around playfully with him at the beach. Amy performs several menial tasks for him. Fran acts like her fiancé has ceased to exist whenever she is in Alex's presence.

Into this scenario comes Barney, an old friend of Alex the composer enlists to help with the arrangement of his musical score. Barney is the antithesis of Alex: contentious, lacking in self-esteem, a perennial outsider. Director Douglas presents this point deftly by framing Alex at the center of Tuttle family functions, while Barney is in the background of several group scenes. Sinatra's performance is especially arresting when considered against the backdrop of the film, since the idyllic elements of *Young at Heart* are precisely the kind of scenarios Sinatra had found himself in as an actor in the '40s. That he is able to so vividly create a character that contrasts these utopian settings and events is a concrete indication that he had moved on to a new, more mature plane in his motion picture career. This is clear from his initial scene, in which Barney first meets Laurie. The cheery, wholesome girl is of the type Sinatra's characters had mooned over in prior musicals. Here, though, there is no simple childlike shyness or confusion from Sinatra's character. Barney is disdainful of her, responding to most of her questions with terse, unfriendly answers. When he does finally begin to open up, it is only to ridicule her optimism, launching into a self-pitying speech about how fate has it in for him. He refers to himself as a "stumble-bum." He has no parents, no education, no military service record. Sinatra handles all of this expertly, calling on many of the same mannerisms that served him so well in *Suddenly*, minus the evil edge. Laurie, true to form, tells Barney to quit feeling sorry for himself—and it's clear from that point that these characters are going to fall in love. Then Barney will indeed learn to laugh and thereby become the kind of ideal husband Laurie pines for.

The last time Sinatra had sung on screen, in *Meet Danny Wilson*, his crooning was meant to elicit swoons from his audience, which had been his musical mandate from the beginning of his movie career. In *Young at Heart*, however, he begins a new phase: With selections like "One for My Baby" and "Just One of Those Things," Sinatra exhibits a heretofore unexpressed talent to wring tortured emotion from a lyric. It is certainly no coincidence that his recording career also shifted its tone to this theme at about the same time. Almost all of the songs in the film stem from the characters performing, whether it's Sinatra at a bar or the girls practicing with their father; it isn't like the characters suddenly burst into a song and dance that propels the plot forward, *à la* a prototypical musical. But, as good as he was in those song-and-dance numbers in his previous films,

Sinatra returned to musicals, albeit in a more world-weary role, with Doris Day in *Young at Heart*.

arguably this sort of musical suits Sinatra better. With just him, the piano and his voice, he is able to convey all the emotion the scene requires, without any flashy extras.

While they worked well together on screen, there was some conflict during filming between Sinatra and Day. He was fond of her but became immediately suspicious of her husband Martin Melcher. Although the production was being produced by Day and Melcher's company, Arwin, for Warner Bros., Sinatra still insisted that Melcher be banned from the set, telling Jack Warner he wouldn't report for work otherwise. All studio security guards were told that Melcher was not allowed in. Between scenes, Sinatra tried hard to convince Day that she was being used, but she refused to listen. When Melcher died in 1968, it was discovered he had squandered all the money Day had made in her two-decade film career.

Commercially and critically, *Young at Heart* was a big hit for Sinatra and Day. It was called "a smooth, smartly done production, a family-type piece with appeal to young and old alike"[29] and "a warm, wholesome show that's good family entertainment."[30] It also came at a high point in their music careers. While the picture was in production, an annual poll of 4150 disc jockeys voted them the top male and female recording artists of 1954—Sinatra moving up five spots from the previous year and Day leap-frogging Jo Stafford. The deejays also doled out top male song honors to Sinatra for the film's theme tune while Day earned a spot on the female list for "Secret Love."

As far as Sinatra's acting career went, *Young at Heart*'s success showed that he could comfortably do musicals again. But before he jumped back into that pond, he was already committed to appear in another drama, this one directed by Stanley Kramer.

Not as a Stranger

Produced and Directed by Stanley Kramer
Screenplay: Edna and Edward Anhalt, from the novel by Morton Thompson
Cinematography: Franz Planer (Black and White)
Editor: Frederic Knudtson
Cast: Olivia de Havilland, Robert Mitchum, Frank Sinatra, Gloria Grahame, Broderick Crawford, Charles Bickford, Myron McCormick, Lon Chaney, Jr., Jesse White, Harry Morgan, Lee Marvin, Virginia Christine, Whit Bissell, Jack Raine, Mae Clarke, Juanita Moore, Herb Vigran, Jerry Paris, William Vedder, John Dierkes, Will Wright, Frank Jenks, Harry Shannon, Carl Switzer, Gail Bonney, King Donovan, Paul Guilfoyle, Robert Bailey, John Goddard, Getrude Hoffman, Jack Daly, Earle Hodgins, Harry Lauter, Scotty Morrow, Scott Seaton, Eve McVeagh, Nancy Kulp, Isabel Garcia, Brad Brown, Tom Ferrandini, Franklyn Farnum, Marlo Dwyer, Ralph Brooks, Jimmy Hawkins, Frank Orth, Bob Perry, Mack Williams, Mabel Smaney, Irene Tedrow, Stafford Repp
Released July 11, 1955
Stanley Kramer Productions for United Artists
135 minutes

For a film that was a major hit and based on a best-selling novel, *Not as a Stranger* is one of Sinatra's least known movies. It was United Artists' biggest grossing film up to that time and netted Sinatra a BAFTA nomination. But he plays a supporting role that is decidedly tangential to the main narrative.

The story deals with Lucas Marsh (Robert Mitchum), who since childhood has wanted to be a doctor. Low on money, this brilliant and dedicated medical student marries a nurse several years older than he is, because she can afford to put him through medical school. Nurse Kris Hedvigson (Olivia de Havilland) truly cares about Lucas and supports him financially and otherwise. He is cold and aloof toward her, concentrating fully on his medical work. Lucas is a very stubborn and egocentric person, dismissing Kris, and other doctors, as beneath him in skill and intelligence, even his mentor, Dr. Aarons (Broderick Crawford). Upon finishing his internship, Lucas joins Dr. Runkleman (Charles Bickford), who has heart trouble, is overworked, and needs someone to help with the slew of low-income patients and, he hopes, take over. Stressed out by his situation, Lucas has an affair with rich widow Harriet Long (Gloria Grahame). Kris, now pregnant, leaves him. When he attempts to save Dr. Runkleman's life with a heart operation, he fails and the doctor dies. Riddled with guilt and remorse, Lucas returns to Kris and begs her to take him back.

Sinatra is cast in the supporting role of fellow doctor Alfred Boone, Lucas's best friend. Alfred is loyal to Lucas but also very direct. At one point he confronts the much bigger man and states, "Sometimes I wish I had 75 more pounds. I'd belt you one!" Sinatra's role is far different from any of the roles he had played since shifting gears in the early 1950s and getting away from playing the fresh-faced innocent. However, Sinatra instills elements of those earlier characters in Alfred. Unlike Maggio, Alfred has nothing to prove. He is wealthy, breezy and, in something of a role reversal, it is Frank who plays support to the leading actor and his character is the one who acts as the lead's conscience. He joins Kris and Dr. Aarons in attempting to straighten Lucas out.

Mitchum is almost too cold in his role. As a result, Sinatra gets the opportunity to show a range of emotions, even in a supporting role with less screen time. He can be jokey or tough or concerned, and in each case he makes it believable. It is a very committed performance.

Not as a Stranger was Stanley Kramer's directorial debut, and he also acted as producer. As we can see, Kramer enjoyed working with all-star casts even at the outset of his directorial career. And while his drama is very earnest, having this many egos collected on a set can be daunting. Victoria Amador stated in her Olivia de Havilland biography:

Sinatra (left) and Robert Mitchum played doctors in *Not as a Stranger*, one of Frank's least known films.

The film set was very much a boys' club; all the leading actors were boozers and brawlers. Sinatra and Crawford got into so badly that Crawford ate Sinatra's toupee and almost choked on it. Olivia held her own. She liked Sinatra and recalled that he had "an extraordinarily quick mind, and was always on time and perfectly prepared. He was so professional that it was unnerving. I admired him for his work very much but we had no contact with each other except during the scenes we played together."[31]

It is interesting that de Havilland recalls Sinatra as punctual after his misbehavior on other projects.

Not as a Stranger started out as a novel by Morton Thompson that was a huge hit and was lauded by the Literary Guild. Thompson died in July

1953, missing out on much of his book's success and accolades. By February 1954, Kramer was already receiving publicity for being interested in the movie rights. He had hired his cast by the fall of 1954. The announcement of Mitchum being cast as Lucas resulted in outrage from the book's many fans. Readers wrote in with their own choices for the role, including Montgomery Clift, Farley Granger and Cornel Wilde. Kramer told syndicated columnist Bob Thomas:

> I have talked to many surgeons since I started work on this picture over a year ago and have found that most of them are big rugged men. They are butchers not in the derogatory sense but in the nature of the work they do. It takes a strong man to cut up human beings and to withstand the strain of hours over an operating table. That's why I picked strong personalities—Mitchum, Broderick Crawford, Charles Bickford—to play the surgeons in this picture. I may be wrong about Mitchum. Time will tell.[32]

For his part, Mitchum prepared for his role by observing actual surgeries and studying the doctors involved. Some elements of the procedures depicted in the film itself are real too, like the open heart surgery at the end. It is the first time an actual beating heart was shown in a movie.

Just to be sure, Kramer allowed a few scenes from the film to be shown on Ed Sullivan's popular Sunday night program *The Toast of the Town* at the end of 1954, several months before the movie's release. This was an effort to show that Mitchum settled nicely into the role of Lucas (despite the fact that the "older woman" Kris was played by de Havilland, who was only a year older than the actor).

Sinatra was pleased with his work in *Not as a Stranger,* and, despite it not being a leading role, was happy to be cast in a prestigious drama. When discussing his good fortune with Bob Thomas, Sinatra recalled: "*From Here to Eternity* was the greatest thing in the world for me because it opened up a whole new field. I would never have been offered *Suddenly* if it hadn't been for *Eternity*. And never would have been considered for *Not as a Stranger*."[33] And to columnist Aline Mosby he stated, "Actors who can't sing or dance can't switch to our side, but there's no reason why a singer can't be dramatic. A singer is essentially a performer." Mosby also stressed how important *Eternity* had been to Sinatra: "[He] takes his new success calmly because, he indicated, it took a long pull to get it back. 'The trick,' he said, 'is when you're down, not to quit.'"[34]

Sinatra was attached to a project entitled *Pink Tights* which was to co-star Marilyn Monroe. He believed that he would have real chemistry with Marilyn and was looking forward to it, but it eventually fell through. Because Sinatra had signed on, 20th Century–Fox still had to pay his salary through December 1954. Instead Sinatra was cast in *Guys and Dolls*.

Guys and Dolls

Directed by Joseph L. Mankiewicz
Screenplay: Joseph L. Mankiewicz, based on the play by Jo Swerling and Abe Burrows, from a story by Damon Runyon
Producer: Samuel Goldwyn
Cinematography: Harry Stradling (Eastmancolor)
Editor: Daniel Mandell
Songs:
    "Guys and Dolls," "A Woman in Love," "Overture," "Fugue for Tinhorns," "Follow the Fold," "The Oldest Established (Permanent Floating Crap Game)," "I'll Know," "Pet Me Poppa," "I've Never Been in Love Before," "Adelaide's Lament," "Adelaide," "If I Were a Bell," "My Time of Day"/"A Bushel and a Peck," "Take Back Your Mink," "Luck Be a Lady," "Sue Me," "Sit Down You're Rockin' the Boat"; Music and Lyrics: Frank Loesser
Cast: Marlon Brando, Jean Simmons, Frank Sinatra, Vivian Blaine, Robert Keith, Stubby Kaye, B.S. Pully, Johnny Silver, Sheldon Leonard, Danny Dayton, George E. Stone, Regis Toomey, Kathryn Givney, Veda Ann Borg, Mary Alan Hokanson, Joe McTurk, Kay E. Kuter, Stapleton Kent, Renee Renor, Harry Tyler, Sandra and Sonia Warner, Harry Wilson, John Roy, Norman Stevans, Larri Thomas, George Boyce, Steve Carruthers, Gordon Caveth, Tony Galento, Kid Chissell, Sayre Dearing, Bess Flowers, Russell Custer, Robert Haines, Jack Perry, Stuart Hall, Maurice Marks, Harold Miller, Troy Patterson, Charles Morton, Frank Richards, Sandra Warner, Buddy Spencer, Julian Rivero, Brick Sullivan, Bernard Sell, Edwin Rochelle, The Goldwyn Girls
Released November 3, 1955 (New York premiere). December 23, 1955 (wide release).
The Samuel Goldwyn Company for MGM
152 minutes

When the film rights for the Tony Award–winning smash *Guys and Dolls* went up for grabs in early 1954, it was poetic that the story about gamblers and gangsters with Technicolor personalities turned into a money-flinging affair. All the major studios and name producers wanted a piece of the action attached to 1950's Best Musical of the Year, inspired by a pair of stylish Damon Runyon short stories and given vivid life by Frank Loesser's built-for-star-turns songbook. Most of the studios had hopes of signing the industry's best-known actors and actresses to the already iconic roles.

Press reports reveal Paramount saw the property as the perfect vehicle for Bing Crosby and Danny Kaye. MGM envisioned Gene Kelly and Ann Miller in starring roles. Independent producer William Goetz (who was reported to have anted up $650,000) saw Jane Russell, Clark Gable and Ann Miller headlining his cast—with Betty Grable's name mentioned off and on as well.

Producer Samuel Goldwyn had no stars in mind, at least none he spoke to the columns about, when he laid his cash on the table. But his was the biggest bankroll: the then-record sum of $1 million, plus ten percent of the profits. He hit the jackpot. In explaining his decision to part with so much of his own money, the producer *of Hans Christian Andersen, A Song Is Born* and *The Kid from Brooklyn* said *Guys and Dolls* was by far the "most important and exciting" of any musical he had ever brought to the screen.[35]

That turned out to be more than press-agent spin. At the time, *Guys and Dolls* was the closest thing Hollywood had seen to a live stage musical translated to celluloid, a high-energy feast for the eyes and ears that succeeds as much in spite of itself as because of itself. The wobbliness comes from some musical miscasting at the top of its bill; the richness comes from Goldwyn's spare-no-expense vision for the set designs, Joseph Mankiewicz's deft direction and Loesser's even more muscular music: He cut a pair of numbers from the Broadway lineup and added two others. The combination pulses with the rhythms of Broadway—not just the Great White Way where *Guys and Dolls* was born, but the street in the heart of midtown Manhattan near where the movie's Times Square action takes place.

Sinatra wasn't in the best of moods when he entered the *Guys and Dolls* narrative. Although it was his second of four films in 1955 (a career-high feat he would repeat the next year and never eclipse), the in-demand status fueled by his Oscar win did not shield him from career disappointments. The biggest one before him as he went into filming was the sting of being rejected for the leading role he badly wanted in *On the Waterfront*, which won eight Oscars in 1954, including Best Picture. It also earned a Best Actor statue for Marlon Brando, who got the part of Terry Malloy that Sinatra coveted and said he had been promised. Sinatra sued *Waterfront*'s producers, claiming breach of oral contract, in the midst of filming of *Guys and Dolls*—with Brando alongside him on set. Goldwyn had cast the dramatically intense Brando as *Guys and Dolls*' leading man, the charismatic Sky Masterson. This despite Brando never having sung a note on screen or anywhere else in public. And despite the fact that Sinatra coveted the role, for which Loesser's top songs had been written and which earned Robert Alda a Tony.

Sinatra and Marlon Brando (left) did not get along while filming *Guys and Dolls*—nor in later years, when they often competed for film roles.

Sinatra was instead cast in the supporting role of Nathan Detroit, the purveyor of "the oldest established permanent floating crap game in New York." It was a plum part for a vocalist with Sinatra's versatility and an actor with his relaxed flair for comedy, but it is understandable why he considered it a step down now that he had proven himself capable of more head-of-the-class parts. Third billing two years after earning an Academy Award sat with him as poorly as having to again take a back seat to Brando. While Masterson got the lead vocal on the denouement rouser "Luck Be a

Lady" (named by the American Film Institute in 2013 as the 42nd greatest film song in movie history), most of Detroit's up-tempo songs were ensemble numbers a little too reminiscent of his junior-partner days opposite Gene Kelly. Cementing the point is that he often wears his hat—albeit a fedora rather than a sailor's cap—throughout *Guys and Dolls* like he wore it in *Anchors Aweigh* and *On the Town*, tipped back atop his head so a plume of hair can be spied on top (a bit sparser and a touch grayer though it may be).

"I wanted to play Masterson," Sinatra later told *Newsweek*. "I mean, nothing disparaging about Marlon Brando, but Masterson didn't fit him and he knew it."[36] A Hollywood legend has built up around the duo's distaste for each other: Sinatra's aggravation that Brando's Method acting wasted too much time between takes, while Sinatra preferred the spontaneity of as few calls to "action" as possible. Sinatra referred to the emotive Brando as "Mumbles" behind his back.[37] Brando boasted to friends that his physically slight co-star was "one guy I can flatten."[38] Other epithets said to be exchanged in each other's direction, deeply ingrained in the lore of the film if hard to trace back to contemporaneous sources, involve God: Sinatra allegedly said years later that Brando would turn down playing the Almighty because he would hold out for a bigger part, and Brando apparently contended that Sinatra was the kind of guy who would get to Heaven and be mad at God for making him bald. Jean Simmons, who receives second billing as Brando's love interest, acknowledged in a 1990 interview with author Gary Schneeberger that her co-stars were at odds during filming: "He and Marlon had totally different styles. Frank would be ready like on the first take and Marlon hadn't started building his character yet. So it was a bit hard for both of them."[39]

The billing and Brando tensions weren't the only reasons Sinatra was not thoroughly taken with playing Nathan Detroit. There was also the matter of the inimitable stamp Sam Levene had put on the role during its Broadway run (more than 1200 performances). Despite having a singing voice so limited that his big number was written in a single octave, his performance was regarded as nearly pitch-perfect. Levene captured the bedraggled essence of Nathan so effortlessly and indelibly that Robert Guillaume, who took on the role in an all–African-American revival in 1976, mused about stepping into such formidable shoes: "Levene stands over the role every night like a St. Christopher medal in a car. You can't escape him."[40] Interestingly, one renowned actor who was eager to take on the challenge of matching or besting Levene was Sir Laurence Olivier, who made known his desire to grab hold of Nathan Detroit's dice in a 1970 Old Vic revival of *Guys and Dolls*, calling the play "his favorite musical."[41] Alas, the 63-year-old fell ill and the show was never produced.

Sinatra was aiming elsewhere than Levene in his interpretation of Nathan Detroit. He told the *New York Herald Tribune* News Service from the set that he spent several weeks ruminating on the role before agreeing to do it, precisely because "he was unable to picture anyone in the part but Sam Levene."[42] What finally nudged him to take a shot, he explained, was deciding to give a much different reading of the part. "I've begun to see another way of doing it," he said simply. Sinatra's Nathan Detroit is not a big lug given to cuddly bombast; he's a small-time operator always gunning for a promotion, but he can never catch a break big enough to catapult him there. In his relationship with the sweetly ditzy Miss Adelaide (played by Vivian Blaine, just as she was opposite Levene), Sinatra's Nathan is less put-upon by his paramour as he is hard-pressed by his pals. The winning formula for the film version of Detroit, Sinatra calculated, was to downplay the romantic weariness and dial up the world-weariness. Each characterization must deal both with Adelaide's growing laments about still being just a fiancée after 14 years and the need to score big money in a hurry to find a new spot for the crap game. But Sinatra's Nathan clearly cares more about the latter for most of the film. As the actor explained to syndicated columnist Meyer Beck in 1955: "This is strictly a comedy role. Nathan Detroit is as unromantic as they come. In fact, marriage is the only thing he fears."[43]

Guys and Dolls is essentially two films in one. Both were birthed from an ambitious and dazzling opening set piece from Mankiewicz and Oscar-nominated set designer-decorators Oliver Smith, Joseph C. Wright and Howard Bristol. They put Goldwyn's money to inspired use, setting the high-gloss Technicolor tone for the picture. It cost $250,000 to build on a Goldwyn stage a splashy full-sized model of Times Square, filled with movie theaters, cigar stores, souvenir shops, newsstands and enough neon to light the excitement and seediness that color the 150-minute running time. The goal was to bring Broadway out of the theater and into the real world in a surreal way, and it succeeds splendidly. The gangsters and grifters (dressed as if it were the 1920s) and their gals (in more '50s-stylized attire) dance and prance in and out of the CinemaScope frame to the bouncy lyric-less score (some of it done by later Sinatra musical arranger Nelson Riddle)—the motion picture version of a theatrical overture. The colors are vibrant and exaggerated as the "guys" pick pockets, sell suspect goods to the tourists and study racing forms while the "dolls" buy slacks, pose for pictures and generally try to get the boys' attention. The production laid down 12,000 square feet of asphalt so Mankiewicz could enliven his bustling street scenes with 32 moving cars and trucks.

Sinatra is introduced shortly after the opening wraps, hangdog and harried because his law-enforcement nemesis Lt. Brannigan (Robert Keith) is interfering with business. The lawman is making it known to the city's big and small fish alike that he intends to shut down before it even begins the "oldest established permanent floating crap game" that is Nathan Detroit's calling card. Making it more distressing for Nathan and his right- and left-hand men Nicely-Nicely Johnson (Stubby Kaye, reprising his Broadway role) and Benny Southstreet (Johnny Silver, doing the same) is that there are several high rollers in town looking for action. What's worse, Brannigan's policing has made it all but impossible for Nathan to find a place for the game even if he wanted to risk staging it. As Nathan bemoans his limited options to his friends, the Runyon dialogue patterns reproduced by Mankiewicz in his clever screenplay spotlight another of the film's distinctive notes: tough guys who often talk like literature professors (albeit East Coast ones), eschewing contractions. It's a nice touch that sets up the narrative and the film's signature style of depicting the gamblers as a bit shady but not truly nefarious:

> NATHAN: I am not going to find a place for my crap game because everybody knows Brannigan has turned on the heat and is breathing down everybody's neck.
> JOHNNY: That's what he said.
> NICELY-NICELY: You tried the regular places? Won't they take a chance, seeing it's you?
> NATHAN: Seeing it's me, no. Except one. Joey Biltmore's garage. Joey said he might take a chance... for 1000 bucks.
> JOHNNY: 1000?
> NATHAN: In advance and in cash. He would not even take my marker.
> NICELY-NICELY: This I do not believe. That Joey Biltmore will not take your marker.
> NATHAN: You got no idea what a breath this Brannigan has got. A marker's not just a piece of paper saying: "I owe you 1000. Signed, Nathan Detroit." A marker is the one pledge which a guy cannot welsh on, never. It's like not saluting the flag. It does not seem possible. Me without a livelihood.

When he discovers Masterson (Brando) is one of the top-flight talents in town, Nathan sees his chance. Masterson has become a back-room legend as a gambler of deep pockets and deeper cockiness, a man who never refuses a bet because he never doubts his ability to turn the odds to his favor. So Nathan bets him $1000 that Sky won't be able to whisk away a doll of Nathan's choosing on a date to Havana. Masterson leaps at the challenge, smugly confident in his charms, but the wager turns out to be more formidable than he imagined when Nathan reveals his choice to be Sgt. Sarah Brown (Simmons) of the Times Square Save-a-Soul Mission. The bet splits *Guys and Dolls* into two films: one tracking Sky's attempts to woo Sister Sarah, one following Nathan and his assorted associates and hangers-on as they try to find a site for that floating crap game.

When he's merely acting, not singing, Brando is a fine Masterson. His broad shoulders and up-to-something grin conveying the machismo and under-it-all good-guyness that makes the role the story's lead. His Sky isn't as comedically craven as the other mopes hankering for some action, most played as broadly as they would be from the stage—none more so than Sheldon Leonard's fun but one-note Harry the Horse. Brando makes the audience believe both that Sky would bet a grand on wooing an unknown woman and then soften to her prim charms after putting in the time necessary to win the kitty—in both senses. His non-musical scenes with Simmons play best when they're more flirtatious than romantic. There's real chemistry between the two when Sky pretends he wants the mission's help to quit gambling, engaging her in playful banter that shows he knows his Bible as well as he knows his cards. He cinches the deal when he offers to bring Sarah 12 honest-to-goodness sinners to save—important because salvations are down at the mission—if she agrees to the Havana rendezvous.

It is on that date, though, that the Sky-Sarah half of the picture craters. That's because they stop exchanging dialogue and start exchanging lyrics. Simmons, like Brando, was cast for her acting chops and not her vocal chops, admitting to the Associated Press a few months before the film's premiere that when she sang in a movie at 16, "I did one song and they told me to stick to acting."[44] Brando fares even worse, losing the confidence he carries as an actor in exchange for affectation. "My voice is somewhat akin to the mating call of the dying yak," he told the same AP reporter. "I didn't believe that Goldwyn would have the gall to let the public hear it."[45] The casting of Simmons and Brando wasn't the producer's biggest mistake, though; it was using a musical scene, specifically the new number "A Woman in Love," as the moment they fall for each other. The vocals are flat and tuneless from both; so hushed and whispery are Brando's stanzas that one can easily hear evidence of what the actor wrote in his autobiography: "They sewed my words together on one song so tightly that when I mouthed it in front of the camera. I nearly asphyxiated myself."[46]

Sinatra fares far better, not surprisingly, as the lead of the other half of the film—even if it's a performance he could have given, and occasionally looks like he is giving, in his sleep. Nathan is a man of action but not energy, so the laconic nature of the portrayal serves the narrative well. That Sinatra may be a little bored by what he's asked to do here matches nicely with Nathan's narrative arc: He's weary of trying to stay ahead of the much-different pursuits of Lt. Brannigan and Adelaide. While he plots to piece together the crap game all of New York City's underbelly wants,

Nathan often appears to be the guy least looking forward to it. His feathers don't ruffle any more than Masterson's do. But it's not because he's in command of every situation he finds himself in; it's because he seems not to be concerned whether he's in charge of those situations. Even when the game finally gets underway, Nathan reacts with a shrug, not outrage, when the ominous Big Jule from Chicago (B.S. Pully) cheats him out of thousands. Nathan, it seems, has accepted that he'll never be a big shot on par with Masterson.

Nathan does, as the two halves of the picture join back up for the climax, serve as Masterson's right-hand man. Back from Havana, in love with Sarah, the gambler's gambler now has to make good on his bet: Not the $1000 to Nathan; he pays that without protest. No, he has to round up the 12 sinners for Sarah to save the mission—and the only way to do that is to bet each man at the game on one roll of the dice. If Sky loses, he owes them $1000 apiece. If he makes his point, they have to go to the late-night service at the mission. This is the backdrop to which Brando performs "Luck Be a Lady"—another reedy vocal that underserves the payoff moment of the narrative. Sky's reputation and his romantic future are hanging in the balance, and Brando doesn't deliver at the level demanded by the swinging anthem of every gambler's last best hope. No matter to the plot, though: Sky wins the bet, and Nathan rounds up the ne'er-do-wells on Masterson's behalf and takes them to the mission (where they hear the Good Word preached and Kaye's rollicking version of "Sit Down You're Rockin' the Boat").

Sinatra's musical highlight comes at the end of the picture, when Adelaide finally catches up with Nathan and he realizes it's time to settle down. While there has been zero palpable romance between the two to this point, Sinatra's interpretation and performance of "Adelaide" in a deli is vintage Voice from the bobbysoxer era. Sweeping gestures, precise just-off-the-beat phrasing, smiles for the crowd he plays to throughout—this is the Frank Sinatra that Hollywood came calling for a decade and a half earlier. The song is one of Loesser's additions to the film, created to give Sinatra a standout solo after confining his vocal performances to trios and even full-chorus numbers throughout. All threads tie up tidily at the end with Sky and Sarah, and Nathan and Adelaide, getting married.

Guys and Dolls was an enormous success. In the end, Goldwyn spent $5 million on the production (which was released under the MGM banner) and it brought in $13.1 million. So happy with his male stars was the producer that he praised them roundly in the press in the weeks after the November 3, 1955, premiere. He called Brando "a great actor with great simplicity and humility"[47] and Sinatra "a great artist" who gives "plus value."[48] Critical praise was not quite universal, but the film got some raves,

(Left to right): Marlon Brando, Jean Simmons, Sinatra, and Vivian Blaine on the *Guys and Dolls* set.

including *Variety* calling it "a bang-up film musical in top drawer Goldwyn manner"[49] and *Motion Picture Herald* calling it entertainment of "monumental size, eye-catching opulence and richness of talent and detail."[50] *Labor's Daily* called Sinatra's performance "superb and disarmingly charming"[51] and nationally syndicated columnist Erskine Johnson awarded the crooner honors for "best movie warbling of the month."[52]

The satisfied audiences *Guys and Dolls* left in its wake catapulted Sinatra into *The Tender Trap*, where he once again enjoyed life at the top of the bill and settled into the more comfortable climes of a traditional comedic romantic lead. As for any lingering disappointments over his experience with Brando and Nathan Detroit, Sinatra seems not to have completely shed the sting for the rest of his career. During a June 1984 concert at Carnegie Hall captured on the posthumously released 4-CD/1-DVD live set

New York, he introduces "Luck Be a Lady" with a few barbs in Mumbles' direction:

> It wasn't my good fortune to sing this song in the film because they had chosen the great baritone from the Met, Marlon Brando, to sing the song. Holy geez! He's a hell of an actor, but when it comes to singing—forget it, Charlie! That's not his racket, it's mine.[53]

It was hardly the first time Sinatra aimed to rectify being passed over as the film's leading vocal presence. Two decades before the Carnegie Hall show, in 1963, he released through his record label the ambitious "Reprise Musical Repertory Theatre" four-album set, featuring the songbooks of four hit Broadway shows performed by himself and friends Dean Martin, Debbie Reynolds, Sammy Davis, Jr., Dinah Shore and Bing Crosby. On the *Guys and Dolls* disc, he gave himself all of Sky Masterson's solos—including what would become his signature in-studio take on "Luck Be a Lady."

The Tender Trap

Directed by Charles Walters
Screenplay: Julius Epstein, from the play by Max Shulman and Robert Paul Smith
Producer: Lawrence Weingarten
Cinematography: Paul Vogel (Eastmancolor)
Editor: John Dunning
Song:
    "(Love Is) the Tender Trap"; Lyrics: Sammy Cahn; Music: Jimmy Van Heusen
Cast: Frank Sinatra, Debbie Reynolds, David Wayne, Celeste Holm, Jarma Lewis, Lola Albright, Carolyn Jones, Howard St. John, Joey Faye, Tom Helmore, Willard Sage, Marc Wilder, Jack Boyle, James Drury, Benny Rubin, Wilson Wood, Madge Blake, Bill Baldwin, Stuart Holmes, May McAvoy, Herb Butterfield, Oliver Cross, Sam Harris, Reginald Simpson, Edward Tuttle, Dave White, Gordon Richards, Frank Sully, Dan Quigg, Gustave Lax, Max Power, Don Lynch, George Peters, Erin Selwyn, Max Power, Forrest Draper, Hal Floyd, King Mojave, Michael Kostick, Bette Arlen
Released November 4, 1955
MGM
111 minutes

Sinatra was riding high in 1955 with hit recordings and a flourishing movie career. It is hard to believe that only three years earlier, he was struggling to get by. Now with an Oscar under his belt, and a few critically acclaimed performances, he wanted to explore the comedy genre. Always a strong fan of comedy, he requested to have the Three Stooges appear on one of his television shows a few years earlier, and was an early admirer of Dean Martin and Jerry Lewis. Sinatra's first impression of Martin and Lewis was "the dago's lousy but the little Jew is great."[54] By 1955, Frank was good friends with both men, and he remained so.

In 1954, the opening night stars of the Broadway play *The Tender Trap* were Robert Preston, Ronny Graham, Kim Hunter and Joey Faye. When it closed in January 1955, already there were press reports that it was going to be made into a film. Louella Parsons reported in her syndicated column:

> When Debbie Reynolds returns from New York next week she'll be told that *The Tender Trap* ... has been bought for her. It's a breezy, gay comedy by Max Schulman and Paul Smith. Debbie starts to work in six weeks with Larry Weingarten as her producer. She had this vacation coming to her, and where better could she spend it than near Eddie Fisher? She plans to make as many pictures as MGM has ready for her before she and Eddie take an extended honeymoon in June. Dore Schary, who made the purchase of *The Tender Trap*, said he feels it's just right for Debbie, now one of MGM's most important stars.[55]

Reynolds had indeed been riding high at MGM ever since appearing with Gene Kelly and Donald O'Connor in Stanley Donen's *Singin' in the Rain* (1952). Several hit films followed, including *The Affairs of Dobie Gillis* (1953) and *Susan Slept Here* (1954). By that spring it was being reported that Sinatra had signed for *The Tender Trap* male lead. Hedda Hopper stated in her syndicated column that he would play "an eligible bachelor who escapes the clutches of all the females until *The Tender Trap*, meaning Debbie, catches him."[56] Although it was not a musical, there was a title song, and it became a big hit for Sinatra based on its appearance in this movie.

The opening credit sequence was obviously orchestrated to give Sinatra the opportunity to sing in the film. It starts out with Sinatra singing and walking toward the camera from very far away, the film's title appearing once he gets close to the camera. And then this scene is mirrored at the very end of the movie, but with all four leads.

Sinatra's musical career hit another milestone in 1955 with the release of his first album as a long playing 33⅓ disc, "In the Wee Small Hours." Prior to this, Sinatra's albums were a collection of 78 rpm singles in a booklet, hence the term "album." However, "In the Wee Small Hours" was his first LP. At the time, not all phonographs could accommodate a 12-inch disc, so "In the Wee Small Hours" was also issued on two ten-inch discs and on four four-song EP (extended play) discs. Released in April 1955, right around the time he signed for *The Tender Trap*, it reached #2 on the *Billboard* charts and was his most successful album in eight years.

Having several songs on one disc allowed Sinatra to maintain a consistent theme, or concept, and the tracks contained on "In the Wee Small Hours" dealt with different levels of loneliness and isolation. Sinatra is in top form singing Hoagy Carmichael's heartbreaking "I Get Along Without You Very Well" and Rodgers and Hart's "Glad to Be Unhappy." Other songs included "Mood Indigo," "What Is This Thing Called Love," "Dancing on the Ceiling" and the title track. The album eschewed any tough guy trappings to exhibit a greater depth of emotion, with no fear of expressing sadness.

Just as his records became more mature and dramatic, Sinatra happily entered a movie project that was light-hearted and funny. He was setting out to prove that, along with dramas and musicals, he could also effectively play comedy.

Sinatra is 35-year-old New York theatrical agent Charlie Reader, who has found that beautiful women are plentiful in the Big Apple, especially if they have show biz aspirations and believe Charlie can help get them somewhere. They not only romance him, they do his housework. Charlie is so distracted by his frivolous lifestyle, he doesn't bother reading a telegram that indicates that his childhood friend Joe McCall (David Wayne) is coming for a visit. When Joe shows up, Charlie is delighted. Their backstory is quickly revealed: Charlie had his eyes on a girl named Ethel back in high school, but it was Joe who had the nerve to approach her. They are now married for 11 years and have three children, but decided some time away from each other might strengthen their marriage, which has settled into a rut. Joe is flabbergasted by how easily his old friend attracts young, beautiful women, and he even becomes smitten himself with one of them, classical musician Sylvia Crewes (Celeste Holm).

Charlie is attracted to new client Julie Gillis (Reynolds), a young, pretty and virginal singer-actress. She is much different than the women Charlie has become used to, and that attracts him all the more. Unable to choose between Julie and Sylvia, Charlie ends up proposing to both. He eventually realizes that it is Julie he truly loves, and he lets Sylvia down easy. She, in turn, must do the same for Joe, who has fallen in love with her. Sylvia realizes that Joe still loves his wife and children, and that she is merely a big city distraction. Joe returns home; Charlie leaves all of his women and goes to Europe to clear his head. When Charlie returns, he is invited to Sylvia's wedding (she met a charming man and they fell in love).

Debbie Reynolds and Frank Sinatra in *The Tender Trap*.

Sylvia tosses the bouquet to Charlie, and he in turn tosses it to nearby Julie and proposes. She accepts.

Assessing *The Tender Trap* in the 21st century, what is most interesting is how the film responds to the 1950s culture so completely. Charlie's ease with beautiful women (as much as ten years younger) does not stop at romance. The women insist on also cooking and cleaning for him, exhibiting the traditional domesticity that was expected at the time. While Joe is watching incredulously, a beautiful woman shows up for a visit and immediately insists on straightening up.

The point of the relationship between Charlie and Joe is that each wants what the other has; this grass-is-greener concept often shows up in romantic comedies. Charlie has come to find the women in his life more tedious than exhilarating. There is no challenge, no depth; not even an act of pursuit is necessary. This is why he is so attracted to the uninterested Julie. Joe, whose marriage has reached the same level of tedium to where a two-week separation has been agreed upon, can't understand why Charlie would want to trade this lifestyle for dull domesticity. When Charlie dreamily describes how attractive it is to him to imagine coming home from a hard day's work to a pretty woman and three happy children, Joe counters with a dose of reality: Married with children means new carpeting, braces and other expenses that challenge his income level.

As with most romantic comedies, especially those made as late as the 1950s, everything wraps up neatly and despite some distractions, nobody really does anything wrong before returning to where they belong. Except Charlie. His lifestyle was the one that challenged '50s sensibilities, so it is eschewed for impending domesticity.

Max Schulman's play is pleasant and fun, and the screen adaptation by Jules Epstein (who co-wrote *Casablanca*) retains its amusing dialogue, with Celeste Holm especially scoring with lines like "I have a high I.Q. and a low boiling point" and the self-aware, "Do you have any idea what's available to a woman of 33? Married men. Drunks. Pretty boys looking for someone to support them. Lunatics looking for their fifth divorce! It's quite a list, isn't it?"

Age is a factor that is brought up a few times. It is established that Charlie is 35, considered middle-aged in 1955. His childhood buddy Joe, presumably the same age, followed the societal rules and has a wife and children by this age, while Charlie is still cavorting with younger women, juggling several at a time. At one point, the 33-year-old Sylvia says, "The night is young, and we're middle-aged, anything can happen."

Julie is the character that anchors the proceedings, having a fairy tale idea of meeting the right "fella" and settling down to an acceptable lifestyle with marriage and a family. She is serious, even has a date picked out, and when she meets the right man, it will follow a comfortably predictable trajectory. Charlie, of course, is the polar opposite of what she's looking for, despite his inherent desire for what Joe has. A lot of things have to happen before Charlie ends up with Julie. Joe's infatuation with Sylvia can be just that, but is not acted upon. It goes no further than the level of schoolboy crush before Sylvia straightens him out and makes him realize he belongs with his family.

Sylvia's meeting Mr. Right in the elevator was more a series of chance meetings. She interacted with him several times over the course of the film and it was established that there was an attraction between them, so by the time they meet at again at the end of the movie and the man finally asks her to dinner, it makes sense that he would be the man for her and they would end up together.

Sinatra handily proved he could play comedy, responding well to the comic situations and handling the dialogue well. He presents both the confidence and the longing in Charlie effectively, while continuing to keep things light and amusing. Note the scene where Charlie asks Julie out to dinner and she refuses him and he cannot for the life of him comprehend why. Sinatra played that air of disbelief very well and it gave a lot of insight into the character's state of mind.

Sinatra was very comfortable during the filming of *The Tender Trap*, which must have felt quite good after the conflicts he had with Marlon Brando on *Guys and Dolls*. He and Debbie Reynolds became quite close friends during filming, and he advised her against marrying her current beau, singer Eddie Fisher, because, he warned, singers are nice guys but not good husbands. She did anyway, and Fisher ended up leaving her for Elizabeth Taylor.

Sinatra also enjoyed working with David Wayne, and wanted to work with him again, but by the 1950s, Wayne was concentrating more on TV work. He starred opposite Joanne Woodward in *The Three Faces of Eve* (1957) and with Jerry Lewis in *The Sad Sack* (1957), but most of his work was done for the small screen. Frank did have Wayne guest on his TV show.

Celeste Holm was already a screen veteran of nearly ten years by the time she landed the *Tender Trap* role. She worked with Sinatra and Reynolds again in *High Society* the following year. She may have played one of several women Charlie was courting but her character was much more sophisticated and, with her speech to Joe toward the end, she added a layer of complexity to the women Charlie had no intention of marrying. It is commendable that the movie didn't try to pit any of the women against each other for Charlie's affections; the blame is put on Charlie for his inability to settle.

It is interesting to see actresses like Lola Albright, who opens the film as one of Charlie's girls, snuggling with him on the couch, and Carolyn Jones, who plays a pretty dog walker who is so insignificant to Charlie, he can't always think of her name. The film also features an early appearance by James Drury in a small role. Joey Faye offers an enjoyable comic performance, repeating the role he played in the Broadway stage production.

The Tender Trap was a massive box office hit, profiting beyond its budget by more than a million dollars. Sinatra had successfully accomplished what he had set out to do: excel in a comedy production.

The Man with the Golden Arm

Produced and Directed by Otto Preminger
Screenplay: Walter Newman and Lewis Meltzer, from the novel by Nelson Algren

The Man with the Golden Arm (1955)

Cinematography: Sam Leavitt (Black and White)
Editor: Louis Loeffler
Cast: Frank Sinatra, Eleanor Parker, Kim Novak, Arnold Stang, Darren McGavin, Robert Strauss, John Conte, Doro Merande, George E. Stone, George Mathews, Leonid Kinskey, Emile Meyer, Will Wright, Ralph Neff, Frank Marlowe, Ernest Raboff, Harold "Tommy" Hart, Leonard Bremen, Snub Pollard, Pete Candoli, Shelly Manne, Norman Papson, Jack Mulhall, Paul E. Burns, Herschel Graham, Gordon Mitchell, Joe McTurk, Suzanne Ridgeway, Martha Wentworth, Jeffrey Sayre, Shorty Rogers, Frank Richards
Released December 15, 1955
Otto Preminger Films–Carlyle Productions for United Artists
119 minutes

Sinatra's interest in *The Man with the Golden Arm* made great career sense. The Nelson Algren novel won the prestigious National Book Award (the first time it was bestowed on a work of fiction) in 1950—two years before the novel *From Here to Eternity* won. That the latter film hit theaters two years before the former underscores their vastly different subject matters; and it also spotlights the restrictive influence the Production Code still exerted over Hollywood in the 1950s—at least until *The Man with the Golden Arm*, as defiantly brought to cinemas by director Otto Preminger, and as powerfully performed by Sinatra, helped to break its stranglehold.

Algren's novel was a literary sensation that promised a bold new style of gritty urban noir. The novel, and Algren's talents, were hailed by a who's who of authors whose work still fills university syllabi in American Literature courses. Algren delivered a tale birthed from his own hardscrabble existence in a tenement section of inner-city Chicago, described by one reviewer as "a sordid but compassionate story of a card dealer and dope addict, plus the wretched and degenerate cast of characters along the tough Division Street on (the city's) northwest side."[57] Algren, trained as a journalist though he never worked very long as one, filled the novel with sketches of characters he'd encountered, and earned the nickname the American Dostoevsky for the visceral way he brought their street lives to life.[58]

Frankie Machine (*née* Francis Majcinek) is Algren's protagonist—and the chief reason the first star attached to the project snapped up the film rights. Frankie is a small-time back-room poker dealer (hence the nickname), hooked on morphine as the result of treatment for a war injury (hence the double meaning of his nickname). John Garfield expressed almost immediate interest in turning the novel into a film in 1949, eyeing Frankie Machine as a plum role for himself. He recognized the challenges the Production Code enforcers would present in making a movie with a drug addict at its core, telling syndicated columnist Louella Parsons he thought only one producer could get the job done. "I hope that Darryl Zanuck will make it because he's the only man with sufficient courage to present such a character on the screen," Garfield said. "And I feel it might do a lot of good."[59]

Garfield bought the film rights to *Golden Arm* a year later. At the time, Sinatra was at the nadir of his motion picture (and recording) career. He appeared in not a single movie in 1950, the only year between his film debut in 1941 and his soft retirement in 1970 that he was MIA on screen. Even had he wanted to, he likely could not have afforded the $15,000 Garfield paid to secure the rights.[60]

Garfield's control of the property was beset with problems from the start. He did not corral Zanuck to produce, but Bob Roberts, and Roberts was queasy about the vivid drug themes and the depictions that would be necessary to translate them to celluloid. Garfield wanted Algren to come to Los Angeles to create a script that would navigate around Roberts' concerns; Algren refused because he didn't agree with the sanitizing changes he was asked to make to dodge the inevitable Production Code objections.[61] Columnists reported into 1951 that Garfield was continuing to sink money into the project and hadn't yet even gotten a treatment produced. Then, before any other related activity was documented in the press, the actor passed away at age 39 on May 21, 1952.

At that juncture, *Golden Arm* likely would have left a purely literary legacy if not for Otto Preminger. The maverick producer-director had in 1953 released *The Moon Is Blue* over strenuous and repeated objections from the Production Code office. The film, a romantic comedy based on a successful play of the same name, starred William Holden, David Niven and Maggie McNamara playing the principals of a spirited love triangle. Both male leads, though pals, are in competitive pursuit of the virginity of the female lead—and the censors didn't like the ways it was all talked about. The script was initially rejected in July 1951 because of its "light and gay treatment of the subject of illicit sex and seduction." In December, Preminger submitted a revised script draft that was rejected a month later for its "unacceptably light attitude towards seduction, illicit sex, chastity and virginity." Four days after the second rejection, Preminger advised the Code office he disagreed with its decision and would film the screenplay—and release the result—without further changes.[62]

Preminger brought that took-no-interference mindset to *Man with the Golden Arm*, which he acquired from Garfield's estate in March 1955. He eyed William Holden as Frankie Machine, and told Louella Parsons, "It's as good a man's role as *Lost Weekend*. In the story, the boy gets on

The Man with the Golden Arm (1955)

dope, but in the end he fights until he overcomes it." Alas, as the director bemoaned to the columnist about his would-be-leading man, "everybody else wants [Holden], too."[63] And somebody else *got* him, sending Preminger back to the drawing board. A couple of months later, it was reported that he had put another Oscar winner at the top of the bill: Frank Sinatra.[64]

To land the role, Sinatra had to once again compete with Marlon Brando, his ever-present rival in that era. Preminger had sent a partial screenplay to the agents for both actors. No doubt because he had, in the prior two years, been bested by Brando for a pair of leading roles (Terry Malloy in *On the Waterfront* and Sky Masterson in *Guys and Dolls*), Sinatra took no chances. He signaled his willingness to sign on the dotted line before he'd even read the truncated screenplay's final line—and before Brando's camp had even gotten the script in his hands.[65] Sinatra said, "The picture shows the ravages of the drug habit, people trying to rise out of the slum, skid-row kind of living. I read this thing and fell down. The part is most difficult. This Frankie Machine, the man with the golden arm, is one of the most exciting parts I have ever done or will do."[66]

The script contained some significant differences from Algren's novel—including a new, less downbeat ending and never naming the drug on which Frankie is hooked, although it is widely implied to be heroin, not morphine. The deviations resulted from a clash between Algren and Preminger. The writer traveled to Hollywood to work on the script, presenting the director with a treatment that Preminger promptly threw in the trash. "He had shown me what he thought of me and my people," Algren later said. "And I showed him what I thought of him and his people."[67] The novelist did so by bolting Los Angeles posthaste. Preminger hired screenwriter Walter Newman to write the script.

The picture gets underway in striking fashion that sets its tone and narrative arc before Frankie Machine is ever glimpsed. Preminger weaves a strong cord from two strands to set up the aggressive and discordant story he's telling: Saul Bass' jangly title sequence as unspooled over Elmer Bernstein's driving, horn-heavy opening theme. What viewers see is a cacophony of animated lines moving in abstract ways, personifying the unnerving reality of shooting up before morphing into an arm that looks both less than real and more than real, mirroring the way in which Frankie Machine's life is deconstructed by his addiction. Bernstein's score, which snared an Oscar nomination, pulses beneath the animation, pounding ever more frenetically under the brushes and bass of Shorty Rogers and his Giants with drummer Shelly Manne, until the appearance of that jagged, zig-zagged arm.

Frankie Machine (Sinatra) enters immediately thereafter, stepping out of a bus carrying two pieces of luggage and a wide smile. He looks around the neighborhood he steps into with familiarity and anticipation, his near-galloping eagerness hearkening back to Clarence Doolittle taking his shore leave in Hollywood (*Anchors Aweigh*) or Chip doing the same in New York City (*On the Town*). But those earlier Sinatra characters had no past to speak of, at least not in any way that mattered to their films' narratives. It was as if those men, and really every character Sinatra played prior to *From Here to Eternity*, were born just before the opening credits. And that is definitely not Frankie's story. He has a past. And given the neighborhood in which the bus drops him off, it appears it was not the bright and optimistic one his expression suggests.

Frankie's past is revealed not through exposition or flashback, but through the reactions of those he encounters as he steps back into the downbeat environs he calls home. We learn much about his backstory from the way the other residents seem surprised he's back, some even a little apprehensive at his return, one of the young ladies in a nearby apartment greeting him with a giddy, flirty hello. A beat cop squares up as Frankie passes, eying him warily, and though Frankie walks by with a bounce in his step, he takes a couple of uneasy glances over his shoulder to make sure the law isn't following him. He finally stops outside a bar so nondescript it only blazes BEER from its front window. He looks inside, his face blank, his eyes distant, as if he's remembering something not altogether pleasant, then he spies a small group on a cluster of stools; one group member forces a one-armed patron to dance for a drink. Frankie winces at the mockery, but smiles the next moment when he spies someone else inside. He enters the bar, sneaks up on the slight man and playfully pulls off his eyeglasses. The two, clearly friends, share a laugh and an embrace, then the smaller man asks Frankie how he is in a tone that makes clear it's more than a verbal backslap. The wattage of Frankie's smile dims almost imperceptibly, not in humiliation, it seems, but regret. He replies simply: "The monkey's gone."

In just over two minutes of screen time, Preminger has brilliantly framed up the 117 minutes to follow—and Sinatra has exhibited a subtlety and nuance in physical and emotional expression heretofore unseen in even his best screen work. Frankie is back in his old seedy stomping grounds, where he is well-known if not universally beloved, except maybe by the ladies, after being away to battle an addiction. There's something about the ringleader of those mocking the disabled man he doesn't like, and it stretches beyond the cruelty Frankie just witnessed. And he has a loyal friend in the slight man who asked about his well-being—who just might be Frankie's best chance to continue to outrun the demons he's beaten back.

The Man with the Golden Arm (1955)

Frankie has both big dreams and big troubles as he returns to what we later learn is the wrong side of the Chicago tracks. On the former side of the ledger is what is in one of those bags he was carrying as he got off the bus: a drum kit. He learned to play the skins while he was away at a prison hospital. (Sinatra was tutored himself pre-production by Shelly Manne, who plays on the soundtrack.[68]) Frankie was in prison for his involvement in the illegal gambling ring, in the hospital to undergo rehabilitation for his drug habit. His plans, and the source of his hope as he stepped off the bus, is that a hospital benefactor has arranged an audition for him with a jazz band in need of a drummer. If he lands the gig, he can escape the illegal gambling racket, where his skills as a dealer have earned him an ironic nickname, "the man with the golden arm."

On the troubles side of Frankie's journey are two major players: His wife Zosh (Eleanor Parker, seemingly presaging Joan Crawford's wild-eyed performance in *What Ever Happened to Baby Jane?*), a stripper who wound up in a wheelchair after Frankie, stoned, crashed their car. He then married her out of guilt; since they were paired in dysfunction, she fears he'll leave if the dysfunction does. The other impediment to the fresh start Frankie is after is Nifty Louie (Darren McGavin), the heartless bar bully. Louie has a financial interest in Frankie's golden arm for each of its dual meanings: He holds a stake in the illegal poker game Frankie no longer wants to deal for, and he's a dealer himself in the narcotics that got Frankie sent to rehab.

The story that follows is as jagged and full of sharp, painful turns as the opening credits' animated arm. Sinatra shines as brightly in moments that require desperate actions and careening emotions as he does in expressing the intimate inner life of a man who, ironically given his earned reputation as a winning card dealer, keeps getting dealt a bad hand. Zosh continues to play on his remorse over the accident—an ever-present reminder of the life Frankie wants to leave behind and restriction to him actually doing it. The apartment they share, in a ramshackle tenement house at the top of a staircase Preminger shoots with the most foreboding shadows he employs for any set, offers him none of the hope he wore on his face when he disembarked the bus. He can't even practice the drums there for his big audition: The beats give Zosh headaches, and her complaining about them gives Frankie headaches. Sinatra begins to layer quiet exasperation and sad resignation to Frankie's expressions whenever the two are together; they serve as the starting of a stopwatch that signals to the viewer time is running out on the new life and happier times Frankie Machine envisioned after leaving prison clean and sober.

The stopwatch only speeds up at the bar. Zero Schwiefka (Robert Strauss), Nifty Louie's junior partner, turns Frankie in to the cops on a bogus charge to force the dealer every gambler wants to play against back to the table. During his brief time in jail, locked up with a junkie suffering through increasingly agitated withdrawal, we understand Frankie's monkey won't be gone for good. He's kicked the habit, but not the people who fueled it. He clings to the bars of the cell as physically far away from the addict as he can, and Preminger's camera isolates on his face in the first of an effectively few close-ups. As Frankie tries to drown out his cellmate's pleas for a fix, Sinatra coaxes a pitch-perfect twitch out of his upper lip.

Louie (played by McGavin with preening malevolence but enough self-restraint to keep him short of caricature) is the final needle in Frankie's sobriety coffin. With so many outside forces working against him, Frankie gives in to the inside force gnawing at him. Sinatra is at his minimalist best in the scene of Frankie's initial relapse inside Louie's dank apartment, fidgety and paranoid but mostly wordless—registering shame and desire as Bernstein's score pounds home the on-edge atmosphere of the moment. Preminger opts for a tight shot of Frankie's face as the drugs are administered, and the sadness of the character's fate is depicted through blink-and-you'll-miss-them movements: the arch of an eyebrow, the return of the lip twitch, the steely focus of a hundred-yard stare followed immediately by the eyes' irises receding and falling blank. It is a bravura performance by Sinatra given only in micro-expression.

The only hope Frankie has in fighting through the bad seeds around him and the bad decisions he makes is Molly (Kim Novak), the strip-club waitress he loves. Molly is the only person in the twisted tapestry of Frankie's life who wants more and better for him. Even his quirky little friend from the opening scene, Sparrow (Arnold Stang, an offbeat casting choice since he was then best known for his comic role as second banana on TV's *Milton Berle Show*), is too much small-time hustler and thief to really help his pal and protector crawl out of the ooze. But Molly encourages Frankie's desire to stay clean—from drugs and the influence of the street. Novak brings kindness and earnestness to the part, which is mostly all it requires. She doesn't dramatically hold her own in her scenes with Sinatra, but she does provide a soft backdrop for him to play against, the only outpost where the depth of Frankie Machine's heart can be explored.

That is evident in their exchange after Molly lets him practice his drums at her apartment, down those murky stairs in his own building. It's the only moment in the entire film where Frankie manifests the same easy optimism he displayed in its opening two minutes:

> FRANKIE: I quit the game, Molly.
> MOLLY: It wouldn't have hurt you to wait a coupla days, Frank.
> FRANKIE: I wanted to quit. I'm quitting a couple of things.
> MOLLY: Is it bad?

The Man with the Golden Arm (1955)

FRANKIE: Not too bad.
MOLLY: You shouldn't have started again.
FRANKIE: Who knows why I started in the first place? I guess in the beginning it grew on me for kicks. Louie gave me my first shot for nothin'. I thought I could take it or leave it alone. So I took it and I took again and again. One day Louie wasn't around. I nearly went crazy 'til I found him. Oh, I was sick. I was so sick.
MOLLY: You can't be that sick and live.
FRANKIE: That's why I knew I was hooked. There was a 40-pound monkey on my back. The only way to get along with a load like that is to keep leaning on a fix.
MOLLY: Don't. Don't.
FRANKIE: I'm one of the lucky ones, Molly. I kicked it and I'm not too far hooked to kick it again. I've had my last fix. I mean it, Molly.

He may mean it, but he can't live it. Things fall apart quickly. Frankie fights with Zosh and in his feelings of being trapped gets shot up again by Louie. Molly sees he's high when he visits her at the club, as Sinatra subtly layers more jitters onto Frankie's declining demeanor. She moves to another part of town to get away from him. Zero and Louie entice him back into the card game. He takes another hit to dull the pain of Molly leaving. He then deals for 24 straight hours, and at Louie's urging cheats some high rollers on a winning streak. When he's caught, he's tossed into the street. Exhausted and strung out, he remembers his audition, stumbles in late and plays the drums so poorly that he leaves after only a couple of botched runs. Back to Louie's he goes to dull the pain, but the drug dealer won't give his card dealer any

Sinatra did his heroin withdrawal scene in *The Man with the Golden Arm* in one take. He received a Best Actor Oscar nomination for his performance.

more "candy." Frankie knocks Louie cold and searches vainly for his stash, becoming more frenzied as he first heads home to Zosh and then to Molly's new apartment to find some money for a score.

It is in Molly's apartment that Sinatra secures his Academy Award nomination for Best Actor in a Leading Role. Denied money by his true love, Frankie is left only one choice: to ride out with no medical intervention the ravages of the addiction that has again taken full control of him. To beat the monkey again cold turkey, locked in Molly's bedroom. Sinatra commands every second of the scene as he progresses from swallowing hard to get air, pulling at his clothes, convulsing on the bed, cutting his arm, groaning, crying, begging through the door, breaking furniture, trying to crawl out the window and finally winding up in a fetal position on the floor. Sinatra overplays not a single beat of the scene; his movements are not broad, but intimate. He doesn't emote Frankie's pain as much as experience and embody it. He gives the viewer just enough of the external torture to uncloak the internal agony. The fact that he did it in a single take, with no rehearsals, is astounding.

It was not the way Preminger envisioned the scene. The director, a perfectionist (and often maligned for it), had outlined days of takes, rehearsals and retakes. But Sinatra firmly said no.[69] He did so not because of his well-documented dislike of overpreparing on the grounds it swiped his performance of spontaneity; he did plenty of on-set prep work during the shoot, with *Modern Screen* noting from the set that in another scene, "Frank rehearsed his lines, gradually working his way into the mood of a sleazy, underprivileged small-time hoodlum."[70] Sinatra's reluctance was rooted in confidence. He had spent time at drug rehabilitation clinics studying patients and knew how he wanted to play every harrowing note of the cold-turkey scene, according to Martha Crawford Caratini, Eleanor Parker's stunt double.[71] He told Preminger: "Just keep those cameras grinding."[72]

The Man with the Golden Arm ends on screen in a more upbeat way than it does in Algren's novel, in which Frankie commits suicide. The movie wraps with its antagonists, Louie and Zosh, both dead: She pushed him down that shadowy staircase in her apartment building after he discovered she had been faking her paralysis to hang on to Frankie; then she jumps from the apartment's balcony to her death after her lies are exposed. The final shot shows Frankie and Molly strolling away from the neighborhood that always broke their hearts with blank expressions. Their future may be unknown but at least it includes each other. He looks ten years older than when the audience met him.

It could have been a downbeat ending for the production as a whole if the Production Code office had gotten its way and kept the film out of theaters. Before shooting was completed, the censors cried foul, lambasting the script because it dealt with drug use and addiction, a disallowed subject matter for the movies. The federal Narcotics Bureau threw in with the Code office, arguing that the villain (presumably Frankie Machine) "should have shot himself or ended up in jail" because "dope addicts never get cured."[73] Preminger cared not a whit: "Many people think because I have had censorship trouble, I am in the business to make dirty pictures. This is not true. I want to make *adult* films. And, if necessary, I will fight for the right to make them."[74]

And fight he did. When the Code office refused to give *Golden Arm* its seal of approval, the director didn't flinch. "I feel my picture will not only not have a bad effect; I am sure it will have a good effect, by dramatizing the evils of dope through the medium of entertainment."[75] United Artists, the company through which Preminger released the movie, stood resolutely behind him and it. UA went so far as to resign from the Motion Picture Association of America over the imbroglio. UA president Arthur B. Krim hailed the movie's "outstanding caliber" and called it one of the most important productions his company had ever brought to the screen.[76] The film was released, without the Code seal of approval, on December 15, 1955. Its robust box-office performance added to the industry and cultural voices that predicted and even called for the Production Code's demise. It finally was disbanded in 1968—seven years after retroactively awarding *The Man with the Golden Arm* its seal.

Sinatra earned his best reviews since *From Here to Eternity*—some even stronger—for his embodiment of Frankie Machine. *The Spokesman-Review*'s Dorothy Powers noted, "Sinatra switches his narcotic moods with the finesse of a practiced junkie."[77] Syndicated columnist Louella Parsons, who pursed her rhetorical lips in saying the film "overstepped the bounds of decency," nonetheless singled Sinatra out as giving "a performance that is so real you find yourself wanting to scream with the horror of his battle against dope."[78] Even the buttoned-up Philip Scheuer of *The Los Angeles Times*, who tossed about words like "bitter," "dregs" and "monotony" in his review headlined "Sordid Film on Drugs," praised the leading man: "Sinatra gives a near-great performance."[79]

Sinatra was so spent after *Golden Arm* wrapped that he hightailed it to his home in Palm Springs and slept.[80] "I was absolutely exhausted," he said. "Preminger had put me through a terrific pace."[81] By the time Ernest Borgnine beat him for the Best Actor Oscar a few months later, Sinatra was already not only rested, but finished filming his follow-up feature, which would take far less physical, emotional and dramatic toll on him. He was crooning again with his old friend Bing Crosby in the musical romantic comedy *High Society*.

High Society

Directed by Charles Walters
Screenplay: John Patrick, from the play *The Philadelphia Story* by Philip Barry
Producer: Sol Spiegel
Cinematography: Paul Vogel (Technicolor)
Editor: Ralph E. Winters
Songs:
"High Society Calypso," "Little One," "Who Wants to Be a Millionaire?," "True Love," "I Love You Samantha," "Well, Did You Evah!," "Mind If I Make Love to You," "Now You Has Jazz," "You're Sensational" Written by Cole Porter
Cast: Frank Sinatra, Bing Crosby, Grace Kelly, Celeste Holm, John Lund, Louis Calhern, Sidney Blackmer, Louis Armstrong, Margalo Gillmore, Lydia Reed, Gordon Richards, Richard Garrick, Paul Keast, Reginald Simpson, Richard Keene, Hugh Boswell, Barrett Deems, Edmond Hall, Ruth Lee, Billy Kyle, Arvell Shaw, Helen Spring, James "Trummy" Young, Florence Wix, Murray Pollack, Jeffrey Sayre, Norman Stevens, Paul Power, Leoda Richards, Scott Seaton, Don Anderson, Gene Coogan, Steve Carruthers, Franklyn Farnum, James Gonzalez, Tex Brodus, Philo McCullough
Released July 17, 1956
MGM
111 minutes

High Society was filmed between January and March 1956 during a time when some significant events occurred that impacted Frank Sinatra's career. First was the January 27 release of the song "Heartbreak Hotel" by a new young singer named Elvis Presley. Presley had been recording for two years, initially at Sun, a small Memphis studio. His earthy renditions of the blues songs "That's All Right (Mama)" and "Mystery Train" were both shouting and yearning in the classic blues tradition, and it bridged a gap between the African-American rhythm and blues approach, and the more mainstream country and jazz styles. When Sun sold Presley's contact to RCA Victor, his work exploded onto the mainstream when his first single flew to the top of the charts. "Heartbreak Hotel," with Presley's hollering, hiccupy delivery and Scotty Moore's wham-bam-bam-bam guitar solo was jarring to adults and exhilarating to youngsters. It ignited a cultural revolution that Sinatra eventually had to respond to and deal with.

The next event that stunned Sinatra was more personal. His friend Humphrey Bogart was diagnosed with lung cancer in February. Sinatra was part of a group that met at the home of Bogart and his wife Lauren Bacall. Calling themselves "The Rat Pack," the group also included Judy Garland and husband Sid Luft, David Niven, songwriter Jimmy Van Heusen and writer Nathaniel Benchley. When asked by columnist Earl Wilson what the purpose of the group was, Bacall replied, "To drink bourbon and stay up late."[82] Sinatra idolized Bogart and had gotten close to him, so his diagnosis was very upsetting. Frank visited Bogie whenever possible until the iconic actor died in January 1957.

Despite these events occurring as he filmed *High Society*, the movie retains its light-hearted approach and was a happy experience for all involved. The film was based on Philip Barry's play *The Philadelphia Story*, a Broadway hit in the late 1930s and an even bigger hit as a 1940 movie. Both featured Katharine Hepburn. The movie also benefited from performances by Cary Grant and James Stewart, who garnered an Oscar for his performance. It was the fifth highest grossing film of 1940, a year that also offered such popular films as John Ford's *The Grapes of Wrath*, Walt Disney's *Pinocchio*, Alfred Hitchcock's *Rebecca* and Charlie Chaplin's talkie debut *The Great Dictator*.

High Society transformed the original non-musical play and film into a musical, with songs composed by Cole Porter. Porter had not scored a movie since Vincente Minnelli's *The Pirate* (1948) with Gene Kelly and Judy Garland. None of the songs from that film achieved much notice, but Porter continued to enjoy success on Broadway with *Kiss Me Kate*, *Can-Can* and *Silk Stockings*, all of which were later made into films, *Can-Can* featuring Sinatra. By 1956, Porter's career was nearing its end. His mother had died in 1952, and his wife, Linda Lee Thomas, lost her battle with emphysema in 1954. *High Society* was Porter's penultimate motion picture score (he scored the Gene Kelly film *Les Girls* the following year). By 1958, ulcers in his right leg caused amputation, after which he never wrote another song. He died in 1964.

High Society was shot in Newport, Rhode Island, at Clarendon Court, which was owned by Mae Cadwell Hayward. (It was sold to Claus von Bulow in 1970.) Because of the close proximity to the Newport Jazz Festival, Louis Armstrong got involved with the production along with his band, who play themselves.

C.K. Dexter Haven (Bing Crosby) hovers around the mansion of his ex-wife Tracy Lord (Grace Kelly), who is soon to be married. Because her pending nuptials are considered news, magazine journalist Mike Connor (Sinatra) and his photographer Liz Imbrie (Celeste Holm) wander about the house putting together their magazine feature. Tracy's intended is the successful but dull George Kittredge (John Lund). Confusion reigns when Tracy asks that her Uncle Willy (Louis Calhern) pose as her estranged father, so that when her actual father (Sidney Blackmer) shows up, he can pretend to be Uncle Willy. Mike soon falls for Tracy, who now has three men vying for her. She realizes in the end that Dexter remains the man for her, while Connor ends up with Liz.

Comparisons to *The Philadelphia Story* are natural in that the 1940 film has lived on into the 21st century as a classic, more so than this musical remake. Katharine Hepburn repeated her Broadway role as Tracy in the earlier film, and though she is quite beautiful and appealing. Grace Kelly cannot measure up to Hepburn's performance. There are flashes of Hepburn in Kelly's performance, but she's still too elegant and poised to completely pull off the madcap heiress role. She also barely sings in this film and doesn't have any solo numbers, which is unusual for the leading lady of a musical and speaks to the fact that she was miscast. Kelly may have been distracted enough by real-life events: A month after production concluded, she married the prince of Monaco and left acting altogether.

Crosby is all wrong in the role that had once been played by Cary Grant. While the 36-year-old Grant had no problem playing *The Philadelphia Story*'s handsome, charismatic lead, 53-year-old Bing comes off as a real square pretending to be a handsome rascal. He is eight years older than John Lund, playing his "dull" romantic rival, and 27 years older than

(Left to right): Grace Kelly, Bing Crosby, Sinatra and Celeste Holm in *High Society*.

Kelly. (Grant and Hepburn were three years apart.) While his ability as a singer is still commendable as he smoothly croons the Porter songs, he is far too old for the role. But, because his company, Bing Crosby Productions, had a hand in the making of the film, he was able to secure the lead quite handily. Set aside his musical numbers and Crosby is the weakest part of the movie.

Sinatra, playing a role that had won James Stewart an Oscar 16 years earlier, holds his own spouting the wisecracks from the original play, and Holm, whose forte is dry humorous dialogue, is every bit as great as Ruth Hussey was in 1940. Perhaps the best performance comes from Louis Calhern as the wickedly flirty Uncle Willy, who matches his career-defining comic turn in the Marx Brothers classic *Duck Soup* (1933).

Despite his being miscast, Crosby shows he can still croon, and appears in the movie's two best numbers. A real highlight is when Bing recalls his long ago days on the Brunswick label and performs "Now You Has Jazz" with Louis Armstrong and his band. Another song highlight is "Well, Did You Evah!," a Crosby-Sinatra duet, as it is strewn with wisecracks like similar duets Bing did with Bob Hope in their popular *Road* pictures. At one point when Bing adds one of his "ba-ba-ba-boo" asides, Sinatra responds to it negatively, and Crosby states, "You must be one of the new fellas." Despite what has been claimed in some other studies, Crosby was not aloof and withdrawn during the filming of *High Society*. He and Sinatra got along quite well, and remained friendly thereafter. Their camaraderie is evident when they perform this number. Perhaps the film would have benefited from more numbers featuring Crosby and Sinatra together, because they show off some really wonderful chemistry in their one song number, Frank playing his character as definitely tipsy, Bing a little less so but still amused.

Produced for under $3 million, *High Society*'s box office receipts topped $8 million. It was one of the top ten moneymakers of 1956. It was also nominated for two Oscars, Best Original Score (Johnny Green and Saul Chaplin) and Best Song (Porter's "True Love"). It almost secured a third nomination but that resulted in one of the most delightfully infamous slip-ups in Academy Award history.

Plans were made to nominate the film for Best Motion Picture Story, despite it not being original, having come from a play and a previous film. The writers nominated were Edward Bernds and Elwood Ullman, who had nothing to do with this film, but had penned the screenplay for an unrelated Bowery Boys comedy by the same title, released the previous year. Amused by the error, but not wanting to embarrass the Academy, Bernds and Ullman asked to have their names removed from the ballot. The Academy was relieved as they believed many members might have voted for the

High Society director Charles Walters (left) goes over a song with Sinatra and Grace Kelly.

Bowery Boys movie on a lark, causing further embarrassment if it actually won the Oscar. Ironically, the *High Society* review in *Time* magazine said that Sinatra's performance made him seem like "a Dead End Kid with a typewriter."[83] The Dead End Kids were precursors to the Bowery Boys.

Just as *High Society* filming completed in March 1956, Sinatra's latest Capitol album "Songs for Swinging Lovers" was released. Recorded just before production began on the movie, it benefited from Nelson Riddle's arrangements and featured the popular tracks "You Make Me Feel So Young," "I've Got You Under My Skin," "Pennies from Heaven" and "Too Marvelous for Words." It reached #2 on the *Billboard* charts.

However, by the time *High Society* was released in July 1956, newcomer Elvis Presley had secured four successive #1 hits, include the raucous rocker "Hound Dog," the yearning ballad "I Want You, I Need You, I Love You" and the R&B cover "Don't Be Cruel," along with "Heartbreak

Hotel." Before 1956 was up, Presley had another #1 hit with his ballad "Love Me Tender," which was also the title song of his movie debut. In 1956, Sinatra had no #1 singles at all, and only one that made the Top Ten ("Hey Jealous Lover," which rose to #3 in the late fall).

Rock'n'roll didn't start with Presley. Even the mainstream was already acquainted with this new sound before "Heartbreak Hotel" climbed the charts. In 1955, "Rock Around the Clock" by Bill Haley and the Comets was heard during the credits for the movie *Blackboard Jungle* and was subsequently a hit on the radio. However, when Presley came along with songs that had a strong urban component, it got a reaction from Sinatra. Presley had started a cultural revolution that threatened to overshadow the old style. Sinatra complained in the magazine *Western World*:

> My only deep sorrow is the unrelenting insistence of recording and motion picture companies upon purveying the most brutal, ugly, degenerate, vicious form of expression it has been my displeasure to hear—naturally I refer to the bulk of rock'n'roll. It fosters almost totally negative and destructive reactions in young people. It smells phony and false. It is sung, played and written for the most part by cretinous goons and by means of its almost imbecilic reiterations and sly, lewd—in plain fact dirty—lyrics, and as I said before, it manages to be the martial music of every sideburned delinquent on the face of the earth. This rancid smelling aphrodisiac I deplore. But, in spite of it, the contribution of American music to the world could be said to have one of the healthiest effects of all our contributions.[84]

Presley called a press conference and countered Sinatra in a widely syndicated response:

> It's the greatest music ever, and it will continue to be so. I like it, and I'm sure many other persons feel the same way. I also admit it's the only thing I can do. He has a right to his opinion, but I can't see him knocking my music for no good reason. I admire him as a performer and an actor, but I think he's badly mistaken about this. If I remember correctly, he was also part of a trend. I don't see how he can call the youth of today immoral and delinquent.[85]

Sinatra and Presley's relationship would take several turns over the next few years.

Johnny Concho

Directed by Don McGuire
Screenplay: Don McGuire and David Harmon, from Harmon's story "The Man Who Owned the Town"
Producer: Frank Sinatra

Cinematography: William Mellor (Technicolor)
Editor: Eda Warren
Cast: Frank Sinatra, Keenan Wynn, William Conrad, Phyllis Kirk, Wallace Ford, Dorothy Adams, Christopher Dark, Leo Gordon, Howard Petrie, Harry Bartell, Dan Riss, Willis Bouchey, Robert Osterloh, Jean Byron, Claude Akins, John Qualen, Budd Knapp, Ben Wright, Strother Martin, Joe Bassett, Malcolm Atterbury, Russell Thorson, John Daheim
Released July 27, 1956
Kent Productions for United Artists
84 minutes

Johnny Concho was shot in only 16 days just prior to Sinatra starting work on shooting *High Society*. It was his first Western and the first movie he produced. And it was his first time playing a dislikable character since *Suddenly*. But whereas the assassin in *Suddenly* is cold and heartless to his very core, Johnny Concho is really just a hollow braggart who gets a Western-movie–style comeuppance.

Johnny lives in Cripple Creek, Arizona, and is a man who boastfully struts about, getting his way in whatever situation. The reason is, his brother Red is a much-feared gunslinger, so they feel they need to let Johnny have his way. The one person who loves Johnny is Mary Dark (Phyllis Kirk), daughter of a general store owner (Wallace Ford). Johnny had been regularly winning at cards because he has been allowed to simply state what his hand is without showing it, and then to take the pot. A stranger in town, Tallman (William Conrad), calls his bluff. When Johnny loftily brags who his brother is, Tallman introduces himself as the man who stood up to, and killed, Red Concho. Revealing his actual cowardice, Johnny leaves town. Mary, who still loves him, follows.

Johnny discovers that everyone in nearby towns knows that he is not be trusted or feared. Meanwhile, Tallman takes over Cripple Creek and demands a percentage of every business in town. Johnny later discovers that brother Red was the same sort of hollow braggart he had been, and never really was a gunslinger. He tries to overcome the shame of his past by returning to Cripple Creek and facing Tallman. Tallman wounds him, but is shot dead by Mary's father. Johnny remains ashamed, but the townspeople are impressed by his bravery and he makes a new life for himself with Mary.

As the first movie Sinatra produced and the only film made for his company Kent Productions, it is rather impressive that he chose a story, and a role, that allowed him to challenge another area of his talent. Johnny is not a cold-hearted bad guy, he is an entitled upstart, a sniveling coward

Phyllis Kirk and Frank Sinatra in *Johnny Concho*.

who takes advantage of a status he doesn't deserve—and soon discovers he never really had. He has no problem with being hated, as long as he can take what he wants. At one point as he approaches a blacksmith shop, the blacksmith says, "One of these days, I'll break a yard of his neck!" A townsman states, "Not while Red Concho is alive. Until then, you'll do like the rest of us, smile and hate."

Sinatra pulls out all stops as far as any innate talent or experience he has as a screen actor, showing real emotion as the coward who at once can be a bully and a braggart, and then suddenly the worst kind of coward and wimp. At one point he says to the loyal Mary, "I can't take care of me, let alone take care of you. No food, no money and the sign of a leper on me— is that what you want a part of?" And when he discovers his brother was never who he was believed to be, he tells her, "I'm dead, Mary. I just ain't got the guts to lay down."

Socialite Gloria Vanderbilt was originally cast as Mary. Vanderbilt, who had just started acting in a 1954 stage production, was romantically involved with Sinatra around this time, when she was between marriages to Leopold Stokowski and Sidney Lumet. She left the production and it was rumored her leaving was due to conflicts with Sinatra but, in fact, it was due to conflicts with the film's director, Don McGuire.

She was replaced by Phyllis Kirk, who told syndicated columnist Dick Kleiner[86]:

> Sixteen days to make a picture is too fast. I don't care what anybody says, no actor can do justice to a part in that time unless he has a lot of rehearsing, which we didn't. But Frank was a darling; kind and considerate and very easy to work with and for.

Vanderbilt, who lived until 2019, never acted in a theatrical film. She did some sporadic TV work from 1957 into the 1970s.

Clocking in at a breezy 84 minutes, *Johnny Concho* never feels rushed. With no excess subplots, it is a clear-cut Western about a dislikable figure who realizes and reforms in the end. Sinatra attacks the role with everything he has to offer and comes off quite well. In fact, *Johnny Concho* is a neat little Western drama that further benefits from a strong supporting cast. Unfortunately, it was not a success, grossing less than its production costs. This didn't hurt Sinatra overall as it was easy to overlook amidst a string of successful movies. It came out at around the same time as *High Society* which was a smash.

Johnny Concho is a very unconventional Western, which is maybe why it wasn't a big success and isn't very well-known today. The man who is supposed to be our protagonist isn't the sort of macho hero we're used to seeing, and in fact isn't even very likable. It also isn't very action-heavy, which would be fine except there are parts in the middle where it drags a bit. But Frank remained very proud of the film despite its not performing well at the box office.

Sinatra re-released *Johnny Concho* in 1960 and it managed to generate a small profit during a period when Sinatra had achieved show biz status that was beyond his capacity four years earlier. However, more problems for the movie arose when small-time producer Jack Broder of Realart productions sued for a share of the profits. Broder, who was known for re-releasing old Universal product, and for producing the notorious *Bela Lugosi Meets a Brooklyn Gorilla* (1952), claimed that his company had sold the rights to David Harmon's original story to Sinatra's Kent Productions. Now that the movie was making money in its re-release, Broder believed he was owed somewhere between $20,000 and $60,000. Sinatra settled for an undisclosed amount.

An intriguing item appeared in newspapers at the end of 1955:

> Frank Sinatra, currently the busiest star in Hollywood, is looking ahead to March 1957, in connection with his second undertaking as an independent producer. This will be a musical comedy called *The Jazz Train* in which Sammy Davis is scheduled to co-star with Sinatra. Mervyn Nelson wrote the screenplay in which Davis plans to make his screen debut as the producer and

choreographer of a musical show being put on for the Air Force. Sinatra will appear as the manager of the troupe.[87]

There is no record of this intriguing production to ever have been considered beyond this point. Mervyn Nelson was a vaudeville performer who also acted on Broadway. He wrote several plays, including *The Jazz Train*, but is credited for writing and directing only two films, including the gay-themed drama *Some of My Best Friends Are…* (1971). According to the Global Musical Theater website:

> *The Jazz Train* was "A Musical Dedicated to the Negro People," but was not a conventional book musical. The "train" was made up of "cars" (coaches), each one representing a different period or stage in the evolution of black American popular music as seen through the eyes of Mervyn Nelson, the director and devisor of the show.[88]

The Jazz Train played London's Piccadilly Theatre for 111 performances beginning in April 1955.

Sinatra went from this small-scale, independently produced Western to a big, bloated indie production for Stanley Kramer and with co-stars Cary Grant and Sophia Loren. But *The Pride and the Passion* turned out to be a troubled production.

The Pride and the Passion

Produced and Directed by Stanley Kramer
Screenplay: Edna and Edward Anhalt, from the novel *The Gun* by C.S. Forester
Cinematography: Franz Planer (Technicolor)
Editors: Ellsworth Hoagland and Frederic Knudtson
Cast: Cary Grant, Frank Sinatra, Sophia Loren, Theodore Bikel, John Wengraf, Jay Novello, José Nieto, Carlos Larrañaga, Philip Van Zandt, Paco El Laberinto, Julián Ugarte, Félix de Pomés, Carlos Casaravilla, Juan Olaguivel, Nana DeHerrera, Carlos De Mendoza, Luis Gedes, Carlos Diaz de Mendozza, Xan das Bolas, Adolfo Suarez, Barta Barri
Released July 10, 1957
Stanley Kramer Productions for United Artists
132 minutes

The Pride and the Passion was the one weak film among all the successful projects that Sinatra was engaged in during this period. So many projects came at Sinatra in 1955 and '56, it is impressive that he found time to concentrate as effectively on each one. Every one of them enjoyed some measure of success, even *The Pride and the Passion* despite it not being a very good movie.

As 1955 became 1956, Sinatra was swamped with work in movies and music. As early as January 1956, he was basking in the massive success of three starring films released in rapid succession, *Guys and Dolls, The Man with the Golden Arm,* and *The Tender Trap*—two hit musicals, and a serious drama that challenged his innate acting skill and netted him an Oscar nomination. He was involved in shooting his first self-produced independent movie and was about to start work on another musical, *High Society*, that was also a huge hit. Sinatra's contract to appear in *The Pride and the Passion* was already signed by January 1956, and he was in talks for both *The Joker Is Wild*, an indie musical drama about performer Joe E. Lewis, and *Pal Joey* at Columbia.

And, despite the rise of rock'n'roll and Sinatra's swipes at it in the press, his albums were still nearing the top of the charts. In 1957, his albums "Close to You," "A Swingin' Affair" and "Where Are You?" were in the Top 5. For the most part, the singles he released from those albums failed to chart well, being eclipsed by the popularity of rock'n'roll, as kids usually purchased 45 rpm records rather than LPs. However, in 1957, Sinatra hit Number One with "All of Me" and Number Six with "Witchcraft." The culture appeared to determine that while rock'n'roll might be all the rage with the kids, singers like Sinatra were for grown-ups.

However, Sinatra balked when the press considered his current success a comeback. According to syndicated columnist Erskine Johnson, Sinatra was especially incensed when he attended the *Guys and Dolls* premiere and saw the program describe his career as having "ups and downs matching the steepness of a Himalayan mountain peak. After soaring to what was almost national adulation a dozen years ago, a combination of poor roles, a bad press and other things sent his career zooming downward. He was reputedly washed up. Today his 'second career' is in high gear." Johnson continued:

> The next day Sinatra reportedly blew his top over the wordage about him in the program. He's said to have ranted: "Where do they get that stuff—'He was reputedly washed up.' 'My career zoomed downward.' 'My second career.' It sounds like I'm making a comeback. I've never been away." The year 1953, in which he won an Academy supporting performance award for his non-singing role of little Angelo Maggio in *From Here to Eternity* may have been a career turning point for Sinatra, but he doesn't look back on the film, or the role or the Oscar as a comeback. The Oscar just proved, he contends, something Hollywood had always refused to believe—that Frank Sinatra could act as well

as sing. But since then there's been no doubt about it. *Guys and Dolls* and *The Tender Trap* are current proof. So is *The Man with the Golden Arm* in which Sinatra, playing a dope addict, is in the Oscar race again. Coming up: His first independent production—and first Western—*Johnny Concho*; *High Society*, a musical remake of *The Philadelphia Story*, with Frank co-starring with Bing Crosby and Grace Kelly; Sinatra and Cary Grant in *The Pride and the Passion*—and more movie plans that extend to 1960. Forty-year-old Frank Sinatra is one of Hollywood's all time controversial greats. He's hated and he's loved. He punched a Broadway columnist in the nose. He busted the camera of a news photographer. He fought in a Hollywood café parking lot with a nightclub press agent. He was divorced from his wife Nancy and then married sexy Ava Gardner. Before Ava won a Nevada divorce, the final decree of which she's never bothered to pick up, she and Frank staged domestic battles and reconciliations all the way from Beverly Hills to Spain. Some people find him a gay, fascinating personality. Other people find him surly and unlikable.[89]

As Johnson explains it, Sinatra was responding to his success by becoming the difficult, contentious celebrity. It had gotten to the point where Sinatra didn't want to acknowledge that his career had once been at low ebb.

Although Sinatra had two top stars to work with as well as a top-notch director, *The Pride and the Passion* was still a rather dull, overlong production. And despite its final running time being over two hours, there is little to say about its aesthetics. It is set during the Peninsular War where Royal Navy Captain Anthony Trumbull (Cary Grant) is assigned to find a huge cannon that had belonged to the Spanish army but was abandoned as being too cumbersome for their advancement. Guerrilla warriors headed by Miguel (Sinatra) offer to help the captain obtain the cannon if they can use it to capture Ávila. Trumbull realizes that in order to seize the gun for the British to fight the French, he must team up with Miguel and use the help of the Spanish peasants to restore the gun and use it against the French forces. At the same time, the evil French commander of Ávila, General Jouvet (Theodore Bikel), orders all Spaniards to be forced to reveal information on the cannon or be executed. Meanwhile, there is conflict between Trumbull and Miguel when the latter's girl Juana (Sophia Loren) falls for Trumbull.

Producer-director Stanley Kramer spent a year preparing *The Pride and the Passion*. He arranged for Loren to play the female lead and had her flown in from Italy. This was the actress's first year working in American films; during 1957, she appeared in this movie, *Boy on a Dolphin* with Alan Ladd and *Legend of the Lost* with John Wayne. It has been written that Grant and Loren had a romance during the filming of *The Pride and the Passion* that became quite intense; Grant was reportedly so obsessed with her that she found it unsettling and ended up marrying her agent, Carlo

The Pride and the Passion **was not worthy of the talents of Cary Grant (left) or Sinatra.**

Ponti, not long after filming of this movie concluded. Grant was still married to Betsy Drake at the time.

It has been stated in some previous biographies that Sinatra chose to do the film so he could be near Ava Gardner, who was also shooting in Spain. But other studies claim that he didn't want to do the movie after signing, because his estranged wife was also working in the area and he didn't want to run into her. The latter seems more feasible at this point in their relationship. However, Sinatra was notably difficult during filming. He insisted on his own car being shipped to Spain for his use while working on the movie, even though the studio offered him the use of a $15,000 Mercedes. He also wouldn't stay on location, and insisted on having a suite a nearby luxury hotel. He notoriously refused to do more than one take. He also refused to work after a certain date, even if the movie was still in production, because he had other projects. Despite this, Sinatra got along well with both Loren and Grant, who felt he was miscast. This was Kramer's second directorial effort, after *Not as a Stranger* (1955). With his next film, *The Defiant Ones* (1958), Kramer hit his stride.

One positive thing that came out of *The Pride and the Passion* was Sinatra's friendship with the film's unit photographer Sam Shaw. He and Sinatra shared an interest in art, discussed it seriously and visited nearby museums. Over the years, Sinatra amassed quite an impressive art collection, and also dabbled in painting. This became a plot point on an episode of *The Dick Van Dyke Show* when Rob and Laura accidentally bid on a painting that it turns out Sinatra painted—signing his name backwards.

Despite the troubled production, *The Pride and the Passion* enjoyed box office success, mostly because of the three leads' popularity. Despite Sinatra using an affected Spanish accent throughout (learning it by having Spanish guitarist Vicente Gómez read his lines on tape so Sinatra could copy his inflections), critics generally thought he did well in the role.

For his next film, Frank arranged to portray a personal friend's life story. He had read nightclub comedian Joe E. Lewis's biography *The Joker Is Wild*, written by Art Cohn, and wanted to play the lead in a movie. Lewis had already turned down MGM who had wanted to secure the film rights to his story. But because Sinatra was a friend, arrangements were made. The result was one was another one of Sinatra's finest performances.

The Joker Is Wild

Directed by Charles Vidor
Screenplay: Oscar Saul, from the book by Art Cohn
Producer: Samuel J. Briskin
Cinematography: Daniel Fapp (Black and White)
Editor: Everett Douglas
Songs:
    "All the Way"; Music: Jimmy Van Heusen; Lyrics: Sammy Cahn
    "At Sundown"; Written by Walter Donaldson
    "I Cried for You"; Written by Arthur Freed, Gus Arnheim and
        Abe Lyman

"If I Could Be with You"; Music: James P. Johnson; Lyrics: Henry Creamer

"Out of Nowhere"; Music: Johnny Green; Lyrics: Edward Heyman; Special Lyrics: Harry Harris

"Swingin' on a Star"; Music: Jimmy Van Heusen; Lyrics: Johnny Burke; Special Lyrics: Harry Harris

"Naturally"; Special night club number by Harry Harris

Cast: Frank Sinatra, Mitzi Gaynor, Jeanne Crain, Eddie Albert, Beverly Garland, Jackie Coogan, Barry Kelley, Ted de Corsia, Leonard Graves, Valerie Allen, Hank Henry, Sophie Tucker, Eric Alden, John Harding, Harold Huber, Walter Woolf King, Ned Wever, Eric Wilton, William Pullen, Mary Treen, Wally Brown, Don Beddoe, Len Hendry, Kathleen Gallant, Sid Melton, James Cavanaugh, Bobby Barber, Dick Elliott, Paul Bryar, Shirley Falls, Benny Burt, Jimmy Cross, Phyllis Douglas, Harriette Tarler, Heidi Duval, Florine Carlan, Paula Hill, Lucy Knoch, Bill Hickman, Franklyn Farnum, Joseph LaCava, Edward Ingram, Howard Joslin, Estelle Lawrence, Dorothy Johnson, Larry Knight, Joe Gray, Donna Jo Dribble, Helene Marshall, William Mader, Mabel Rea, Jack Stoney, Brick Sullivan, Alan Paige, Billie Bird, Kit Guard, Regina Gleason, Forbes Murray, Carl M. Leviness, Harold Miller, Art Lewis, Dave White, Edna Ryan, Cosmo Sardo, Oliver McGowan, Kenner Kemp, Russ Bender, Jeffrey Sayre, Pat Moran, Dennis McMullan, Lorna Jordon, Elliott Sullivan, Mike Mahoney, Kay Tapscott, Arturo Petterino, George Offerman, Jr., Reita Green, Bill Baldwin (voice), Bing Crosby (voice)

Released October 25, 1957

Paramount

126 minutes

The story of singer-comedian Joe E. Lewis, who had a serious altercation with one of Al Capone's men in the 1920s but enjoyed the support of Capone himself, was compelling enough to become a popular book, published at the beginning of 1955. In his *Los Angeles Times* column "Book Report," Robert Kirsch wrote, "Art Cohn's *The Joker is Wild*, the story of Joe E. Lewis, the comedian and character par excellence, is likely the best show business biography written in the past 20 years."

MGM offered $150,000 for the film rights, but Lewis had retained control over the material and turned them down. However, Lewis was more comfortable with his friend Frank Sinatra's pitch to play the role, and an independent production was set up with Lewis, Sinatra, Cohn and director Charles Vidor. Each was paid a six-figure sum and given a percentage of the film's profits. Paramount acted as their studio and distributor.

Vidor was an established director who was at the height of his powers when signed to do *The Joker Is Wild*. At Columbia, where he frequently clashed with Harry Cohn, he directed Rita Hayworth in the classics *Cover Girl* (1944) with Gene Kelly and the noir classic *Gilda* (1946) with Glenn Ford. Vidor scored big with Samuel Goldwyn's production of *Hans Christian Andersen* (1952) with Danny Kaye and enjoyed great success at MGM with *Love Me or Leave Me* (1955) featuring Doris Day and James Cagney, the latter giving an Oscar-nominated performance. *Love Me or Leave Me* was a drama with music about real-life singer Ruth Etting and her relationship with gangster Moe "The Gimp" Snyder. Vidor's understanding of the material made Sinatra realize that he'd be the best choice to direct Joe E. Lewis' similar story.

The Joker Is Wild begins in the 1920s when Lewis is asked by mobsters to work their clubs. Joe, already booked elsewhere, insists on honoring his commitments and turns them down. The mob then attacks him, smashing in his skull and slitting his vocal cords. After hours of surgery, Joe awakens, unable to talk, his head heavily bandaged. Realizing his career as a singer has ended, he reinvents his act as a sharp, witty nightclub comic. But his demons are plentiful and he descends into a self-destructive life of bitter alcoholism. When he finally hits rock bottom, he decides to clean up his life.

The Joker Is Wild was a project that Sinatra truly believed in and, as a result, he pulls out every stop as far as his acting talent is concerned, just as he would always do with roles that particularly resonated with him. It is especially remarkable, coming off something as wrongheaded as *The Pride and the Passion,* that Sinatra would choose a role that was equally challenging. Although he had far more in common with an old nightclub entertainer who got mixed up with the mob than he did with the Spanish agitator he played in his previous effort, both roles offered challenges.

Joe E. Lewis, like most successful performers, had a set delivery, a certain method with his vocal inflections, in song and in speech and mannerisms. He performed differently when he was drunk than when he was sober. He did not carry this style into his real life, where he sometimes lacked confidence but still exuded a street-wise toughness. It would have been easy for Sinatra to simply read the lines with conviction when playing Lewis the man, and simply ape his mannerisms when portraying Lewis the comic. But Sinatra mines the character very deeply and captures every nuance with a naturalness that is skilled and impressive.

The film opens with Sinatra, as Lewis, belting out "All of Me" with the utter confidence that a successful nightclub entertainer would exude. (In fact, his performance of "All of Me" not only made it a hit, it also won the

Sinatra gives one of his best performances as Joe E. Lewis in *The Joker Is Wild*.

Oscar for Best Song.) When Lewis gamely tries to work after his injury, all he can manage to get is working in cheap burlesque houses doing hoary routines.

The most fascinating aspect of this part of the movie is Sinatra's flair for comedy within the context of a style he didn't usually do. Donning a loud suit, a wig and the customary baggy pants, Sinatra presents Lewis struggling to retain composure as he performs the old "Don't Play That Music" routine, variations of which had been done by everyone from Abbott and Costello to Clark and McCullough. Being comically slapped by a cop and doused with seltzer water, Lewis powers through the humiliation and Sinatra brilliantly conveys his suppressed desperation. The comparison from the pre-injury Lewis, with his boisterous and powerful singing voice, and his true slumming after his injury is as heartbreaking as it is compelling.

When Sophie Tucker (playing herself) recognizes Lewis and presents him to the audience, he attempts to sing "All of Me" again, but his voice won't reach the high notes that once came so easily. It is another challenging aspect of the character that Sinatra handles masterfully. Lewis noted some titters of derisive amusement from the audience and started making self-deprecating wisecracks about his situation. The audience laughed and he became a hit in spite of himself. This is what led the entertainer back into the better clubs. Then when he'd belt out one of his old tunes, the gruffness and cracking of his voice became a part of the act. Sinatra shows Lewis' tentativeness gradually evolving into confidence.

There are two particularly daunting scenes that really test Sinatra's mettle as an actor. The first is shortly after Lewis wakes up in the hospital, after the attack has resulted in a fractured skull and the slicing of his vocal cords. Realizing his plight, Joe tries to communicate but can only let out a series of anguished wails that increase as he also reacts violently and needs to be sedated. It takes a great deal of emotional power to effectively convey this state, and Sinatra once again rises to the occasion. It is one of the most stunning scenes he would play in his entire screen career.

Another especially impressive sequence, among many, is when Lewis has increased his drinking before showtime and is performing while clearly inebriated. Sinatra maintains the usual gestures and inflections, accurately presenting Joe's jokes and delivery, but more slurred and staggering. Lewis keeps up his wisecracks to cover his inebriation, and makes it look like a part of the act. Sinatra once again presents this very effectively.

The supporting cast is strong, with Eddie Albert especially fine as the low-key counterpart to Sinatra's unbridled charisma, playing Joe's long-suffering accompanist. Jackie Coogan, playing a man who books shows and bets, also exhibits a level of loyalty and friendship that Joe seems to inspire.

Jeanne Crain is both attractive and captivating as Letty Gray, a woman of some means who falls in love with Joe. He feels inferior to her and avoids the relationship she truly wants. When he does finally decide to propose, it is after returning from a tour of entertaining servicemen in dangerous situations. He discovers she is already married. Her later appearance at one of his shows, the one where he is clearly too drunk to perform, causes sadness for her and a certain volatility in Joe, who stops his act and stumbles off stage, injuring himself in a fall on some steps.

Mitzi Gaynor offers perhaps her career-best performance as Martha Stewart,[90] the woman Joe did marry, the film seeming to indicate that he was rebounding. His marriage to Martha didn't last, and the scene where she tearfully ends their relationship while Joe is preoccupied at a crap table is one of the most stirring scenes in the film.

The only drawback in *The Joker Is Wild* is the anticlimactic ending. Joe has lost everyone, even his loyal accompanist, whom he accidentally punches during a violent reaction to a heckler at one of his shows. He is walking alone, flooded with memories, and visited by his conscience who appears as a reflecting image in the store windows he's passing. It basically represents Joe's decision to clean up his act, and that is what he sets out to do as the film ends. The last shot shows Joe headed to the Chez Paree in Chicago, getting ready to perform once again. Because Joe E. Lewis lived another 14 years, it was impossible to conclude a life that was still going on. The film does the best it can under the circumstances.

Vidor's direction is typically great, as he follows his master shots with medium shots and intimate closeups that allow the actors to convey the nuance of their characters, especially Sinatra. Perhaps his most impressive visual takes place just after Joe is attacked in his room. The gangsters hurry out of the hotel where Joe is staying, leaving him for dead. After a few beats, Vidor shows Joe's door open and his bloodied hand coming into the frame. As Sinatra slowly crawls out, splattered with blood and barely

Gag shot of Sinatra (right) and Joe E. Lewis, the entertainer he portrayed in *The Joker Is Wild*.

alive, Vidor fixes the camera on him and allows his body movements to be the only action in the frame.

The Joker Is Wild was a hit and pleased the critics. Because he had a stake in the production, Sinatra did not make the same sort of demands as he had when filming the big studio production *The Pride and the Passion*. There was a light-hearted approach to some of the filming. At one point, during a scene between Sinatra and Jackie Coogan, a photo of Sinatra's friend Bing Crosby was put on the wall of what was supposed to be Lewis' dressing room. When Sinatra went to point at something as part of the scene, he saw the Crosby photo and broke out laughing.

Sinatra had played in light musicals and straight dramas with success, and now did an exceptional job in a musical that also had a strong dramatic narrative. As a result, he was drawn to a similar project with his next film, *Pal Joey*.

Pal Joey

Directed by George Sidney
Screenplay: Dorothy Kingsley, from the musical by John O'Hara
Producer: Fred Kohlmar
Cinematography: Harold Lipstein (Technicolor)
Editor: Viola Lawrence, Jerome Thoms
Songs:
"There's a Small Hotel," "I Could Write a Book," "The Lady Is a Tramp," "My Funny Valentine," "Zip," "What Do I Care for a Dame," "Great Big Town," "I Didn't Know What Time It Was," "That Terrific Rainbow," "Bewitched"; Music: Richard Rodgers; Lyrics: Lorenz Hart
Cast: Rita Hayworth, Frank Sinatra, Kim Novak, Barbara Nichols, Bobby Sherwood, Hank Henry, Elizabeth Patterson, Barry Bernard, Ellie Kent, Mara McAfree, Ernesto Molinari, Bek Nelson, Frank Wilcox, Robert Anderson, Gail Bonney, Rudy Diaz, Tol Avery, Snub Pollard, Frank Sully, Robert Reed, Eddie Bartell, Al Nalbandian, Joe Miksak, Al Bain, Lessie Lynne Wong, Barbara Yung, Jean Nakaba, Elizabeth Fenton, Nellie Gee Ching, Hermes Pan, Bert Stevens, Betty Utey, Hermie Rose, Leoda Richards, James Seay, Frank Wilimarth, Michael Fereris, Patty Lynn, Bob Glenn, Everett Glass, Ellie Kent, John Hubbard, George Ford, Cheryl Kubert, Leota Larraine, Allen Gin, Jo Ann Smith, Mitchell Rhein, Stephen Soldi, Robert Piperio, Howard Sigrist, Ilsa Ostroffsky, Philo McCullough, Raymond McWalters,

Bobbie Jean Henson, George DeNormand, Bob Glenn, Darlene Engle, Michael Ferris, Sam Harris, Helen Elliot, Sue Boomer, Jane Chung, Barrie Chase
Released October 25, 1957
Columbia
111 minutes

Sinatra's career was at its chrysalis moment when this screen adaptation of John O'Hara's book and Broadway play about a low-wattage show biz rapscallion hit theaters in October 1957. The bobbysoxers who more than 15 years earlier squealed at the sight of Sinatra had sons named Bobby now, and those boys were listening to Elvis Presley and Little Richard on their transistor radios. The fathers of those boys did not swoon at Frankie the way their wives had; they swung with him, baby. *Pal Joey* would be a motion picture of note if all it had to recommend it was documenting the cultural moment that the Voice metamorphosed into the Chairman of the Board as Technicolorfully as a caterpillar transforms into a butterfly. But it has much more going for it than that, singled out by one critic as "the quintessential Sinatra film musical."[91]

The material—in its rawest, original form—made a star out of Gene Kelly on Broadway in 1940. O'Hara had concocted the character of Joey Evans in the late 1930s, in a series of short stories composed as letters in *The New Yorker*; he later compiled them into a novel. The Joey of the written word is a calculating louse, a Chicago nightclub entertainer of low morals and lofty ambitions.

Pal Joey **might feature Sinatra's finest all-around screen performance.**

Readers came to know his venality in notes he swapped with his "Friend Ted"; he signed them "Pal Joey." Kelly was plucked from the chorus and minor roles to be the star of the musical play O'Hara created in collaboration with songwriters Richard Rodgers and Lorenz Hart. Key to Kelly's landing the role was his youthful energy and undeniable charm: Joey was still a rat, but as brought to life by Kelly a more likable rat than on paper. As the star noted to his hometown newspaper the *Pittsburgh Post-Gazette*, "We've softened him up so that he isn't too offensive."[92]

That said, the plot still revolves around Joey cravenly starting an affair with a bored socialite (Vera Simpson, played by Vivienne Segal), who he manipulates into giving him the money to open his own club and the fashionable clothes and accessories to look the part. Even as he's playing Vera, he's cavalierly toying with a good girl in the chorus. It all comes crashing down when the ladies compare notes on Joey's snaky behavior, and the curtain drops with him penniless *because* of how he treated the women and remorseless *about* how he treated the women. As *The Brooklyn Citizen* summed up, even after referring to the show as "a joy to behold": "It is a bitter, merciless portrait of a punk."[93]

A tidy success, the play ran for 374 performances. Columbia chief Harry Cohn quickly snatched up its rights for the big screen. Right out of the gate, the gossip columns were filled with speculation about who wanted, and who should land, the title role. James Cagney and Cary Grant were considered.[94] George Raft and Robert Montgomery were both said to want what was considered throughout the industry "a good part for whoever gets it."[95] Kelly, who segued seamlessly into the movies after *Pal Joey*'s Broadway run, was even attached to the project twice—first in 1944, after his star turn in *Cover Girl*, then in 1952 after a Broadway revival of the play regenerated buzz about the film project. The first attempt fizzled when MGM, the studio that held Kelly's contract, raised his loan-out price; the second because of the Production Code office and its jittery censors. Dorothy Kilgallen documented the formidable problems facing Cohn years into his journey of trying to make a movie of the property he just had to have: "That was an excellent musical comedy but it was no more film material under the then or present Johnston office standards than page 364 of the Manhattan telephone directory."[96]

But in 1953, the logjam broke—or at least the legendarily bombastic and bullheaded Cohn plowed forward as if it had. The columns were filling up not just with speculation that Marlon Brando would assume the role, but ruminations from him about it. "The film script has gone back to the original story," he told the Associated Press. "Joey is supposed to be a fifth-rate dancer, and I can dance well enough for that. It would be ridiculous to cast an able dancer like Kelly."[97] Also ridiculous, at least to Mae

West, was the notion that she would be the ideal Vera Simpson. "I was offered the matron's role in *Pal Joey* opposite Marlon Brando but I turned it down," the 60-year-old star said in 1954. "Joey makes a sucker out of this dame and that's against my whole concept of handling men."[98] The phantom picture even had a director attached, and an unlikely one at that: Elia Kazan, fresh off his Oscar win for *On the Waterfront* with Brando as his star.[99]

Plans yet again stalled. It wasn't until Columbia commissioned a script that siphoned off some of the rye from the ribald goings-on that the green light stayed lit. Cohn enlisted director George Sidney, a musical maestro who had helmed the 1951 *Show Boat*, *Kiss Me Kate* and *Anchors Aweigh* (first of the three Kelly-Sinatra song-and-dance team-ups). Kirk Douglas was reported to be the lead, an offbeat casting choice to be sure, but one taken quite seriously by Douglas. He devoted weeks of song-and-dance lessons to preparation, only to discover that the studio was using him—in classic Joey Evans fashion—to get what it really wanted: Frank Sinatra. When Sinatra signed on in March 1956, an unnamed Columbia executive told a reporter to "please phone Kirk Douglas and tell him thanks, we got Sinatra."[100]

Sinatra was then so in-demand as a film talent that production on *Pal Joey* had to be postponed until early 1957 while he wrapped up other projects. He landed a $150,000 payday plus 25 percent of the profits for signing on the dotted line, sweet vindication given his previous work with Cohn. When the producer signed him as Maggio in *From Here to Eternity*, at the nadir of Sinatra's acting career, the contract was for just $10,000 with an option for another picture at the same price. Cohn didn't pick it up—even after Sinatra won his Best Supporting Actor Oscar. Perhaps Cohn was flashing back to that moment his star could have seen as a slight when the *Pal Joey* contract was signed. Cohn had already inked Kim Novak to play the sweet chorus gal who falls for Joey and Rita Hayworth as Vera Simpson. (Though five years younger than her leading man, she was to play 20 years older.) The latter casting resolved a longstanding contract dispute between the studio and the actress who had starred in some of its biggest hits of the last 15 years, *You'll Never Get Rich*, *Cover Girl* and *Gilda* among them. So there was tension among executives as Sinatra, one of Hollywood's hottest properties, agreed to appear in a film with Hayworth, whose star had begun to fade. Some accounts of the resolution of the discomfort are short and to the point: Sinatra magnanimously insisted Hayworth take the top of the bill: "She is Columbia Pictures."[101] Others drag the moment out, suggesting that Sinatra leaned into the uneasiness with self-satisfaction. "Well, you've got something else on your mind," he reportedly said. "I can guess what it is—billing. It will read: Rita

Hayworth, Frank Sinatra, Kim Novak. I don't mind being in the middle of a nice sandwich. If I'm good, people will remember no matter where the name is." It was said that Cohn let out a cheer.[102]

Sinatra wasn't just good. He was self-assuredly stellar, hoisting the film on his still narrow shoulders and casually romping through it with style and heart. Heart was a new wrinkle to the story, and came courtesy of the script by Dorothy Kingsley. She exhibits a deft touch with double entendre and the back-slapping speech of the era's pallies, middle-aged men who regale each other with quips about the "built" on the "mice" in their orbit. Yet she also gives Joey something he never received at the end of John O'Hara's pen: a conscience and vulnerability he can't completely conceal with his bravado. Sinatra praised both aspects of Kingsley's work as he brought it to life. He called the screenwriter "a gentle girl" who nonetheless "did the roughest script I've ever read, with lots of good native humor in it."[103] The star waxed more philosophical in comments to the Associated Press: "They had some trouble with the script, but that is all fixed now. They didn't know whether to keep Joey a heel…. They decided to give him a chance. That'll be all right."[104]

It was far more than that. That Joey's racket was changed from hoofer to crooner fit Sinatra's talents. He is at the height of his powers as a dramatic and comic actor and a singer of up-tempo sextet swing and tender ballads. The intangible glue that holds his performance together, though, emanates more from the man than his increasingly impressive talents. *Pal Joey* is the closest thing viewers had gotten to date, and certainly the closest thing they would get in the years that followed, to seeing the real Frank Sinatra on screen—warts and all. Joey Evans is the Sinatra they knew from albums and concerts, smooth and confident behind the microphone; he's the Sinatra they'd come to know from TV appearances and gossip column tales of his consorting with his buddies—good-naturedly cocksure, the charming leader of the pack even before it was called the Rat Pack, spouting a lexicon of with-it lingo (one of the film's promo spots was Sinatra defining Joey-isms like "gasser" and "poppin'"); and the Sinatra they imagined he had to be from his volcanic affair with Ava Gardner, his many dalliances with starlets endlessly bandied about the press, his all-too-frequent battles with the scribes of that press. Sinatra by 1957 had a reason and a right to be world-weary, traveling in less than a decade from all-but-forgotten to ceaselessly in-demand. The emotional complexity, sometimes volatility, those years had stamped into his psyche were now as indelible a part of him as the baritone that launched his career. He brought it all to *Pal Joey*.

Joey Evans lives by many mottos, not his least practiced being, "Treat every dame like a lady and every lady like a dame." Viewers meet him in the back of a police car, picked up, we learn by the time it drops him off at the train station, for entertaining an underage girl who happened to be the mayor's daughter. The train deposits him in San Francisco, where he knocks about town half-heartedly looking for a performing gig before he discovers an old friend/antagonist is headlining the house band at the Barbary Coast Club, one of the City by the Bay's seediest nightspots. Ned Galvin (Bobby Sherwood) tries to rebuff him, but Joey's a hard one to rebuff. When the house emcee fails to show, Joey snatches a mic, jumps on stage to tell a few jokes nobody laughs at, then launches into a song that brings down the house. Dyspeptic club owner Mike Miggins (Hank Henry) offers him a job, and the plot is off and running.

It's not a complex story. Joey settles in as if he owns the place, playing romantic angles with pretty much every chorus girl. He takes a particular shine to Linda Fisher (Novak, wooden to the point that it requires Herculean suspension of disbelief to think Joey would ever fall for her). But then the house band plays a private Nob Hill show, a charity auction for Vera Prentice-Simpson (Hayworth), a former stripper who married for money and respectability. In Vera, Joey sees his ticket out of the small-time, so he seizes the moment when the bidding falls short of its goal to jump uninvited into the auctioneer's role. He remembers Mrs. Prentice-Simpson from her days as "Vera Vanessa the Undresser"—and offers one of her old burlesque performances to the highest bidder. The scene gives viewers the first glimpse inside Joey's bruised soul, and Sinatra plays it with silent, subtle aplomb. As Vera suggestively sings her old take-it-all-off calling card "Zip" (not Hayworth on vocals but the dubbed Jo Ann Greer), George Sidney's camera alternates between her sultry swayings and Joey observing them. His reactions are not those of a guy playing an angle to bed a "mouse," or even a heel trying to embarrass a socialite as a lark because her kind always looks down on him. They reveal the wistful, wheels-turning thoughts of a small-timer who finally sees his ticket to the big time. Mrs. Prentice-Simpson, he determines, is going to bankroll his dream: a club of his own, Chez Joey.

There's an inspired gag that spotlights the transparency into his real life that Sinatra brings to his reel life. It occurs when Vera looks to return the embarrassment Joey visited upon her at the auction. She shows up with a couple of stuffy blue-bloods, and Joey tries to impress them with tall tales of his show biz successes, and by ordering a bottle of the house's best champagne for the table. When it arrives, Joey asks the waiter to ensure him the bubbly is top-shelf, and he is told it is of 1950 vintage. Joey mutters in response that 1950 "may have been a good year for the grape, but it was a lousy year for emcees." That year, of course, was Sinatra's worst professionally. He was taking a pounding in the press for leaving his wife and three children for the very public affair with Ava Gardner, his records had stopped flying off the shelves and he didn't appear in a single film. Given the wide reports that Sinatra ad-libbed extensively during the shoot, it's a reasonable conclusion that he added the aside as a dollop of additional insight into the personal demons he shared with his pal Joey.

Some of Sinatra's best acting, and a vivid example of his transformation from the Voice into the Chairman of the Board documented by the film, comes in a pair of musical set pieces. The first is "I Could Write a Book," a solo number for Joey before he introduces the chorus girls. He owns every inch of the club's small stage, employing the sideways downward glance and upward-facing-open-palmed spreading of his arms that started the bobbysoxers fainting in the aisles. But he adds to his repertoire a restrained sensuality that screams "This is not the 1940s any more!" It reveals itself vocally—the baritone is deeper, more resonant in its smoothness than it was when he was a teen idol, the just-off-the-beat phrasing of key lyrics that had increasingly come to characterize his 1950s output with Capitol Records more evident and effective than ever.

This new, not-necessarily-suitable-for-teens Sinatra was also on display in the physicality of the performance—how he sidles up to, drops down on and hops off of the stage stool and the hypnotic way he slowly makes eye contact with (we presume because Sidney's deft camera never leaves him) the ladies in the crowd. He softly snaps his fingers to the rhythm of the band synched to his movements across the stage, pointing his finger with quiet come-hither command at more females enraptured by the velvet in his voice. The camera only switches off him when he spots Linda among the chorus girls in the wings. She smiles awkwardly at his look—a glance, not a gaze. but nonetheless unnerving to the innocent. He gently pulls her onstage, telling the crowd a love song needs a girl, then draws her in tight as they sway to the music, her pained discomfort gradually giving way to the wonderment of being before an audience. By the time they duet on the closing line—"How to make two lovers of friends"— it's clear that's precisely what Linda wants to happen.

Even more impressive is "The Lady Is a Tramp," the number in which the Chairman bursts from his cocoon in all his ring-a-ding glory. Vera drops into the club just after closing time, and Mike tells Joey to sing the lady a song. He slides behind the piano and taps out the opening notes to the Rodgers and Hart showstopper, written two decades earlier for the Broadway musical *Babes in Arms*. The song is rendered with equal parts sexuality and almost-imperceptible smirk as Joey tries to alternately offend and woo the K-L-A-S-Y (a Joey spelling) broad. Sinatra is effortlessly magnetic as he draws on a cigarette, the smoke billowing all around him as he stands up, drops the butt on the floor and stamps it out in perfect syncopation to the music. Sinatra then gently pushes the piano away with his foot without looking at it—his eyes bored into Vera as he devours the song while conveying Joey's clear desire to devour her. Hayworth does her best acting of the movie here as well, communicating with only micro-changes to her face and body language that Vera can't quite figure out whether to be insulted or titillated by the performance—so she settles on infatuated. Sinatra's best vocal choice here isn't vocal at all: Where the lyrics call for him to sing "It's oke" after noting the lady is broke, he simply shrugs his shoulders in "who cares?" fashion. The essence of Joey Evans. It is not surprising that the three-minute, 19-second sequence has been called "the finest Frank Sinatra performance ever filmed."[105]

The plot hits familiar beats as it plays out: Vera funds Chez Joey while keeping its frontman on her yacht as her boy toy. Linda falls more deeply for Joey while he tries unsuccessfully to avoid falling for her. It all comes to a head when Mrs. Prentice-Simpson demands he either fire or demean the "mouse" by forcing her to perform a striptease. Joey, declaring "Nobody owns Joey but Joey," chooses to forego his ill-gotten gain and treat the gal he loves right. Even so, he has too much heart, and self-awareness, to expect them to live happily ever after. When Linda suggests they flee San Francisco and start an act of their own, Joey lectures her with words they

Sinatra falls in love with Kim Novak in *Pal Joey*.

Pal Joey (1957) 121

both quickly ignore ... and which Gene Kelly's iteration of the character would have never thought, let alone spoken:

> Are you out of your mind or something? Know what you're getting into? I'll brush you off before the station. Why don't you beat it? Look, l have no desire to be hemmed in. ... Why don't you get out while you got the chance?

Pal Joey was another hit for Sinatra, raking in $4.7 million on the star power of the leads and Columbia's vaunted publicity machine. Studio flacks generated coverage for a Hollywood-wide contest to find the perfect Snuffy, Joey's pet dog, whose qualifications included eating the food Joey favored (lox, cheese blintzes, bagels). Director Sidney made clear, though, the winning mutt mustn't "mistake Sinatra for a bone—or a lamppost."[106] A pound-abandoned Cairn terrier just days away from execution landed the part—and the $500-a-week contract that came with it.[107] (Another nugget passed around the press was that Sinatra was treated to 35 full costume changes in the film, to the tune of more than 200 yards of wool suits and tuxedos. By contrast, the studio noted, he wore one khaki outfit in *From Here to Eternity*, priced at $8.95.[108])

Perhaps the most offbeat promotion came courtesy of the Three Stooges, longtime Columbia stalwarts. Sinatra was a fan of the slapstick trio, and had them guest star on a 1952 episode of his TV show when Shemp Howard was part of the act with brother Moe Howard and Larry Fine. Shemp had died in November 1955 and was replaced by Joe Besser in 1956 to fulfill the final two years of their Columbia shorts contract. In their 1958 two-reeler *Outer Space Jitters*, the Stooges state that they are "bewitched, bothered and bewildered"—at which point Larry looks straight at the camera and says, "And don't forget to go see *Pal Joey*, folks!"

The movie earned some "gasser" reviews, with *The Los Angeles Times'* Edwin Schallert calling it "bright, sharp and ingenious"[109] and *The New York Times* "a swiftly moving, cheerful and adult musical play that is one of the season's best."[110] According to Edith Lindeman of *The Times-Dispatch*, it hit all the right notes, and she added, "[Sinatra] is Joey, the brassy heel, on the prowl for every skirt and confident of his prowess in the boudoir. ... He punches out a potent performance, glib, irreverent, at once nonchalant and authoritative."[111]

The *Abilene Reporter-News* tossed even more bouquets at Sinatra, and concluded that *Pal Joey* "may well be the best thing Sinatra has ever done. The role calls for feeling and interpretation which exceed anything Sinatra has tried—even including his Academy Award part in *From Here to Eternity*."[112]

Leonard Maltin put the whole production into historical context when he reminisced about hosting a *Pal Joey* screening at the Los Angeles Theatre in the early 2000s:

> To see *Pal Joey* in that setting, with a packed house of nearly 2000 people, was amazing; there was electricity in the air. When Frank sang "The Lady Is a Tramp," it was as if he was standing there in person, and when he finished, there was a spontaneous burst of applause. That film (like several others during his career) deliberately blurred the line between Sinatra's public persona and the particular part he played. The word that came to my mind as I watched him was *swagger*. What a perfect vehicle, tailor-made for him—and presenting him at the peak of his vocal powers.[113]

Joey Evans netted Sinatra a Golden Globe for Best Actor—the only honor he ever earned for a leading performance. His music career got a shot in the arm, as well. His next two albums, "Come Fly with Me" (released in January 1958) and "Frank Sinatra Sings Only for the Lonely" (released in September 1958) both reached No. 1 on the *Billboard* charts. They were the first #1 albums he had since his debut, in 1946.

Kings Go Forth

Directed by Delmer Daves
Screenplay: Merle Miller, from the novel by Joe David Brown
Producer: Frank Ross
Cinematography: Daniel Fapp (Black and White)
Editor: William Murphy
Cast: Frank Sinatra, Tony Curtis, Natalie Wood, Leora Dana, Karl Swenson, Ann Codee, Eddie Ryder, Jacques Berthe, Mark Patscott, Cyril Delevanti, Marie Isnard, Pete Candoli, Mel Lewis, Red Wooten, Richie Kamuca, Red Norvo
Released June 28, 1958
Frank Ross-Eton Productions for United Artists release
109 minutes

With *Kings Go Forth*, Sinatra chose to confront a controversial subject within the context of a military drama. Set in 1944, the film attempts to balance the military drama with the subject of interracial relationships and how the culture, and society, responds to them.

Sinatra plays Sam Loggins, the lieutenant in charge of a U.S. artillery observation unit stationed in the Alps between France and Italy. Their mission is to ferret out German soldiers who are stationed in a small village. New recruits arrive, including Corporal Britt Harris (Tony Curtis),

Kings Go Forth (1958)

Sinatra conflicts with Tony Curtis (right) in *Kings Go Forth*.

whose experience as a radio man comes in handy as the unit has just lost theirs. Harris is a man of privilege, courageous in certain situations, but also a ladies' man who cons his way into easy situations. On leave, Loggins meets Monique Blair (Natalie Wood), an American-born girl who grew up in France. As they become more involved, Monique reveals that her father was black, and the bigotry she has experienced. Loggins is torn by this due to the basic bigotry that is a part of the culture, but decides his love matters more and he overrides any prejudices he might have had. The two go to a jazz club where they find Harris sitting in with the band. Impressed by his musicianship, they ask him to join them. Harris and Monique are immediately attracted to each other. Loggins realizes this and is asked by Monique to tell Harris about her father being black. When he does, he discovers that Harris has no problem with it. Harris and Monique become more involved, much to Loggins' chagrin. Harris tells Loggins that he has proposed to Monique, which breaks Loggins' heart. But he remains tough and tries to be supportive. Harris picks up the paperwork to fill out for permission to marry, but never does anything with it. Loggins is angered to discover that Harris is going around saying it was all a big joke. Loggins has Harris tell this to Monique, who runs off crying. Harris is aloof, stating that it was "a kick," a novelty to propose to a girl of mixed race.

Loggins, consumed with anger and hatred, punches him. Monique tries to drown herself, but is rescued. The conflict between Loggins and Harris becomes serious, each vowing to kill the other. However, they are forced to work together and when Harris is shot, Loggins drags him to safety. An explosion kills Harris and seriously wounds Loggins, who is found alive and hospitalized. His right arm is amputated. He receives a letter from Monique, who tells him she knows Harris is dead, and indicates that her mother has also died. When Loggins gets out of the hospital, he goes to say goodbye to Monique before returning to the States.

The film's narrative is much different than Joe David Brown's novel. In the book, Harris is a Southerner who rejects Monique immediately when he discovers her father was black, and it drives her to suicide. Loggins is then consumed by hatred for his fellow soldier, while Harris reveals himself to be a phony and a coward in battle. The film has the same masculine drama, but avoids the melodramatic finish, offering something more Hollywood, and relatable to moviegoers.

Producer Frank Ross bought the movie rights to Brown's novel in January 1957. Sinatra was already involved. *The Los Angeles Times* reported:

> Frank Sinatra, who has been using his own organization, Kent Productions, actively in connection with his picture career, reached a new plateau. He has joined with Frank Ross, producer of *The Robe*, in the planned filming of *Kings Go Forth*. This is Joe David Brown's novel about two American paratroopers in France who fall in love with the same girl, only to discover her father is a Negro. Sinatra's Kent organization produced his own independent film *Johnny Concho*, which enjoyed marked success, and it will figure in a projected TV series with ABC. However, *Kings Go Forth* probably will prove the biggest test of this company's operations, because the picture, to be made In France, is budgeted at $1,300,000.[114]

Sinatra suggested Charles Vidor as director. Vidor had a reputation for being quite difficult, but Sinatra was very pleased with his direction on *The Joker Is Wild* and was eager to work with him again. However, at the time, Vidor was involved with *A Farewell to Arms* and couldn't accept the job. *Kings Go Forth* did not begin shooting for some time due to a series of unforeseen complications. However, by then, Delmer Daves had signed on to direct. Sadly, Vidor and Sinatra never worked together again, as the director died of a heart attack on the set of his next film *Song of Norway*.

Sinatra originally wanted Audrey Hepburn for the role of Monique, and was disappointed when her work on Billy Wilder's *Love in the Afternoon* kept her from taking the job. Because the character was interracial, there was some discussion of Dorothy Dandridge playing the role, but it ultimately went to Natalie Wood. Tony Curtis took the role of Harris.

While both agreed to be in the movie, each had another project they had to finish. Not wanting to lose either, Ross and Sinatra did their best to work around them. According to *The Los Angeles Times*:

> Producer Frank Ross finds himself in the peculiar position to which he has had to adjust himself "uncomfortably and expensively" of having had to stop production less than halfway through *Kings Go Forth*. Natalie Wood is unavailable and so is Tony Curtis, busy all over Europe in *The Vikings*. So Ross and his director, Delmer Daves, shot their exteriors for two weeks in France with Sinatra alone. That was in early September. Sinatra returned to his TV series and the Ross company has closed down till November 11, on which all three stars are at last expected to get together. "It's becoming 'increasingly difficult' to make a picture when there are so few successes; he [the producer] has to hit on the piece of chemistry that will bring people into a theater," said the erstwhile maker of *The Robe*. "In this case I took a chance in buying Brown's novel and having a screenplay developed by Merle Miller. But with it I was able to attract Sinatra and from then on it was relatively simple. Frank shares production and United Artists provides the balance of financing. Our picture has a great deal to offer in star names alone. Frank, even though not young, has an appeal for the young as, of course, do Natalie and Tony. The combination of their names, plus the strength of the story, should make for that magic chemistry. But it took a year of my life just getting the contracts signed."[115]

Kings Go Forth, even beyond its controversial nature, has a real strength from its performances. Curtis does a nice, smooth job as the conniving, womanizing soldier whose courage in battle conflicts with his disregard for the feelings of others in regular life. Wood is a very appealing actress and her French accent throughout sounds genuine.

However, *Kings Go Forth* is another example of how exceptional Sinatra continued to be as an actor when he had a good script and director. He plays it especially low key, always being jealous of the Curtis character even when he is forced to admit that he's a good soldier. His approach makes it especially effective when he seethes with anger at Harris' manipulation of Monique. When he explodes "*Tell her!*" with a forcefulness not revealed up to this point, it is jarring, as is his sudden punch to Harris. During their final battle scenes, time is taken for Harris to offer an introspective monologue that helps Loggins understand him. Curtis says the lines with conviction, while Sinatra sits quietly and stoically, letting the other actor take the scene.

Sinatra's acting continues to offer a great deal of subtle nuance, especially in scenes where he tags along on the "dates" between Harris and Monique. Even when he isn't speaking, the jealous resentment is plain on his face. It manages to be both a little comical and sad. It's unusual to see Sinatra not playing the romantic lead: Throughout the film, Monique admits that she only loves him as a friend, nothing more, and they don't end up together, but their relationship is still satisfying to watch develop.

Sinatra told interviewer Bob Thomas, a *Kings Go Forth* set visitor:

> [N]ow I know that I can only do one thing at a time. Oh, when I think of the energy I wasted ten years ago trying to do everything at once and getting nothing done really well! Now I know what I'm doing. All of today, I'll devote my time to this picture, giving it all my concentration. Then I'll go have dinner and go to a recording session from nine to midnight at Capitol Records. In the time I'm going there, I'll adjust my thinking to the making of records. I was under analysis for six months once. The reason was that I had a couple of specific problems I had to work out. I got them off my chest and that was that. I know a lot of people who use psychiatry as a crutch. They can hardly wait to get on that couch and tell something new that has occurred to them. I used it more as a way to talk out my problems. It's the same thing you do with a close friend. But in show business it's hard to have close friends, and I don't feel I should burden them with my problems.

The Thomas story continued:

> Frank conceded that success had a lot to do with ironing out his conflicts. Nothing quite succeeds like it, and he has had plenty of success in the last two years. His pictures, for example, now earn him more than a salary. He is a partner in each of them. He figures to make a pile from *The Joker Is Wild* and *Pal Joey*, both of which are cleaning up at the box office. "And I think we'll do well with *Kings Go Forth*," he said. "It's being made at a sensible price and the script is terrific. Plus it will come out right after Natalie Wood has been seen in *Marjorie Morningstar* and Tony Curtis is out with *The Viking*. We should cash in nicely on their success."[116]

While it was not a box office disappointment, *Kings Go Forth* was not the success *Pal Joey* had been. It did moderately well, but should have done better due to its stars. The critics were reserved in their praise, and, in retrospect, it might be due to the subject matter. *Kings Go Forth* received its stronger accolades in the African-American press.

Sinatra had hoped the film would achieve greater success and was rather proud of its confronting a serious issue. In a widely syndicated article, his feelings about this were revealed:

> Frank Sinatra, who thrives on controversy, believes movies could die if devoted only to non-controversial subjects. "The first duty of an actor is to entertain and that the place for sermonizing is in the pulpit," but he adds, "[A] story that has nothing to say has got to be dull. Any story that makes people think for themselves is good and I'm for."

Sinatra continued, "We didn't make [*Kings Go Forth*] as a sermon. It's a love story. Some people won't understand this picture. We hope the public will accept characters as human beings, not as white, grays, blacks or polka dots. Love must be accepted as a very personal relationship between individuals, for that is what it is."[117]

Kings Go Forth is a much different film when seen in the 21st century. The fact that Natalie Wood plays a woman of mixed race and is courted by two white men was controversial in the 1950s. Today viewers would have misgivings over the fact that a white actress was cast. However, even the black press seemed to understand this situation in the 1950s and were pleased that Sinatra confronted it in a film. This movie was hardly the only time Sinatra tried to do something about it. Jerry Lewis told author James L. Neibaur in a 1993 interview:

> You don't understand what it was like back then. Dean and I worked with a dance act called the Step Brothers who were not allowed to leave their dressing room, even to eat. We told the management that we wouldn't perform unless they were allowed to eat in the restaurant and gamble in the casino. When Sammy Davis, Jr., wanted to marry May Britt, Frank Sinatra and I held him as he cried. We told him, "You marry the woman you love! We'll build a wall around you. We guarantee you'll get work." That's how bad those times were.[118]

Sinatra was proud to serve as best man at Davis' November 1960 wedding to May.

The Production Code, while on its way out, also had certain rules about portraying interracial relationships on screen, which is likely why a black actress like Dorothy Dandridge wouldn't have been cast as Monique. The film's frank presentation of racism (Monique doesn't even consider a relationship with Loggins would be possible initially) and Loggins' acceptance of Monique regardless of her heritage is something we don't see a lot in films from this era and it still feels quite sincere today, even if the casting of Wood in and of itself negates much of its message.

By now Sinatra was riding high at all levels, and his next film would be a lavish Sol Spiegel production for MGM with Vincente Minnelli directing. However, once again, it would not be a musical, but another straight drama. And *Some Came Running* would turn out to be one of Sinatra's best films with one of his finest performances.

Some Came Running

Directed by Vincente Minnelli
Screenplay: John Patrick and Arthur Sheekman, from the novel by James Jones

Producer: Sol Siegel
Cinematography: William Daniels (Metrocolor)
Editor: Adrienne Fazan
Cast: Frank Sinatra, Dean Martin, Shirley MacLaine, Martha Hyer, Arthur Kennedy, Nancy Gates, Leora Dana, Betty Lou Keim, Larry Gates, Steve Peck, Connie Gilchrist, Ned Wever, George Cisar, Sheryl Deuville, Anthony Jochim, George Brengal, Don Haggerty, John Brennan, Carmen Phillips, Denny Miller, Paul Jones, William Schallert, George E. Stone, Geraldine Wall, Scott Seaton, Albert Viola, John Wurtz, Jan Arvan, Dave White, Steve Carruthers, Joe Gray, Franklyn Farnum, Tom Buening, Stuart Holmes, Roy Engel, Donald Kerr, Len Lesser
Released December 25, 1958
MGM
137 minutes

James Jones had written *From Here to Eternity*, and when that achieved success as a novel, and later a film, he went right to work on *Some Came Running*. It was completed and published four years later. MGM bought the movie rights as a vehicle for Sinatra, believing the work of the same writer could allow lightning to strike twice. Sinatra agreed, especially after reading a script treatment, and signed to play an ex–G.I. who returns to his small town.

MGM began casting the film, with formidable names like veteran actor Arthur Kennedy, and comparative newcomer Shirley MacLaine, who was making a significant impact since her 1955 movie debut. The casting and plans for production was getting the MGM promo treatment, including write-ups in syndicated newspaper columns and articles in the trades. One of the characters, 'Bama, had not yet been cast.

Dean Martin had only known Sinatra casually by 1958. He had broken up with longtime partner Jerry Lewis two years before, but his solo career wasn't exactly taking off. Dean had made two movies—*Ten Thousand Bedrooms* and *The Young Lions*. The first was a flop that was savaged by critics. The second was better, but still unremarkable. Meanwhile, Lewis' first few solo films were massive hits. Many had predicted that when the team split, comic powerhouse Lewis would go on to bigger and better things, and Martin's career would fizzle. It looked that way in 1958.

Martin saw an article in one of the trades and was attracted to the *Some Came Running* part of 'Bama, which he knew he could pull off. Since his *Ten Thousand Bedrooms* bomb was for MGM, he was sure the powers-that-be would not be interested in casting him. But he thought perhaps Sinatra would consider it. As the story goes, Martin and Sinatra were both at the same function while the casting of *Some Came Running* was still going on. Dean went to greet Frank, who shook his hand. Dean then shoved Frank playfully and said, "You son of a bitch!" Frank, playing along, asked, "Now what I have I done?" Dean said, "You have a role in your next picture about a guy who drinks, gambles, and speaks in a drawl and you don't think of me?" Sinatra stood there for a minute and said, "Y'know, that does make sense." Sinatra spoke to the producers and Dean was cast as 'Bama.

Sinatra was pleased to be reunited with Nancy Gates, with whom he appeared in *Suddenly* a few years earlier, but the producer was reticent about casting Martha Hyer because she had appeared opposite Jerry Lewis in *The Delicate Delinquent*, his first solo effort without Dean. It was assumed that Dean might have misgivings about working with an actress who had appeared successfully with his partner, especially since the duo's breakup was believed to be acrimonious. But Dean had no such reservations.

Vincente Minnelli was assigned to direct. Early in his career, he had been a costume designer and set designer before MGM's Arthur Freed unit hired him to direct. Minnelli had an excellent visual sense, using color cinematography to its greatest effect, and quickly mastered filmmaking in the widescreen process. There is a cinematic term, *mise en scène*, which refers to how scenery and objects are arranged within a film's frame. This is the area where Minnelli's talents were most impressive. Having directed comedies and melodramas as well as musicals, Minnelli's direction promised that *Some Came Running* would be a visually affecting film.

A drama set in 1948, *Some Came Running* stars Sinatra as Dave Hirsh, an Army veteran who wakes after a drunken night and finds himself on a bus pulling into his hometown, Parkman, Indiana, which he left 16 years earlier. Ginny Moorehead, a dumb but earnest prostitute, is with him, insisting that he invited her to come with him while he was drunk the night before. Dave clears his head and tries to let Ginny down easy, giving her money to return to Chicago. She refuses, wanting to avoid a violent ex-boyfriend in that city. Furthermore, she has fallen for Dave. Before the war, Dave was a novelist with two books to his credit. Despite his success, and honorable service in the war, he is a cynical man, stemming from his childhood: An orphan, he was placed in an asylum rather than taken in by his much older brother Frank (Arthur Kennedy), whose wife objected. In the years that Dave has been gone, Frank has inherited his wife's father's jewelry business and sits on the board of one of two local banks. When Dave arrives, he deposits his money—$5500—in the rival bank. This looks bad for Frank, so he reaches out to Dave, inviting him to the house for dinner, much to his wife's chagrin. Their guests also include a professor and his teacher daughter Gwen (Hyer). Dave is immediately smitten with

Gwen because she has the erudition that a writer would seek in a companion—a refreshing change from the airheaded bimbos he's used to, as represented by Ginny. Gwen is also attracted to Dave, but has misgivings about his sordid past. She encourages him to offer his latest story for publication. Dave also becomes friendly with a drifter named 'Bama, a Southerner who drinks, gambles and coasts easily through life.

Brother Frank's conservatism is belied by the fact that he is having an affair with his secretary. When Frank's daughter Dawn finds out, she runs away and starts seeing an older man. Dave intercedes and straightens out Dawn, who is acting out of frustration. Dave's story is published in *The Atlantic*, so he and 'Bama go on a gambling trip with Ginny in tow. While they are playing cards, Gwen phones Dave and indicates she loves him. The card players believe that he's cheating, a fight ensues and 'Bama is stabbed. A doctor discovers that 'Bama is a diabetic and must stop drinking. He refuses. Ginny goes to see Gwen and proclaims her feelings for Dave. When Gwen realizes that Dave had been seeing Ginny, she assures her there is nothing between them. Rejected by Gwen, Dave agrees to marry Ginny despite her intellectual shortcomings, realizing her love and her loyalty. Shortly after marrying in front of a judge, Dave and Ginny attend a town carnival where they are confronted by Ginny's violent old boyfriend. He tries to shoot Dave, but Ginny steps between them and is killed.

One of the strongest dramas in Sinatra's film career, *Some Came Running* gave him a role where he could be understated and call upon his gift for nuance and the subtlety of facial expressions in nearly all of his scenes. Dave is literarily talented and brilliant, cynical and sarcastic, but still genuinely cares about others. Sinatra's talent seems to be buoyed by a top cast of supporting players who are performing at their very best.

As Ginny, Shirley MacLaine manages to balance between earnestness, overpowering passion and tragic desperation. While Dave recognizes her devotion, he tries to avoid exhibiting any affection toward her due to his misgivings about her being so beneath his intellectual level. This is why he becomes attracted to the pretty, but rather cold, Gwen. He longs for the intellectual stimulation as much, or maybe even more, than the sexual satisfaction. 'Bama constantly referring to Ginny as "a pig" ('50s movie slang for "whore") doesn't help. 'Bama also exhibits his disdain when Dave finally agrees to marry Ginny, realizing his chance with Gwen has vanished. Dave is shot to death in the novel, but Sinatra decided himself to change that conclusion. MacLaine would always insist that Frank's decision to have Ginny become the victim while trying to shield Dave is the reason she received an Oscar nomination. MacLaine really is great in this movie, especially considering how easy it would have been to overplay

Some Came Running (1958)

Shirley MacLaine turns in perhaps the best performance in *Some Came Running*, and it enhances Sinatra's work as well.

her character. She might perpetuate—or even have instigated—the "prostitute with a heart of gold" stereotype, but she makes her character easy to love, and her love for Dave comes across as very sincere amidst all the drunken giggling and fraternizing.

Martin's relaxed, carefree performance as 'Bama might be the most important one in his solo film career. There is a running gag in which his character never removes his hat—not even when he is at home shaving. However, at the end of the film, as he stands looking saddened at Ginny's funeral service, 'Bama slowly removes his hat and holds it in front of him. It is the last shot of the film and its impact causes Martin's appealing portrayal to resonate strongly as the movie concludes. This performance led to his appearing opposite John Wayne in Howard Hawks' *Rio Bravo* the next year. Martin's solo career in movies was set.

Sinatra had, by now, fully mastered the craft of movie acting. While he would notoriously shrug off his ability in a few years as moviemaking became a lark, he is fully committed in *Some Came Running*. We truly feel Dave's bitterness about being back in his small town, back in the presence of his blowhard older brother Frank who acquiesces to his haughty wife's

Sinatra (left) and Dean Martin became pals while working on *Some Came Running*. The friendship lasted.

every demand. The fact that this has led Frank to an extramarital affair shows Dave that his brother's lofty position in society belies his tenuous position in his home. Kennedy plays Frank in a stressed-out way that effectively conveys all of the character's conflicting demons.

Sinatra also allows Dave to open up to his own prejudices about Ginny. He knows who she is and what she once was, and in his attempt to conflict with her unbridled devotion, he spits out insults that make her weep. Sinatra manages to convey that Dave really wants Ginny's devotion and happy spirit, and Gwen's cultured intelligence, and is frustrated that he cannot have both.

While she has the less flashy role of Gwen, Hyer does an exceptional job as a very staid individual from an academically based family. This is a bit of an extreme as to what Dave desires, and her attraction to him is purely visceral despite his literary achievements.

One of the real assets to the aesthetic success of *Some Came Running* is Minnelli's remarkable direction. This is especially borne out in the climactic carnival sequence where the director's use of the widescreen process is extraordinary. As he shoots from overhead, crowding the frame with people, rides, vendors and games, we see Ginny's angry boyfriend shoving his way through the people while holding a gun, while 'Bama is trying to maneuver through the masses to warn Dave. Every bit of the

Some Came Running (1958)

frame is filled with color and movement. When Minnelli cuts back to Dave and Ginny, they are walking along unhurried, oblivious to danger, deciding how to spend their wedding night.

Despite his great skill, Minnelli wasn't well liked by Sinatra. Minnelli's setting up shots and filming objects to cut into the scene to help with its pacing, was a long, arduous process that the impatient Sinatra found

Some Came Running director Vincente Minnelli (right) and Sinatra didn't get along well, but the film is among each man's best.

frustrating. At one point, Sinatra and Martin left the set and went back to Los Angeles to do some carousing while Minnelli "directed the furniture." Sinatra may have been unsettled by this sort of pacing, and Minnelli was certainly chagrined at the actor's insistence on shooting only one take, but the end result is what matters. An early scene of Dave, first arriving in town, taking out several literary classics by the likes of Hemingway and Fitzgerald from his bag, and then pulling out a folder of papers called "Unfinished Manuscript" tells us all we need to know about the character's backstory, without any dialogue or further plot exposition.

Along with MacLaine's Oscar nomination for Best Actress, Arthur Kennedy was nominated for Best Supporting Actor and Martha Hyer for Best Supporting Actress. None of them won, but the Academy Awards meant a lot in 1958 and it benefited all of their careers. The box office returns for *Some Came Running* more than doubled its production costs.

As indicated earlier, *Some Came Running* is also significant for the friendship that developed between Frank and Dean Martin. The two men had a lot in common. Both were singers with acting aspirations. Both loved the booze and the broads. They were each from working class towns and backgrounds. They were of Italian heritage. The two men became so close that even as late as the 21st century, Dean's surviving children refer to Sinatra as Uncle Frank, and the Sinatra daughters fondly recall their Uncle Dean. They would appear in more movies together. MacLaine would also become a friend, even sort of a mascot to the Rat Pack.

For his next film, Sinatra would be directed by veteran filmmaker Frank Capra and star opposite one of Sinatra's favorite actors, Edward G. Robinson. However, with *Some Came Running*, Sinatra had just completed his second film that took advantage of his acting ability but didn't give him a chance to do any singing. As he began work on *A Hole in the Head*, his album "Come Dance with Me" was released. It became the most successful album in his recording career. As a result, in *A Hole in the Head*, Frank would get the opportunity to introduce another hit song.

A Hole in the Head

Directed by Frank Capra
Screenplay: Arnold Schulman, from his play
Producers: Frank Capra and Frank Sinatra
Cinematography: William Daniels (Color)
Editor: William Hornbeck

Songs:
"All My Tomorrows," "High Hopes"; Written by Sammy Cahn and Jimmy Van Heusen
Cast: Frank Sinatra, Edward G. Robinson, Eddie Hodges, Eleanor Parker, Carolyn Jones, Thelma Ritter, Keenan Wynn, Joi Lansing, Connie Sawyer, James Komack, Dub Taylor, George DeWitt, Benny Rubin, Ruby Dandridge, B.S. Pully, Joyce Nizzari, Pupi Campo, Emory Parnell, Sam McDaniel, Robert B. Williams, Selma Minden Grenald, Ralph Moratz, John Orland
Released July 15, 1959
SinCap Productions for United Artists
120 minutes

Before he started work on *A Hole in the Head*, Sinatra planned to take an around-the-world trip with Peter Lawford and his wife, then play a supporting role for Howard Hawks in *Rio Bravo*, a John Wayne Western. But he had been pushing himself too hard, and finally collapsed with exhaustion. This is how Dean Martin ended up with the *Rio Bravo* role. In Sheilah Graham's syndicated column, she stated that the ailing actor "has canceled his around-the-world trip that was to have started last week. Instead, Frankie will spend the next two months 'doing nothing' in his Palm Springs home. ...[He] plans to rest except for a few personal appearances, until the fall, when he stars for his own company in *A Hole in the Head*."[119]

A Hole in the Head had been a Broadway production, opening at the Plymouth Theater on February 28, 1957, and running for 156 performances. Sinatra and director Frank Capra secured the film rights for their company SinCap Productions. Capra had not directed a film since 1951's *Here Comes the Groom* with Bing Crosby. Capra was then (1951) 53 and he planned on retiring from feature filmmaking and instead spent the next several years producing science-related subjects for the Bell System Science series. (These films were shown in schools into the 1970s.) Sinatra admired Capra's work and coaxed him out of retirement, and the two formed SinCap. *Hole in the Head* playwright Arnold Schulman was getting into Hollywood screenplays and teleplays at about this time, and he was hired to adapt his play into a movie.

Sinatra was interested in casting one of his favorite actors, Edward G. Robinson, as his brother. Robinson was more than 20 years older than Sinatra, so it is a bit awkward, but it somehow still works. (On Broadway, the role Sinatra played was done by Paul Douglas, who was in Robinson's age bracket.) Sinatra asked his friend Carolyn Jones to join the cast. She told the press that the script was "a lulu": "Imagine playing opposite Frank Sinatra and being directed by Frank Capra!"[120] Eddie Hodges was cast as

Frank's son. Hodges was "discovered" after an appearance on the CBS game show *Name That Tune* and scored on Broadway in the original production of *The Music Man*.

The cast also included such appealing performers as Eleanor Parker (from *The Man with the Golden Arm*), Thelma Ritter, Dub Taylor, Keenan Wynn, Joi Lansing and comical newcomer James Komack. The play's setting was Miami so arrangements were made to shoot there, beginning in October 1958. At one point, the decision was made to call the film *All My Tomorrows* (the title of a song written for the film) but eventually the original title was retained in the belief that the Broadway show was notable enough to warrant it. According to James Bacon's syndicated column, "Sinatra's next project after *A Hole in the Head* might be *Can-Can*. If that isn't enough, Sinatra put in a sizable bid for the film rights to *The Music Man*, the current Broadway smash."[121]

In *A Hole in the Head*, Sinatra plays Tony Manetta, who grew up in the Bronx slums and moved down to Miami with two friends. One became a millionaire businessman. The other became a cab driver, perfectly happy with his work and the steady paycheck. Tony remained a dreamer with big ideas that never materialized. Although he was never wealthy, he overspent to give that appearance. Now, 20 years later, he is a widower with an adoring young son, Ally (Hodges). He is also broke, and the hotel where he lives is threatening to evict him. He phones his brother Mario (Robinson) in New York for a loan, lying that Ally is ill and he needs it for medical bills. Concerned, Manny and his wife Sophie (Ritter) fly to Miami and discover that Ally is just fine, and slacker Tony is just plain broke again. Mario agrees to give Tony the money and even set him up in business, if he agrees to settle down into a life of gainful employment and marriage to a sensible girl. They even have one picked out, Sophie's widow friend Eloise (Parker). Tony had been seeing Shirl (Jones), a barefoot, bongo-playing free spirit who does not meet with Mario's approval. Tony approaches meeting Eloise with cynicism, planning to pretend to accept her in order just to get the money. When he finds that Eloise lost both her husband and young son, who drowned in a camping accident before her eyes, he becomes ashamed of himself and reveals his cynical intentions. Preparing to leave, Eloise asks Tony to stay, indicating she has been so lonesome, she doesn't mind being needed by someone, even under those conditions.

Tony is invited to a party by his millionaire friend Jerry, who is visiting the Miami area. While there, he excitedly tells Jerry about a Disneyland based in Miami, and Jerry seems to respond favorably. But during a trip to the dog track, Tony wins big and then loses it all; Jerry recognizes that his friend is just a penniless dreamer and brushes him off. Tony confronts him and is punched by his bodyguards. Returning home, he walks into a surprise party organized by Ally, who always believed in him and was certain he'd pulled off a big deal with Jerry. Tony decides it would be in Ally's best interests to live in New York with Mario and Sophie, so he has the proper opportunities. Tony stands on the beach and watches them drive away in a cab. But Mario and Sophie have second thoughts, and Ally comes running back to Tony and Eloise.

A Hole in the Head gave Sinatra one of his most appealing characters. Tony Manetta truly believes in his dreams, really thinks his ideas will not only be successful, but will make a generous contribution. (Coincidentally, Walt Disney's company apparently agreed with the concept of extending Disneyland to Florida—they opened Disney World in Orlando in October 1971.)

Bosley Crowther in *The New York Times* stated: "Mr. Sinatra makes the hero of this vibrant color film a softhearted, hardboiled, white-souled black sheep whom we will cherish, along with Mr. Deeds and Mr. Smith, as one of the great guys that Mr. Capra has escorted to the American screen."[122] Tony's relationship with his son, filled with wisecracks, songs, trivia questions and genuine affection, is one of the most inspiring things about his character. That he ends up almost losing even that, only because of an unbridled enthusiasm, is heartbreaking.

Edward G. Robinson, as Mario, manages to effortlessly and effectively steal every scene in which he appears. Angrily fed up with his brother's lies, schemes and impossible dreams, Mario has apparently never refused to throw money Tony's way and allow him to continue pursuing his lifestyle. But he has reached his limit. Sardonically funny, clearly annoyed, Mario's genuine love for his brother comes out more than once and manifests itself even more strongly at the end when Tony is finally ready to give up and call himself a failure. The scene where he and Tony fall weeping into each other's arms is one of the emotional highlights of the movie.

Eddie Hodges began his comparatively brief movie career with this movie. Appealing and genuine, he has many strong moments throughout. His amused reaction to his father's brusque comments and their funny and loving exchanges, his duet of "High Hopes" with Sinatra, and his emotional scenes when he is to be taken away are all highlights. But perhaps his greatest moment is his first reaction to seeing Eloise. His face shows an immediate attraction and connection. Sinatra told the press, "Most child actors are insufferable; Eddie is a wonderful, well-behaved boy. And what a great performer! Eddie is as bright and natural as you'd want a boy of 11 to be. Credit must go to his parents."[123]

Hodges and Sinatra work really well together; their father-son

Sinatra (left) and Eddie Hodges made a fun team in *A Hole in the Head*.

dynamic is convincing. Audiences had not seen Sinatra play a father or act so extensively opposite a child yet in his career but he is wonderfully affectionate. It's a nice counter to the more irresponsible side of his character's personality. Hodges went on to appear in *The Adventures of Huckleberry Finn* (in the title role) and the drama *Advise & Consent* and had a couple of hit records as a teenager. He later served in Vietnam, and eventually became a mental health counselor.

Thelma Ritter plays against type as Mario's emotionally overwrought wife. Usually the dry, wisecracking presence in a film, Ritter reveals another layer of her skills as Sophie worries about her husband, about Tony, and about Ally. Carolyn Jones has less screen time, but resonates deeply as Shirl, the sort of free spirit that would attract a man like Tony.

She has no problem with his irresponsibility, and supports his dreams at face value. Shirl just wants a good time, which Tony provides. When her heart is broken by the entrance of Eloise, Ally tries to comfort her by bringing flowers to her room. The look on Shirl's face, tears streaming down her cheeks, is yet another emotional moment in a movie that is filled with them. Jones later became famous as Morticia Addams on TV's *The Addams Family*.

Eleanor Parker as Eloise has perhaps the most difficult assignment among the actresses. She is not as emotionally overwrought as Sophie nor as flashy as Shirl. She is the grounded, sensible counterpart to the narrative and its characters. Eloise cares about Tony and recognizes the good in him, despite his failures.

There is a scene in the movie that does not appear in the original play, when Tony is invited by his friend Jerry to a party and naively believes he can talk him into a partnership on the Disneyland idea. Keenan Wynn's performance as Jerry is forceful and blustery, brimming with entitled actions and lofty enthusiasm. He treats Tony as an equal, a potential partner, which excites him to the point that he phones Ally and tells him he's won enough money to pay for the hotel and adds, "When I get home I'll tell you the rest. It's a biggie!" But while Ally arranges a party, Tony loses the money he has won and gets brushed off by Jerry. His old friend's change of attitude is abrupt, and Tony is both hurt and angry.

Sinatra's performance opposite Wynn at the party is another highlight of the film. He convincingly works through a wide range of emotions in the span of a few minutes: He appears nervous to broach the subject of his idea with Jerry; then when Jerry seems interested, he immediately latches onto that and is unabashedly enthusiastic, before showing some disappointment and nervousness when Jerry suggests they talk it over more at the track.

One of the more amusing elements of this pivotal scene is Jerry's girlfriend, played by the beautiful Joi Lansing, a close friend of Sinatra's who did a lot of movie and TV work in the '50s and '60s. Lansing is very funny as a demanding sexpot who argues with the carefree millionaire. According to her partner and biographer Alexis Hunter, "Joi loved working with Frank. She loved being near him. And she loved doing comedy. She was a very funny person offscreen." According to Hunter's book *Joi Lansing: A Body to Die For*, Frank and Joi had an affair.

The film further benefits from some creative turns in smaller roles by Dub Taylor, Connie Sawyer, Benny Rubin and B.S. Pully, most of whom were friends of either Sinatra or Capra. Taylor, for instance, was in Capra's Oscar-winning 1938 feature *You Can't Take It with You*.

Capra's direction adds just the right touch to the proceedings. Always

(Left to right): *Hole in the Head* director Frank Capra, Sinatra and Edward G. Robinson pose for a gag shot.

responding well to idealistic characters who challenge the norm, Capra presents an atmosphere of happy poor and angry rich in his best tradition. Just as Mario says at the end, "They're not poor. They may be broke, but they aren't poor. *We're* poor." It is the underlying message in so many of Capra's classic films. And it settles comfortably here.

A Hole in the Head is something of a *tour-de-force* for Sinatra. It calls upon him to be funny, emotionally overcome, seething with anger, offended, ashamed, carefree, enthusiastic, loving and kind. And despite the complexity of this character, Sinatra plays him in a lovable, breezy manner that causes us to champion his dreams and forgive him his faults. He is surrounded by top-level supporting players all working at or near their best. *A Hole in the Head* remains one of his most appealing movies.

At this point in his career, both movies and music were consuming Sinatra's time to the point where he no longer wanted to do a regular TV series. He turned down an offer of a million dollars, quite a sum in the 1950s, and decided to concentrate only on records, live appearances and films.

Never So Few

Directed by John Sturges
Screenplay: Millard Kaufman, from the novel by Tom T. Chamales
Producer: Edmund Grainger
Cinematography: William Daniels (Metrocolor)
Editor: Ferris Webster
Cast: Frank Sinatra, Gina Lollobrigida, Peter Lawford, Steve McQueen, Richard Johnson, Paul Henreid, Brian Donlevy, Dean Jones, Charles Bronson, Philip Ahn, Robert Bray, Kipp Hamilton, John Hoyt, Richard Lupino, Whit Bissell, Aki Aleong, John Bryant, Ross Elliott, Bong Nam, James Hong, George Takei, Irene Tedrow, Maggie Pierce, Mako, Paul Maxwell, Leon Lontoc, Peter Miller, Allan Liu, Dale Ishimoto, Noel De Souza, Rollin Moriyama, Morgan Jones, Isabel Cooley, Spencer Chan, Rayford Barnes, Leo Needham, Charles Bateman, Lawrence Ung, Marie Tsien, George Khoury, Bhupesh Guha, Reginald Lal Singh, W.T. Chang, William Smith, Guy Lee, Jay Lee, Kei Thin Chung, Roy Taguchi
Released December 7, 1959
MGM
125 minutes

Sinatra continued to take it anything but easy in choosing his next film. The same actor who in just the prior few years had played leading roles in movies about drug addiction, a boozy nightclub performer undone by his mob ties, and interracial love turned his attention to a war picture with paradigm-shifting themes for the genre. *Never So Few* capped Sinatra's most prolific, artistically diverse and celebrated decade on the big screen with a story that strayed from Hollywood's standard World War II fare. Its military and political perspectives are more ambitious, and darker, than a typical Allies-vs.-Axis outing of the era. *Never So Few* doesn't always hit its target, but it reveals a Sinatra still aiming to create movies that offer audiences stories and performances that defy their expectations.

The film is based on the popular debut novel of former U.S. Army 2nd Lieutenant Tom T. Chamales, published in 1957. The novel recounts an underreported campaign in the early days of the war, when a small band of about 800 Kachins, the indigenous people of the Burmese hills and jungles, stood against the 40,000 Japanese who invaded the area to close off access to supplies in China for the Allies. The Kachin despised the Japanese, whom they regarded as savage; that opened the door for the U.S.

and British forces to serve alongside them, gathering intelligence, staging guerrilla actions, identifying targets for the Army Air Force to bomb, and rescuing downed Allied airmen. Chamales served with the unit that directed the Kachin, Detachment 101 of the Office of Strategic Services (O.S.S.), commanding a force of Kachin himself.

Chamales was so moved by what he experienced in Burma that after the war he penned *Never So Few*. It levels a serious charge against the leader of China, Chiang Kai-shek: The O.S.S. discovered that independent Chinese warlords, operating under license from Chiang along the China-Burma frontier, were raiding American convoys, murdering guards, selling the loot to the Japanese, and splitting the take with Chiang. The accusations were made in a work of fiction, yet certainly carried startling and politically provocative implications considering they were directed at a man who was still a major player on the global stage when the book was published.

Hollywood came calling for Chamales before *Never So Few* was published. MGM snapped up the film rights in January 1957 for $300,000, the highest price at the time paid by a studio for an author's first book.[124] So hot for the property was MGM, it anted up after only seeing the galley proofs.[125] Hollywood gadfly Louella Parsons was soon gossiping that Walter Chiara—the boyfriend of Sinatra's ex-wife Ava Gardner—was set to star in the film, though in what role she never got around to mentioning.[126] In the end, the leading role went to Sinatra, as part of a three-picture deal he signed with MGM in 1958—eight years after the studio dropped him when his film career hit the skids. It was his performance in the first movie he made under the new contract, *Some Came Running*, that earned him the lead in *Never So Few*. MGM president Joseph Vogel was so impressed by Sinatra's work in *Some Came Running*—calling it one of the best pictures he had ever seen—that he wanted him for the *Never So Few* lead.[127]

Sinatra was inked as O.S.S. Col. Tom Reynolds, the committed leader and caretaker of the Kachin. The star told his director, John Sturges, that he studied Millard Kaufman's screen adaptation of Chamales' novel until he had absorbed the character.

> Frank admits he never memorizes lines, "Only the characters. Thoughts and feelings," he said in a recent interview. "Sometimes, I change the lines after discussion with the director, but never the thought, only the lines, so that they fit me and the character."[128]

But Sinatra's interest in the project, it is clear, was not simply because he wanted another starring role in another war picture. (By the time his movie career concluded, the actor had portrayed nine active-duty U.S. military men—the profession he inhabited most on screen. Cop/private detective came in second with four appearances.) Sinatra also signed on as co-producer, through a one-shot company he called Canterbury Productions. He jumped into his duties behind the camera with gusto—perhaps more gusto than he spent on his duties in front of it. MGM was chasing after stunt casting early on, with rumors suggesting that the company planned to try to convince Ava Gardner to star opposite her ex; she laughed at the thought and said, "Nobody has even mentioned it to me."[129] But when the smoke of those rumors cleared, Sinatra got to work packing the film with his closest Hollywood pals and some industry up-and-comers.

Press reports during pre-production indicate that, at one time or another, the star-producer seemed to envision *Never So Few* as the first Rat Pack movie, before *Ocean's 11*, which was already on his filming schedule. Dean Martin was mentioned as a co-star in late 1958, though he did not appear in the movie.[130] Sinatra also threw his considerable non-physical weight around by adding Peter Lawford to the bill. Lawford was his co-star in *It Happened in Brooklyn* more than a decade earlier and had since become brother-in-law to Massachusetts Senator John F. Kennedy, whom Sinatra liked and admired (and endorsed and campaigned for, when JFK launched a bid for president in early 1960). As Harold Heffernan recounted in his syndicated North American Newspaper Alliance column: "The hitch is that Lawford, who hasn't appeared in a film feature in nearly seven years, won't be able to wrap up the last segment of his *Thin Man* television show for another two months. So Frank is determined to wait for him."[131]

Not only was Sinatra willing to wait, he was keen to make sure Lawford got handsomely compensated for his role as the suave, idealistic O.S.S. doctor. MGM initially offered Lawford $1500 a week for three weeks work, but Sinatra pressured the company to pay him ten times that amount.[132] He wasn't worth the investment, as it turned out. Not because his performance as the urbane Capt. Gray Travis is flawed, but because the role is wafer-thin.

A third member of the Rat Pack was also attached to a pivotal role: Sammy Davis, Jr. But, like Martin, Sammy never stepped before the camera. While Martin was only briefly mentioned in connection with the project in a gossip column, Davis had a signed contract for the pivotal role of Corporal Bill Ringa, an on-the-make jack-of-all trades who earns Reynolds' trust so completely he becomes the colonel's right-hand man and eventual second-in-command. Sinatra brushed aside MGM brass to get his friend the role and the $75,000 payday that came with it. When the studio objected to Davis' casting by saying, "Frank, there are no Negroes in the Burma theater [of operations]," Sinatra replied, "There are now."[133] To ensure it, he had the part, written as a Caucasian in both Chamales' novel and Kaufman's screenplay, rewritten.[134]

The story of Davis' dismissal has blossomed into lore that feeds the "Sinatra was not always a nice man" narrative that followed him throughout his career. While performing in Chicago in January 1959, Davis gave a radio interview in which he said his friend Frank had abused the fame that the ticket- and record-buying public had bestowed upon him; that Frank wasn't "a happy guy," and that he hated to be alone because "he doesn't want time enough to sit and think quietly." When asked who he thought the #1 singer in the country was, Davis named himself. "Bigger than Frank?" came the follow-up. "Oh, yeah," said Davis.[135]

Sinatra got wind of the interview, and Davis got his walking papers. Enter Steve McQueen. At 28, he wasn't Hollywood's typical nascent newcomer: He had knocked about for several years in minor roles on the New York stage before moving to California to scout out film work. He landed top-billed roles in *The Blob* and *The Great St. Louis Bank Robbery*, then made his first indelible mark on the viewing public as bounty hunter Josh Randall in TV's *Wanted: Dead or Alive*. *Never So Few* was his first A-list feature, and he displayed the dynamism that led to his reputation as Hollywood's "king of cool" both in the role of Ringa and in discussing it with the press. "It's nice," he said from the set when asked about working with Sinatra. "Like, I'm playing a soldier in this picture, man. You might say it's a change from the Western thing I'm doing, right?"[136]

Sinatra quickly became a big fan of his unexpected co-star. Perhaps he recognized a little of his younger self in both McQueen's off-screen demeanor and on-screen performance. And McQueen, though a poster boy for the young Hollywood set that would shrug off Sinatra in just a few years, thought the leader of the Rat Pack was still plenty cool, as evidenced by an interview he gave after shooting wrapped: "Frank Sinatra kept saying, 'Give the close-up to Steve.' He went out of his way to give me breaks. And what a swinging, meaty role. ... 'It's your picture, kid,' Steve said Frank told him.[137]

Sinatra's assessment is roughly half true. McQueen does stamp his every scene with his emerging magnetic presence, from his first appearance as Reynolds' driver, removing the gum he chews with cocksure insouciance to stick it to his Jeep's windshield frame as he bounds out of the driver's seat. It's just unfortunate that he—and fellow relative newcomers like Charles Bronson and Dean Jones, who play G.I.s with no love lost for each other—are not in more scenes. That's because half the picture is soap opera–quality romantic melodrama concerning Capt. Reynolds' wooing of pampered socialite Carla Verasi (Gina Lollobrigida), whose address on easy street is funded by wealthy merchant Nikko Regas

(Paul Henreid, in a role nowhere near as rich and a performance nowhere near as arresting as his turn in *Casablanca*). Reynolds and his British co-commander Danny DeMortimer (an enjoyable Richard Johnson) encounter the couple on a visit to Army headquarters in Calcutta, just a short plane ride from the jungle battlefront. Reynolds is smitten from the moment he first spies Carla—quite literally. When she removes her shawl as the group sits around a barroom table, her ample cleavage assumes center stage—and director Sturges makes sure his camera lingers first on it, then on Reynolds' lascivious reaction.

At least that moment, sexist as it is, reads authentically. Little else in Reynolds and Carla's interplay does. They dance. He comes on strong. She not only rebuffs him but mocks his American provincialism. Reynolds is conveniently ordered by brass to take two weeks' leave. He and Carla cross paths again at a party thrown by Nikko. They get some alone time when her boyfriend (or is he just her benefactor?) is called to China on urgent business. They see some sights together, once with Danny, once on their own. Carla remains aloof. Reynolds remains in amorous pursuit. Though they've shared not a single tender moment, he has fallen in love with her. Kaufman's screenplay, limp throughout this part of the story, eventually gets around to her succumbing not so much to Reynolds' charms as to his relentlessness. But not a single spark of chemistry emanates from their interactions—not even when Carla toys with Reynolds by inviting him into her bathroom while she bathes. Sinatra plays the scene with discomfort that seems to indicate dissatisfaction with the material, including an affected stutter—as if seeing a pretty lady covered by bubbles would rattle such a been-there, done-that soldier. Sinatra lobbied MGM when he landed the part to get the international sensation Lollobrigida for the role. It's difficult to see why from the tepid results.

Perhaps there is some marginal chemistry between Sinatra and Lollobrigida on screen, mainly as a result of Carla appearing both reluctant to engage with but simultaneously intrigued by Reynolds. The main issue is that their scenes together (particularly the "will they? won't they?" conflict driving their relationship) aren't as interesting as the war scenes. It might have been more effective had it been more of a B plot in this movie, but it feels like as much time is spent on the romance as the war.

The war portion of the picture is its redemption, despite Sinatra's first several scenes featuring him wearing an out-of-time and out-of-character beatnik goatee—the only time in his film career he sports facial hair. That fleeting fashion *faux pas* aside, Sinatra fills Reynolds' combat boots effortlessly. He plays him not as world-weary, or even particularly war-weary, but simply resigned to the violent task before him and committed to completing it with integrity and capping it with victory. The success of the wartime plot is in large part due to the political narrative woven into what could have otherwise been a boilerplate Hollywood treatment of World War II. It's on display first in the care Reynolds musters for the Kachin under his command. The relationships the commander has with his native men is no less protective than those for the enlisted U.S. and British soldiers in his unit. In fact, when his Kachin aide is badly wounded with no hope of survival in the film's first battle sequence, and the unit has no doctor yet to treat him nor morphine to ease his pain as he dies, Reynolds orders the other men out of the hospital tent and shoots him dead to end his pain. It is a shocking act, certainly not the kind seen in most war pictures of the era, and certainly not involving "foreign" troops. But it spotlights that in Reynolds' view, the Kachin are among his band of brothers.

Sinatra plays an army captain in the jungles of Burma in *Never So Few*.

Some of Sinatra's best acting comes in a similar scene, when Reynolds and several Kachin land in an army hospital after another Japanese sneak attack. Reynolds leaves his private room, a perk of rank, to visit his native men crammed tightly into a communal room. He grows angry when he sees that the food they are being served is insufficient for their recovery. He marches to the colonel's office with the men in tow, arguing above his rank that the Kachin need to be fed not hospital rations, but the food that has sustained them since birth in Burma. The natural actor in Sinatra shines here, resting in the easy authority of being responsible for these men and conveying committed, righteous anger that seethes with control rather than roiling with rage. Reynolds knows what the Kachin need because he cares enough to notice and humanize them, unlike his superiors who see them only as a means to an end. Sinatra's earnestness here is evocative and restrained. The result leaves the audience feeling that Reynolds isn't just arguing for a change in food for the Kachin, but a change in the way his military bosses view the group of men so critical to their war aims in the Pacific.

Sinatra's finest onscreen moments come in the film's final reels. The OSS is sent on a mission to destroy a Japanese airfield in nearby Ubachi, but its supplies, to be delivered by Allied forces from the Chinese, never arrive. Reynolds heads into battle anyway, discovering the convoy carrying the missing supplies was attacked. The evidence the OSS finds as they search the carnage indicates Chinese warlords were behind it. Reynolds indignantly disobeys orders and pursues the marauders into China—where they are rounded up and killed by Ringa on Reynolds' orders. McQueen owns every closeup Sinatra makes sure he gets in this scene, as the unit's most efficient enforcer. And Sinatra demonstrates once again his command of understated physical acting. He hunts down the enemy wordlessly, his commitment to seeing justice done on his terms conveyed in small, meaningful glances, cocks of the head, crouches and raps on walls with his rifle. He is like a cat in purposeful pursuit of a mouse, and director Sturges stages the minimalist action for maximum impact. Along the way, the force finds evidence of the crimes against the Allied troops and China's complicity in them: dozens of dog tags of military personnel slaughtered in the convoy raids, and orders from Chiang Kai-shek giving warlords near the Burmese border free rein to loot and pillage U.S. and British troops.

Sinatra delivers work reminiscent of his best performances when Reynolds returns to Calcutta to face the consequences for his actions. He is arrested and charged with murder in the deaths of the Chinese, publicly an ally of the U.S. in the fight against Japan. The military powers-that-be try to force him to plead mental diminishment due to battle fatigue, but he'll have none of it. Then a well-respected, highly decorated general confronts him. Through all the pressure to cave, Reynolds is resolute. Sinatra plays the scene pitch-perfectly; no outrage or outburst, just the confidence of a man with a clean conscience. Reynolds empties the dog tags on the table in front of the general, which when paired with the copies of Chiang's orders empowering the warlords leads to his exoneration. It's clear the whole travesty will be swept under the rug in the interests of U.S.-Chinese relations, which would still have a few years of public goodwill. But Reynolds, and his values, are the clear winners. It all smacks a bit of *deus ex machina* but for the era, it is a brave and worthwhile effort.

Never So Few has a stellar supporting cast and perhaps we could have seen more of the likes of Bronson and Jones as opposed to Lollobrigida (their characters were just more interesting, whereas she played a very standard love interest). It is especially interesting to see Jones playing this tough sort of role, since he became known for the light-hearted family films he made for Walt Disney a little later in his career. His performance is quite impressive. Richard Johnson plays his relationship with Sinatra as a precursor to the kind of ring-a-ding-ding camaraderie to be celebrated in the Rat Pack films to follow.

Never So Few received mixed reviews and did not enjoy the success of Sinatra's recent vehicles. *Variety* called it "one of those films in which individual scenes and sequences play with verve and excitement," but added, "[W]hen the relation of the scenes is evaluated, and their cumulative effect considered ... the threads begin to unravel like an old, worn sock."[138] The *Spokesman-Review* was more charitable, declaring that "Sinatra is becoming a legend [and] *Never So Few* is incontrovertible evidence."[139] McQueen fared even better: "He could easily get an Academy nomination for his portrayal as the mad young corporal-chauffeur who puts his training in the Brooklyn jungle to good use in the jungles of Burma."[140] It is hard to imagine Sammy Davis, Jr., pulling off the role so notably.

Sinatra began 1959 telling the *Los Angeles Times* that as television continued to take a bite out of box office receipts, he envisioned a splashy return of the motion picture musical: "Give the public a real dandy musical with two or big three stars," he said, "and you'll get them out of their houses and into the theaters."[141] He was to do just that in 1960, joining Shirley MacLaine and Maurice Chevalier in a hit adaptation of the Broadway play *Can-Can*.

Can-Can

Directed by Walter Lang
Screenplay: Dorothy Kingsley and Charles Lederer, from the musical by Abe Burrows
Producer: Jack Cummings
Cinematography: William Daniels (Technicolor)
Editor: Robert Simpson
Songs:
"I Love Paris," "Maidens Typical of France," "Can-Can," "C'est Magnifique," "Apache Dance," "Live and Let Live," "You Do Something to Me," "Let's Do It," "It's All Right with Me," "Come Along with Me," "Just One of Those Things," "Garden of Eden," "Montmart"; Composed by Cole Porter
Cast: Frank Sinatra, Shirley MacLaine, Maurice Chevalier, Louis Jourdan, Juliet Prowse, Marcel Dalio, Leon Belasco, Nestor Paiva, John A. Neris, Jean Del Val, Ann Codee, Wilda Taylor,

Can-Can (1960)

Carole Bryan, Jane and Ruth Earl, Barbara Carter, Vera Lee, Lisa Mitchell, Darlene Tittle, Wanda Shannon, Eugene Borden, George DeNormand, Peter Coe, Mary Stewart, Lili Valenty, Maurice Marsac, Edwin Rochelle, Alphonse Martel, Arthur Tovey, Michele Montau, Kay Tapscott, Victor Romito, Marc Wilder, Marcel De la Brosse, Wilbur Mack, Jack Deery, Edward Le Veque, Sam Harris, Renee Godfrey, Eddie Le Baron, Jonathan Kidd
Released March 11, 1960
20th Century–Fox
131 minutes

Can-Can is a watershed moment in Sinatra's film career. This is true not because it is his finest performance, or even his best work in a musical. Nor is it true because he again tackles, as he had throughout much of the 1950s, a character that allows him to grow and sharpen his talents as an actor. It is true because, for the first time since his film debut in *Higher and Higher*, he plays, in essence, himself. His character's name may be Francois Durnais, but he doesn't embody a rakish French lawyer in 1890s Paris. He embodies Frank Sinatra in 1960, the brightest, swingingest star in Hollywood. The singer singularly focused for two decades on proving that his abilities in front of a camera were as formidable as those behind a microphone had determined his point was made. He would only a few more times over the next 20-plus years muster the motivation to subsume his stardom, and the image he wore so comfortably as the result of it, to deliver an acting performance that challenged his skills.

This is not to say that Sinatra never made a winning, entertaining or interesting film during the remaining portion of his movie career, only that he increasingly viewed moviemaking as a lark and, as a rule, stopped stepping into roles or projects that challenged him. Francois Durnais and *Can-Can* vividly illustrate that truth.Loosely based on the musical play by Abe Burrows with a songbook by Cole Porter, the story had no meaty or age- and attitude-appropriate role for Sinatra. So it was rewritten by Charles Lederer and Dorothy Kingsley (who did yeowoman's work adapting *Pal Joey* from the stage) to add the Durnais character specifically for him. Francois is lawyer and lover to Simone Pistache (Shirley MacLaine playing a part that is a composite of two characters from the play), the owner of and featured talent at the Bal du Paradis, a cabaret popular and scandalous for the same reason: the dance of the title. Director Walter Lang swipes a trick from the original *King Kong* in revealing the "monster" to viewers only after characters talk about its shocking nature numerous times. It's a sharp technique to build speculation about the dance's "lewd and lascivious" nature, for which it has been banned by the French government.

Before filmgoers see the can-can, all the characters do, including a pair of judges: Chief Magistrate Paul Barriere (Maurice Chevalier) and Associate Magistrate Philippe Forrestier (Louis Jourdan). Barriere is a friend of Durnais, older but only slightly less a raconteur, while Forrestier is an unbent arrow, law-and-order all the way. The latter has the entire dance company arrested and the former slyly finds cause to dismiss the charges. The charmingly slithery Durnais makes it easier for Barriere to free his lover with his courtroom machinations. Forrestier senses something may be amiss with his mentor and colleague, so he goes undercover at the cabaret to gather evidence of wrongdoing (and wrong-dancing), but he upends his own plans by falling for the free-spirited Simone. His affections set up an ages-old love triangle as he tries to steal her from the marriage-phobic Durnais with a proposal and the promise of making a respectable woman of her. After the expected will-she-or-won't-she, Simone chooses Francois, who finally realizes he loves her enough make her his wife—after some low-wattage flirtation with chorus girl Claudine (Juliet Prowse, in her billed-performance film debut).

Sinatra assumed more than the lead role in *Can-Can*, signing on to produce the picture through another vaguely British-sounding one-shot production house, this time called Suffolk Productions. Although his co-producer Jack Cummings was initially after Marilyn Monroe for the role of Simone,[142] Sinatra had his eyes on his *Some Came Running* co-star MacLaine, and spared no headaches for others in making his wish a reality (waiting for her to fulfill other commitments cost the production time and money). He was clearly feeling the oats of his stardom.

Sinatra played off the challenges with humble-brag nonchalance, telling Hedda Hopper, "[I]t wasn't easy but everybody was so nice. I guess along the way I've made some friends for which I'm very grateful."[143] In getting MacLaine, the star-producer-Hollywood shot-caller was not just—or even mostly, it seems—flexing his industry muscles. He also wanted to help ensure the shoot would be, in Rat Pack parlance, "a gasser." MacLaine was, after all, a women's auxiliary member of the swaggering boys' club (she'd make a cameo in *Ocean's 11* later in the year). Having her on set and before the cameras ensured a good time—if not perfect casting for a piece set in turn-of-the-century Paris and co-starring suave Frenchmen Chevalier and Jourdan. MacLaine's broad comedic acting and disinterest in feigning the slightest hint of a French accent did not serve the role, or the film, well.

Sinatra's displayed equal disinterest in making Francois even vaguely French. In his initial encounter with Jourdan's Forrestier, he inexplicably refers to the morals of "your countrymen" to the judge although he is, in fact, supposed to be French himself. Soon thereafter, while encouraging the

Can-Can (1960)

jurist to let his hair down through singing "Le Magnifique" while adorned in a bevy of rotating beauties, Sinatra slips into Porter's well-known number the lyrical ad lib "ring-a-ding-ding-ding." Tossing one of the favorite phrases he famously shared from the stage and in the clubs with Dino and Sammy served notice that film audiences would from now on get less acting, and more *being*, from his on-screen work.

> It may just be one ring-a-ding-ding, but it is a significant moment in Sinatra's film career, because after appearing in forty films, it's the first time Frank Sinatra doesn't bother to try. As the king of show business in 1960, Sinatra had, by this time, firmly passed from stardom into the land of legend. And with the interpolation of "ring-a-ding-ding" he is, in effect, saying. "Hey, I'm Frank Sinatra—I'll coast along here on my charm. I don't need to act and work at a genuine characterization." He's taking his pleasure and winking at the audience.[144]

Make no mistake, the audience gets its fair share of pleasure from *Can-Can*, and from most of the films that followed in which Sinatra brought his personality to a role more than a true performance. His interpretations of some of Porter's best-known compositions are, not surprisingly, top-drawer. His duet with MacLaine on "Let's Do It," while it seems

Sinatra and Shirley MacLaine give disappointing contemporary performances in the period musical *Can-Can*.

more appropriate for a contemporary Broadway stage with its pantomiming playfulness, is energetic fun that offers the audience a good time in part because the performers are having such a good time. The best number, though, is "It's All Right with Me," which Francois sings to Claudine during one of his off-again moments with Simone. It's the romantic Sinatra of the era—not 1890s France, but 1960s America—at his best. The whiskey-weary baritone conveys a wounded heart devoid of bravado. It's no wonder, seeing their chemistry in this scene, that Sinatra and Prowse were an item for the next couple of years.

Can-Can earned some solid reviews—the *Tampa Bay Times* called it "colorfully lavish and lively"[145] and *Film Bulletin* said it was "certain to entertain every spectator in the theater."[146] But *Variety* labeled the whole affair only "serviceable" and called out as "jarring" the "juxtaposition of Sinatra and MacLaine on the one hand, and authentic Parisians Maurice Chevalier and Louis Jourdan on the other." (It added, correctly, that the allegedly scandalous dance of the title "is fun, but about as lewd and lascivious as a Maypole dance.")[147] The film was also a hit, topping the box office for all films released in 1960, coming in second for the year only to 1959's *Ben-Hur*.[148]

But it did not please all audiences. *Can-Can*'s most famous detractor was Soviet premier Nikita Khrushchev, who as part of an American goodwill tour in September 1959 stopped by 20th Century–Fox studios for lunch and a chance to see a film being made. *Can-Can* was that film. The Russian leader and his wife had lunch with a who's who of Hollywood including Edward G. Robinson, Judy Garland, Shelley Winters, Gary Cooper, Kim Novak, Dean Martin, Ginger Rogers, Kirk Douglas, Jack Benny, Tony Curtis, Zsa Zsa Gabor and Marilyn Monroe, who studio chief Spyros Skouras made triply sure was on time, which was not her professional or personal calling card. News came while everyone was eating that the Khrushchevs would not be able to go to Disneyland due to safety concerns. Sinatra, sitting next to David Niven, whispered into Niven's ear, "Screw the cops! Tell the old broad that you and I will take 'em down there this afternoon."[149]

Alas, the dashing leading men did not follow through, so the Khrushchevs had to settle for seeing the can-can production number performed. While the premier seemed to enjoy himself during the run-through, clapping and tapping his feet, the next day he dropped some choice rhetorical bombs—that served double duty as publicity gold for the production. "It was immoral," he hectored. "Humanity's face is more beautiful than its backside. Only people who are over-satiated like such things and similar pornography."[150]

"Over-satiated" was precisely the feel Sinatra would go after with his next film. *Ocean's 11* would be the first big-screen outing of his group of show-biz friends known sometimes as the Clan or the Summit but ultimately as the Rat Pack. It would hardly aim to be high art, but rather a high time—when the cameras were rolling and when they weren't.

Ocean's 11

Directed and Produced by Lewis Milestone
Screenplay: Harry Brown and Charles Lederer, from a story by George Clayton Johnson and Jack Golden Russell
Cinematography: William H. Daniels (Technicolor)
Editor: Philip W. Anderson
Songs:
 "Ain't That a Kick in the Head"; Written by Sammy Cahn, Jimmy Van Heusen
 "Eee-O-11"; Written by Sammy Cahn, Jimmy Van Heusen
 "I'm Gonna Live Until I Die"; Words by Al Hoffman; Music by Walter Kent and Husband Curtis
Cast: Frank Sinatra, Dean Martin, Sammy Davis, Jr., Peter Lawford, Angie Dickinson, Richard Conte, Cesar Romero, Patrice Wymore, Joey Bishop, Akim Tamiroff, Henry Silva, Ilka Chase, Buddy Lester, Richard Benedict, Jean Willes, Norman Fell, Shirley MacLaine, Clem Harvey, Ronny Dapo, Hank Henry, Lew Gallo, Red Skelton, George Raft, Don "Red" Barry, Marjorie Bennett, Norman Brooks, George Fenneman, John Indrisano, Pinky Lee, Jack Perrin, Forrest Lederer, Jack Perry, Nelson Leigh, Steve Pendelton, Louis Quinn, Red Norvo, Tom Middleton, Goerge E. Stone, H.T. Tsiang, Richard Sinatra, Fred Rapport, Maurice Marks, Norma Yost, Shiva, Hoot Gibson, Nicky Blair, Murray Alper, Joseph Glick, Robert Bice, Helen Jay, Buddy Shaw, Gregory Gaye, Boyd Cabeen, Paul Bryar
Released August 4, 1960
Dorchester Productions for Warner Brothers
127 minutes

"That Big One!" was the tagline Warner Bros. attached to Sinatra's first non-musical film of the 1960s. And a large, attention-grabbing undertaking it was. *Ocean's 11* was generating buzz two years before its release, for the big names in the cast as well as those rumored to be joining them. The excitement over the production wasn't hurt by the fact that Sinatra's co-star, Peter Lawford, also happened to be the brother-in-law of Senator

John F. Kennedy, whose political star was beginning the meteoric rise that would land him in the White House. As if that wasn't enough, the movie boasted an audacious story, an Oscar-winning director and a glamorous location—Las Vegas—that Americans had heard and even dreamed about but most had not yet seen up close and *en masse*. *Ocean's 11* was primed to be a "big one," indeed.

But only to a segment of American pop culture. The schism that had developed when Sinatra and his brand of crooners-swingers was pushed down the popular music charts by rock'n'roll was coming to a close. And Sinatra would play a role in its re-emergence. As Elvis Presley neared the conclusion of his military service, his manager, Colonel Tom Parker, was surprised to be contacted by Sinatra, who indicated he was preparing a TV special for May 1960 and wanted Elvis as the star attraction. He even suggested the show be called *Welcome Home Elvis*. The program would be shot in March, shortly after Presley received his honorable discharge and returned home from Germany. Parker realized the exposure would be great, something Elvis needed to rekindle his career. While a backlog of songs was released over the two years he had been in the army, this pre-recorded material was becoming quite scarce in the days leading up to Elvis' discharge. Immediately upon coming home, he was whisked into production of *G.I. Blues*, the album "Elvis Is Back" and the single "Stuck on You," which was not among the tracks on the album.

Parker saw the wisdom of promoting these releases on a big TV special with the two greatest singing stars in the world appearing together. But both Parker and Presley still remembered Sinatra's criticisms of Elvis, and rock'n'roll in general. Parker charged Sinatra $125,000 for a ten-minute appearance—an outrageous amount for the time. Sinatra agreed to the price. In fact, he had changed the pitch of his tune, if not the tune itself, regarding the music of those "cretinous goons." "I still don't like it," he said of rock'n'roll. "But, after all, the kid's been away two years, and I get the feeling he really believes in what he's doing. I think he really loves it, and that's the secret of his success."[151]

On the show, Elvis performed his new hit "Stuck on You" as well as another, "Fame and Fortune," and plugged his movie, which was due for November release. He also had a fun bit with Frank where Sinatra sang Presley's 1956 hit "Love Me Tender" while Elvis crooned the Sinatra song "Witchcraft," both camping it up throughout. Still, there is a discernible awkwardness. Elvis was on for roughly eight minutes; the rest of the hour special featured Sinatra, his *Ocean's 11* co-stars Sammy Davis, Jr., Joey Bishop and Peter Lawford, plus Frank's daughter, Nancy, who would later co-star with Elvis in the movie *Speedway* (1968). Upon conclusion of the show's taping, Elvis disdainfully said to friends, "To my face, they couldn't have been nicer to me!"[152] During the filming of *G.I. Blues,* Sinatra often visited the set, as he was then seeing co-star Juliet Prowse. He would sometimes stop in Elvis' dressing room to say hello. Elvis crony Lamar Fike stated, "Elvis was never paranoid about Sinatra, or afraid of him, either."[153]

Sinatra had reason to feel the same about the King, given the exalted place the Chairman held in Hollywood and on the charts among music fans more seasoned than Presley's. The chief reason for all the anticipation for *Ocean's 11* was, ironically, also the chief reason it was not a particularly good film. The movie brought before the cameras Sinatra's version of Humphrey Bogart's old Rat Pack, the core of which was Sinatra himself (known as the Leader in the context of the group) along with Dean Martin and Davis (whose feud with Sinatra that got him bounced from *Never So Few* two years earlier had been patched up). Secondary members, because they weren't song-and-dance men, were Lawford and comedian Bishop. The quintet tried to be known as the Clan or the Summit but could never shed the Rat Pack label, even though Sinatra didn't care for it.

The group arrived in Las Vegas in early January 1960. Their first order of business, though, was not to begin making a movie. They initially took to the stage at the Sands—a pretty clear sign that they viewed moviemaking as the less important, or at least not the most important, reason for being in the desert. As Sinatra biographer James Kaplan summed it up: "No plan, no script, no starting pistol. Nobody ever preconceived the idea of rolling out these five guys and their bar cart on the stage of the Sands' Copa Room that January as shooting for *Ocean's 11* began."[154]

Vegas had never seen anything like it. In early February, as word of the on-stage hijinks spread, the Sands had 18,000 reservation requests for its 200 rooms; fellow Hollywood A-listers scrambled for tickets, Cary Grant, Rosalind Russell, Kirk Douglas and Gregory Peck among them. What was all the fuss about? A chance to see the ultimate bourgeois boys club, who had been devising their own chic lingo ("a little hey-hey" meaning sex, "the big casino" meaning death) and carousing through Hollywood's trendiest night spots for a couple of years.

That devil-may-care bonhomie, packaged with a bit of middle-aged naughtiness, was what Sinatra and Lawford hoped to bring to movie houses. Jack Kennedy's sister's husband had bought the rights to the story of *Ocean's 11* in 1957 from an aspiring director no one really heard of before or after. Lawford, who didn't have the Hollywood juice to get the movie made on his own, shared the idea with his friend and *Never So Few* co-star, Sinatra. Sinatra loved it: One-time heroes of World War II, aging members of the Army's 82nd Airborne, regroup for one last mission: to "liberate" millions of dollars simultaneously from five Las Vegas casinos on New Year's Eve. Sinatra saw it as the perfect vehicle to play with pals and make a movie. The nightclub shindig was the unexpected cherry on top, a way to ensure what Sinatra of the era craved: non-stop action. The shows and extracurricular activities would begin in the wee hours and extend well into the next day, with on-set work after "action" rarely getting underway before late afternoon.

Sinatra is Sgt. Danny Ocean, mastermind of the elaborate scheme and leader of the ten-man outfit. The character is an extension of the real-life Sinatra: a garrulous hipster given to playful practical jokes who receives unquestioned devotion from all around him. The part did not require him to act so much as *be*. Similarly, the rest of the Rat Pack walk breezily through their roles, in which they also play incarnations of themselves. Jimmy Foster (Lawford) is the charming Englishman who joins up seemingly to escape the boredom of his breeding; Josh Howard (Davis) is the agreeable mascot, quick to entertain his brethren with a song and a dance and laugh at their jokes; Mushy O'Connors (Bishop) is the sad-faced sidekick seemingly just happy to be in such luminous company. And Sam Harmon (Martin), Danny's second-in-command, is almost as fast with a quip and a smirk, almost as irresistible to the "dames," and the only one whose opinion and approval Danny occasionally courts.

The Rat Packers are joined by pros Richard Conte (as the team's electrician whiz) and Cesar Romero (as a gentlemanly mobster with designs first on Jimmy's mom [Ilka Chase] and then his loot). They were almost joined by a whole lot more. In 1958, Jackie Gleason was being wooed by

(Left to right): Richard Conte, Buddy Lester, Joey Bishop, Sammy Davis, Jr., Sinatra, Dean Martin, Peter Lawford, Akim Tamiroff, Richard Benedict, Henry Silva, Norman Fell, and Clem Harvey pull a heist in *Ocean's 11*.

Sinatra to join the cast—the Great One in That Big One.[155] Robert Wagner was on the wish list in August 1959.[156] Jack Lemmon and Tony Curtis were sought for cameos (in drag, *à la Some Like It Hot*) in December '59. The most intriguing bit of casting almost involved Steve McQueen, who had launched his film career by taking over a role originally earmarked for Davis in *Never So Few*. McQueen was said to be locked up to play the heist mastermind—until he got offered a role in *The Magnificent Seven*. Akim Tamiroff, at 60 twice the age of McQueen, stepped in as Spyros Acebos.[157] One wild casting story involves Henry Silva, who plays Roger Corneal, one of Ocean's 10 (Ocean himself is the eleventh). Sinatra, a fan of the actor's work in *Hatful of Rain*, offered him the role at a stoplight in Los Angeles by screaming out his car window, "I think you're a gasser."[158]

The screenplay, by Harry Brown and Charles Lederer, was hyped by Lawford early and often. "I know it sounds wild, but we have a script that makes your ears stand up," he said in 1958. "We plan to show it to the sheriff of Clark County and let him go over it for any possible slips. I think he'll get quite a charge out of it."[159] So much of a charge, the gossip columns reported a year later, that there was some doubt the movie would even get made because "the film would show how a hold-up of a gambling casino was planned and pulled off."[160] An even more colorful story, from Lawford's lips to Erskine Johnson's ears, involved studio chief Jack Warner hatching a heist plan of his own. "Wait a minute, Frankie," he is said to have told Sinatra. "Let's get 12 instead of 11, forget about making the movie and take the script to Vegas and try it."[161]

Ocean's 11 would be a much better movie if it were quickly to establish the stars' personae and get on to the details of its rather complex storyline, which involves everything from rewiring of casino vault doors to transporting the loot out of the city via garbage truck. However, the screenplay repeatedly scuttles the narrative to spotlight the interplay of its cast. It works for viewers who would rather see Sinatra and his pals cavort about with lit cigarettes and full highball glasses than see Danny Ocean and his war buddies intricately burgle the Sahara, Riviera, Desert Inn, Sands and Flamingo. That's not to say the film is without narrative merit: the ending, a wicked bit of comeuppance for the crew that offers a jolt of legitimate surprise, is well-staged and well-played. The two songs—one for Martin (the up-tempo "Ain't That a Kick in the Head") and one for Davis (the mid-tempo "Eee-O-Eleven")—are standouts that serve the plot. Lewis Milestone's direction is also top-drawer, particularly his presentation of the neon glitz and energy that was Las Vegas in its early days. The man who earned two Best Director Oscars (*Two Arabian Knights* and *All Quiet on the Western Front*) and coaxed an Oscar-nominated performance out of Adolphe Menjou in *The Front Page* doesn't have much to work with cast-wise, because no one besides Davis and occasionally Martin (as the one old soldier who initially doubts the merits of the plan) is doing much acting. Sinatra does flash one bit of the nuance that made his breakthrough '50s performances so rich: subtly fingering a booze bottle at the back of the frame as if weighing it as a weapon while Romero's Duke Santos extorts the men of their ill-gotten gains.

The female roles are particularly thankless. Sinatra signaled the film's sexist point of view when he responded to Hedda Hopper's question about whether the film would have any dames: "Oh, naturally," he said. "But they'll be incidental."[162] Right he was. Shirley MacLaine turns up in a drunken cameo outside one of the casinos, spilling out of her car to be kissed and then spurned by Harmon to keep the boys' plan on schedule. In another scene, Ocean berates his estranged wife (a radiant but underused Angie Dickenson) after she rejects his crude suggestion that they partake of a little "hey-hey"; later, Dickinson's character is seen literally waiting by the phone for his call. Even more alarming: Sam proposes that politics is a noble pursuit, especially since it would allow an office-holder the opportunity to "repeal the 14th and 20th amendments—take the vote away from women and makes slaves out of 'em." The racial jokes are equally wince-worthy. As the boys are making their getaway in Josh's garbage truck, they apply dark makeup to make themselves harder to spot at night. Josh gets a chuckle out of watching his friends conceal their skin tone and says, "I knew this color would come in handy one day." Jimmy responds, "How do you get this stuff off?"—and Josh begins to answer before catching himself, the double butt of the joke.

Ocean's 11 does by and large follow the blueprint for a heist movie (gathering the team, forming the plan, executing the plan; the fact that the audience is supposed to root for the con men and that they don't face any serious consequences at the end is a big factor as well). But much of it has not aged well. It frequently works much better as a time capsule, lending insight as to how the Rat Pack interacted and to what Las Vegas looked like in the early '60s, than it does as a movie. It seems like there is much more time spent on unnecessary exposition than the heist, which should be the highlight of the film but gets lost in everything else.

Ironically, or perhaps intentionally, *Ocean's 11* was a hit with audiences for the very same reasons it wasn't a particularly distinguished film. Many moviegoers of the time were fascinated with the private lives of these entertainers, and the picture did give Rat Pack fans an idea what their offscreen get-togethers were probably like. *Variety* hit the critical nail on the head: "Laboring under the handicaps of a contrived script, an uncertain approach and personalities in essence playing themselves, the production never quite makes its point, but romps along merrily unconcerned that it doesn't."[163] Playing a casually cool version of himself devoid of heavy lifting as an actor suited Sinatra fine, so much so that he would reassemble with some mix of the Pack for three more pictures over the next four years. Each was well-received by moviegoers, if not in the critical press. In the early 1980s, Burt Reynolds revived the Rat Pack formula with *The Cannonball Run* and its sequel; the latter reunited Sinatra, Martin, and Davis (along with MacLaine) for exploits which seemed especially foolish now that they were all in their 60s. As expected, however, these sophomoric road-race comedies also attracted a large audience.

An even bigger hit was the full-on 2001 reboot of *Ocean's Eleven* (spelled out, not numerical). Starring A-listers George Clooney (as Danny Ocean, the only character reprised from the original), Brad Pitt and Matt Damon, the movie again centered on a Las Vegas heist—this time on the night of a major championship fight. With the cast invested in portraying three-dimensional characters and the intricacies of the plot executed as the centerpiece of the action, the movie was a critical and popular hit. Dickinson and Silva, the last of the original's main cast still living, had cameos as fight fans. The movie spawned a pair of direct sequels (*Ocean's Twelve* in 2004 and *Ocean's Thirteen* in 2007) and led to the all-female reboot *Ocean's 8* (back to numbers) in 2018—with Sandra Bullock playing Danny's sister Debbie. More box office gold.

Back in 1960, Sinatra pocketed the gold and goodwill that came his way from the original *Ocean's 11* and snapped up the chance to work with a Hollywood legend from the era of the original Rat Pack's leader. He'd play opposite Humphrey Bogart contemporary Spencer Tracy in his next film, the adventure drama *The Devil at 4 O'Clock*. It was hardly a momentous occasion.

The Devil at 4 O'Clock

Directed by Mervyn LeRoy
Screenplay: Liam O'Brien, from the novel by Max Catto
Producer: Fred Kohlmar
Cinematography: Joseph F. Biroc (Eastmancolor)
Editor: Charles Nelson
Cast: Spencer Tracy, Frank Sinatra, Kerwin Mathews, Jean-Pierre Aumont, Gregoire Aslan, Alexander Scourby, Barbara Luna, Cathy Lewis, Bernie Hamilton, Martin Brandt, Louis Merrill, Marcel Dallo, Thomas H. Middleton, Ann Duggan, Louis

Mercier, Michele Montau, Nanette Tanaka, Moki Hana, Warren Hsieh, Jean Del Val, Robert M. Luck, Max Dommar, Tony Maxwell, Eugene Borden, Earl D'Eon, Janine Grandel, Robin Shimatsu, Pearl Rose, Ma Ma Loa, William Keaulani, Norman Wright, Guy Lee

Released October 18, 1961

Fred Kohlmar Productions and Mervyn LeRoy Productions for Columbia

126 minutes

An action movie that also ushered in the concept of the disaster film, *The Devil at 4 O'Clock* was a disaster in and of itself. The most expensive production Columbia had ever produced, it lost more than a million dollars. It was promoted in the same breath as the films *The Bridge on the River Kwai* and *The Guns of Navarone*, but was not a war picture as both of those were. And its two stars were not particularly fond of each other.

Originally the film was going to be made with Spencer Tracy and Sidney Poitier. But a pending Screen Actors Guild strike caused the project to be shelved. When it was reactivated, Poitier was no longer available, and that's when Sinatra got involved.

Initially it didn't seem like there would be a conflict. Both Tracy and Sinatra would as a matter of routine stipulate in their contracts that they were to receive top billing for any movie in which they appeared, but for *Devil* Sinatra agreed without hesitation to take second billing to Tracy. However, Tracy was old and in poor health by the time he appeared in this movie, so he could only work in the mornings. Sinatra, however, spent his mornings flying around the islands on a private plane he hired, trying to convince islanders to vote for John F. Kennedy in the next presidential election. By the time he got to the set, Tracy was finished working for the day. Director Mervyn LeRoy was forced to shoot around him, or to have someone hold a broom opposite Tracy, who would say his lines to the broom, while a script girl read Frank's lines. For a serious actor like Tracy, considered by some to be the finest screen actor in movie history, this was not acceptable.

Another problem was Katharine Hepburn, who was extremely watchful over Tracy. Actor Kerwin Mathews, a supporting player in *Devil*, recalled for Tracy's biographer James Curtis:

> The first day on location on Maui—standing exactly where the first pilgrims landed on a Hawaiian island—I met the Hepburn thing. I had a present for her—a book to read, *Hawaii*, which would explain so much about the islands. I gave it to her. She walked out on a pier and threw the book in the ocean, saying, "Who wants to know anything about this awful place?" Because she was

Spencer Tracy (left) is considered the actor's actor, but he couldn't save the lackluster *The Devil at 4 O'Clock*.

always next to Spence, no one had a chance to talk to him. No one got to know him, even though I tried constantly.[164]

The Devil at 4 O'Clock came along near the end of veteran filmmaker Mervyn LeRoy's career. He had helmed such enduring classics as *Little Caesar* (1931) and *I Am a Fugitive from a Chain Gang* (1933), as well as films featuring such diverse stars as James Cagney, Joe E. Brown and Greer Garson. He had already worked with Tracy on *Thirty Seconds Over Tokyo* (1944). He also contributed to the direction of *The Wizard of Oz* (1939). In his autobiography, he recalled *Devil*:

> What made it a problem was that the climactic scene involved a volcano, and that's the kind of thing you have to worry about and plan for with extreme care.... It was done partly on a Hollywood sound stage, partly in the Hawaiian Islands. And we also used miniatures extensively. Mostly, though, we shot in Lahaina, on the Hawaiian island of Maui. We built a lovely set there—an entire village, complete with a street, a church, and even a jail. Even though we were shooting in one of the most beautiful places on earth, it was a tough picture.[165]

Tracy is well cast as alcoholic priest Father Doonan, who works on a Pacific island until he discovers there is leprosy among its children—a fact the islanders want to keep secret. He creates a leper colony near a volcano and is forever seeking donations from the islanders. A younger priest (Mathews) shows up to take over for Doonan. Sinatra is Harry, a convict headed for Tahiti with two others (Gregorie Aslan, Bernie Hamilton); the three stop on the island. When the volcano erupts, Father Doonan wants to rescue the children, and the convicts offer to help, believing it could lead to their sentences being commuted. There is also a tangential romance between Harry and a blind girl (Barbara Luna in her film debut). The Bernie Hamilton character becomes a hero by holding up a collapsed wooden bridge and allowing the youngsters to escape.

The Devil at 4 O'Clock had its share of its technical mishaps. According to a *Miami Herald* story:

> Columbia Studios electrician Zlarvin Tweiss is not a believer in the old adage that lightning never strikes twice in the same place. Tweiss was operating a lightning machine for a storm sequence ... when he miscalculated the distance and the bolt of lightning struck him in the back. He guessed wrong the second time too and he was struck in the same area.[166]

Tracy turns in quite a good performance as the irascible priest who has lost his faith as a result of the suffering he has seen. Sinatra, in devil-may-care mode, is effective but with a less demanding role. With leprosy, blindness and an erupting volcano, A.H. Weiler in *The New York Times* stated: "[T]here is enough martyrdom here to interest a saint. And, even if our tough convicts reach Paradise and a state of grace helping unfortunates, it still makes for unconvincing, manufactured melodrama."[167]

The Devil at 4 O'Clock is certainly one of Sinatra's least interesting films and performances. Perhaps it is because he was distracted, or perhaps because the character of Harry offered the seasoned actor no challenge. Sinatra walks through his part with a discernible indifference. On top of that, the film is dull—certainly for an action-adventure film. The random dollops of excitement and suspense are thwarted by a protracted running time and a romance that disrupts from the rhythm and pace of the narrative.

The special effects are reasonably impressive, particularly the volcano eruption. The volcano was man-made, and an ill-timed explosion very nearly took out the helicopter from which the cameraman was filming. It's a great shot, though. Sinatra is able to effectively and subtly show how his character softens over time, to the point where even Tracy's character (who initially dislikes him) comes to realize it. A lot of the problems stem from the lackluster script that seems like it tries to drum up as much melodrama as possible. The romance between Harry and Camille feels especially contrived.

John F. Kennedy was elected president on November 8, 1960, after which, according to Curtis, "Sinatra lost what little interest he retained in *The Devil at 4 O'Clock* and the gulf between him and Tracy widened." Mathews told Curtis, "By the end of *The Devil at 4 O'Clock* Tracy was barely tolerating Frank." Tracy himself was shaken up by the passing of his old friend and co-star Clark Gable on November 16, 1960.

Along with the distraction of the presidential race, Sinatra was also distracted by running his own record label, Reprise Records, which he founded in 1960. His first Reprise album, "Ring-a-Ding-Ding," came out in March 1961 and rose to #4 on the charts by the time he was filming *Devil at 4 O'Clock*. He had also recorded a heartfelt tribute to bandleader Tommy Dorsey, "I Remember Tommy," consisting of re-recordings from his years singing for Dorsey's band, including "I'll Be Seeing You" and "I'm Getting Sentimental Over You"—two wartime classics, the latter of which had been Dorsey's theme song.

Sergeants 3

Directed by John Sturges
Screenplay: W.R. Burnett, based on Rudyard Kipling's poem "Gunga Din" and the screenplay of the 1939 movie.
Producer: Frank Sinatra
Cinematography: Winton Hoch (Technicolor)
Editor: Ferris Webster
Cast: Frank Sinatra, Dean Martin, Sammy Davis, Jr., Peter Lawford, Joey Bishop, Henry Silva, Ruta Lee, Buddy Lester, Phillip Crosby,

Dennis Crosby, Lindsay Crosby, Hank Henry, Richard Simmins, Michael Pate, Armand Alzamora, Richard Hale, Mickey Finn, Sonny King, Eddie Little Sky, Rodd Redwing, Dorothy Abbott, Madge Blake, James Waters, Charles Horvath, Harry Wilson, Robert Robinson, Danny Sands, Al Haskell, Rudy Sooter, Billy McCoy, Mack Gray, Susan Woods, Leon Alton, Frank Ellis, Rudy Bowman, Walter Merrill, Danny Borzage

Released February 10, 1962

Essex Productions and Meadway-Claude Productions company for United Artists

112 minutes

When *Ocean's 11* became a hit, Sinatra was chagrined that he hadn't produced it himself. A movie that was really just a light-hearted lark turned out to be one of the top 15 grossing films of 1960. So when Sinatra gathered up his Rat Pack cronies for another movie, he produced it for his own company.

In 1939, director George Stevens made a feature-length adventure movie based on Rudyard Kipling's poem "Gunga Din"; the screenplay was by Joel Sayre and Fred Guiol, based on a story by Ben Hecht and Charles MacArthur. The script was rewritten and revamped by a number of other writers, including William Faulkner, before it was finally filmed with Cary Grant, Victor McLaglen, Douglas Fairbanks, Jr., and Sam Jaffe. Sinatra got the idea to take this story and rewrite it into a Western. He hired W.R. Burnett to write the screenplay. Burnett had scripted such Westerns as *Dark Command, The Westerner, Yellow Sky* and *The Badlanders*. Sinatra then asked John Sturges to direct. Sturges had helmed *Gunfight at the O.K. Corral, Last Train from Gun Hill* and *The Magnificent Seven*. However, after making these commendable choices, Frank got indulgent. He found roles for cronies Buddy Lester, Henry Silva, Mack Gray, even Bing Crosby's three younger sons. Ruta Lee was the only woman co-star. According to a promotional article in the *New York Daily News*[168]:

> Sinatra produced with Howard W. Koch acting as executive producer. Exteriors were shot on location near Kanab and at Bryce Canyon National Park, Utah. A working company of 250 arrived on the location site in Utah from Hollywood. This contingent included production staff, technical crews, production staff for the Technicolor-Panavision cameras and a large acting group. Later, hundreds of local citizens from nearby towns and Indian reservations were added. Not far from Kanab, on the abandoned town site of Parie, the Hollywood unit constructed a brand new town, which they called Medicine Bend. Since it is in a wild and almost inaccessible section of the country, the crew had to build a hard road to transport equipment and personnel to the shooting site.

Dean Martin arrived on location for the first week of location filming; Joey Bishop was not yet needed. Dean sent Bishop a postcard with a view of the city. Bishop responded by sending Dean a CARE package.

Frank wanted to call the movie *Soldiers 3,* but he discovered that MGM owned the rights to that title, having produced their own adventure based on *Gunga Din* in 1951 with Walter Pidgeon, Stewart Granger and David Niven .

Sinatra, Martin and Peter Lawford play the title characters Mike, Chip and Larry, serving in the cavalry in Indian Territory. When his hitch is up, Larry plans to leave the Army and marry a beautiful woman (Ruta Lee). Sammy Davis, Jr., plays Jonah, a former slave who connects with the trio when they come to his aid as he is being terrorized by outlaws in a bar. Mike and Chip spike the drink of an uptight, brown-nosing soldier (Bishop), which forces Larry back onto the job and away from his girl. He is tricked into signing a re-enlistment paper with the promise that it will be destroyed after the next mission. There is more action, the sergeants are captured, and Jonah saves the day by blowing his trumpet as a warning. The sergeants are decorated, Jonah is allowed to join the troop, and because Larry's re-enlistment paper was not destroyed, he must serve another hitch with the others.

(Left to right): Dean Martin, Sinatra and Peter Lawford remade *Gunga Din* as a Western in *Sergeants 3.*

Westerns were central to the development of cinema. One of the earliest movies to use editing to tell a story was Edwin S. Porter's one-reel Western *The Great Train Robbery* (1903) with G.M. Anderson; as Broncho Billy, he would become the screen's first cowboy hero. Wildly popular from the silent era into the 1940s, the Western became less so after World War II. Then in 1950, Anthony Mann's *Winchester '73* with James Stewart became a hit, and then TV ushered in a myriad of cowboy shows.

Sinatra's approach was in response to the Western's popularity with all ages. While grown-ups enjoyed a serious story and some romance, children wanted action and comedy. Sinatra believed that his screenwriter and director could craft a solid Western feature, containing both action and a compelling narrative, while his Rat Pack could effectively offer action and humor. Using Kipling's "Gunga Din" as the basis enabled the Rat Packers to indulge in comedy within the context of the action, as Grant, McLaglen and Fairbanks did in 1939. But that wasn't particularly easy to do.

For example, there is a barroom brawl within the first ten minutes of *Sergeants 3* and while a similar scene in *Gunga Din* came off like carefree heroics, this film more closely resembles the type of movie Elvis Presley was making during that era. The brawl features bombastic slapstick comedy instead of breezy antics. Sinatra, Lawford and Martin fight a bar filled with imposing cowboy "varmints" who stagger comically when hit with a bottle or chair, swing and miss repeatedly while *getting* hit, and accidentally hit one another. It is the sort of scene that would delight children, which was Sinatra's intention.

Within the first half-hour, the boys are involved in an Indian attack that runs a full 12 minutes of relentless action. This is played more seriously, with brief cutaways to the guys winking, shaking hands or offering smart quips. The sequence is quite violent, with arrows piercing chests and guns blazing. Dino casually ignites dynamite sticks with the lit cigar in his mouth, tossing them into the outdoor action from the safety of a building.

There are some elements of humor that fall flat. Dino enters an abandoned saloon that has a sign which states, "No Licker Sold to Soldiers." The gag is that liquor is spelled as it is. But a more challenging word like "soldiers" being spelled correctly negates the purpose of the joke.

Because of director Sturges' experience filming Westerns, he makes excellent use of the locations in his establishing shots. Beautiful scenery framing the actors. And because the film's leads had already established themselves as entertainers, they don't venture too far from their noted selves. Dino has a drawl, Sammy is sharp and physically agile, Sinatra is focused and commanding. Peter Lawford, a semi-skilled laborer from the old MGM musical ranks, spent his career being carried by better actors. *Sergeants 3* is no exception. He is given the least to do among the leads.

Sergeants 3 (1962)

The real problem is that *Sergeants 3* is structurally uneven. The romance, comedy, action and narrative don't flow as seamlessly as they should. But at the same time, the performances are appealing, the narrative is simple and easy to follow, and the action sequences offer genuine excitement.

Because he was the producer as well as the star, Sinatra contributed to the marketing of *Sergeants 3*. He even hosted a special screening for underprivileged children at a New York theater:

> Frank Sinatra will personally serve as host to some 2500 orphans and handicapped children at 10:00 a.m. premiere performance of *Sergeants 3* at the Capitol Theatre Saturday, February 10. On that morning, come rain, snow or sleet, Frank will be in the theatre lobby to greet the hordes of happy, shouting children as they arrive from all parts of the city in a fleet of 60 deluxe buses. The Capitol Theatre has set aside seats for 2500 young guests from children's homes, settlement houses, welfare agencies and hospitals. For many, this will be the first time they have ever attended a Broadway motion picture theater, and for nearly all, meeting a big name star of the entertainment world such as Sinatra will be nothing less thrilling than the experience of a lifetime.[169]

Next-day reports in the press indicated that the children were so boisterously appreciative of the movie's action scenes, their cheers and laughter could be heard by passersby outside the theater.

Critics were not impressed with *Sergeants 3*. According to *Variety*,

> *Sergeants 3* is warmed-over *Gunga Din* in a westernized version of that epic, with American-style Indians and Vegas-style soldiers of fortune. The essential differences between the two pictures, other than the obvious one of setting, is that the emphasis in *Gunga* was serious with a tongue-in-cheek overtone, whereas the emphasis in *Sergeants* is tongue-in-cheek with serious overtones.[170]

Exhibitors writing to the trade papers stated that the film went over well with their audiences. One stated: "A wonderful comedy—nice color, scenery and buffoonery." Another chimed in with "Here is the kind of picture that we need more of. Lots of action, comedy, and everything that young people like."

Sergeants 3 made a commendable $4.3 million, so Frank considered it a success. Personal life events made this a bit of a milestone in that it is the last film with all five members of the Rat Pack. Peter Lawford was married to President John F. Kennedy's sister, and it was planned that when the president visited the West Coast, he would stay with Sinatra. Frank even built an addition onto his house for security purposes, including a place for the Secret Service to stay. But JFK's brother, Attorney General Robert Kennedy, nixed the idea due to Sinatra's alleged ties to underworld figures.

JFK ended up staying with Bing Crosby. Sinatra cut ties completely with Lawford. Years later, Jerry Lewis seemed to think this was of little consequence, stating, "[Lawford] would have been a *Star Search* loser." Because of the success of *Sergeants 3*, Sinatra planned future Rat Pack ensemble films, including *Robin and the 7 Hoods*. Lawford, originally set to be in that movie, was replaced—with Bing Crosby.

Sinatra next took on a serious role that tapped into his talents as an actor. And almost half of the $2.2 million budget for *The Manchurian Candidate* went to pay his salary.

The Manchurian Candidate

Directed by John Frankenheimer
Screenplay: George Axelrod, from the novel by Richard Condon
Producers: George Axelrod, John Frankenheimer
Cinematography: Lionel Lindon (Black and White)
Editor: Ferris Webster
Cast: Frank Sinatra, Laurence Harvey, Janet Leigh, Angela Lansbury, Henry Silva, James Gregory, Leslie Parrish, John McGiver, Khigh Dhiegh, James Edwards, Douglas Henderson, Albert Paulsen, Barry Kelley, Lloyd Corrigan, Madame Spivy, Irving Steinberg, Reggie Nalder, Helen Kleeb, Robert Riordan, Miyoshi Jingu, John Francis, Paul Frees, Mimi Dillard, Merrit Bohn, Nicky Blair, James Casino, Robert Burton, Joe Adams, Harry Carter, Ray Nailey, George DeNormand, Nick Bolin, Albert Cavens, Minta Durfee, Estelle Etterre, Tom Harris, Bess Flowers, Lee Tung Foo, James Gonzales, Stuart Hall, Wesley Gale, Wilbur Mack, Julie Payne, Charles Perry, Marquita Moll, Tom Lowell, Karen Norris, Jean Vaughn, Bert Stevens, Raynum K. Tsukamoto, James Yagi, Anton von Stralen, Alyce Allen, Evelyn Birdy, Lana Crawford, Mickey Finn, Benjie Bancroft
Released October 24, 1962
United Artists
126 minutes

While there were some instances around this time of Sinatra taking a less serious approach to movies, this is belied by his performance in *The Manchurian Candidate*, another top title in his screen career. A psychological drama that takes chances and challenges its audience, it was based on Richard Condon's novel and directed with style and flair by John Frankenheimer. Screenwriter George Axelrod had been known for lighter fare, including the scripts for *The Seven Year Itch* and *Breakfast at Tiffany's*. He rises to the occasion with this tense drama. And Sinatra, once again involved with producing the film, should be commended for taking on such an offbeat production.

Hedda Hopper's column was already talking about the project just after the new year in 1962:

> Starring will be Sinatra, Laurence Harvey, Janet Leigh and a new girl, Claire Griswold. This is Claire's first film, and she signed a five-picture deal with Frankie and Frankenheimer. She's a New York model who has done TV....[171]

Actually, TV actress Griswold debuted in Blake Edwards' *Experiment in Terror* a few months before *The Manchurian Candidate* was released. It was to be her only feature film, as she was replaced in *Manchurian* by Leslie Parrish before filming commenced. Griswold was married to director Sydney Pollack for 50 years until his death in 2008.

Other articles from the same time focussed more on Sinatra's personal life. Juliet Prowse was prepared to fly home to South Africa to plan their wedding while Frank was busy working on *The Manchurian Candidate*. But the wedding had been called off by March 1962, as Juliet was not in agreement with Frank's expectation that she would end her career once they were married.

The Manchurian Candidate went before the cameras in February 1962. It stars Sinatra as Captain Bennett Marco, who, with Staff Sergeant Raymond Shaw (Laurence Harvey), are part of a platoon captured by the Soviets during the Korean Conflict. Upon returning to United Nations command, Marco recommends Shaw for the Medal of Honor, which he receives. Shaw returns to the States and is used by his manipulative mother (Angela Lansbury) and stepfather, a Senator (James Gregory), to advance the latter's career. Shaw was

Sinatra turned in another fine performance in *The Manchurian Candidate*, one of his best films.

brainwashed while a captive and has become an assassin being used by the Communists, his brainwashing having programmed him to act unwittingly. Both the Chinese and the Soviet Union employ him in their attempts to take over the U.S. government. When asked about Shaw, the others in the platoon, including Marco, also brainwashed, coldly recite, "Raymond Shaw is the kindest, bravest, warmest, most wonderful human being I've ever known in my life."

Marco, now a major working with Army intelligence, has a recurring dream where Shaw murders two missing members of their platoon during their captivity and brainwashing. Another soldier (James Edwards) has the same dream. An investigation is launched. Shaw becomes involved with the beautiful daughter (Parrish) of his conservative stepfather's liberal rival (John McGiver). It is discovered that Shaw's mother is involved in his programming and programs him to kill the rival Senator. The daughter is also liquidated. The mother then directs Raymond to attempt an assassination of the presidential candidate. He appears to be just about to do so, but then instead kills his mother and stepfather. When Marco bursts in on him, he turns the gun on himself.

The Manchurian Candidate was released during the Cuban Missile Crisis so despite its challenging the narrative's linear structure, it was found to be compelling and absorbing by audiences. It more than tripled is production costs at the box office, while Angela Lansbury was nominated for a Best Supporting Actress Oscar.

There were some interesting casting choices that Sinatra suggested during pre-production. One was Jackie Gleason for the role of the Senator (ultimately played by James Gregory). Gleason had shot two features for 1962 release, both coming out in the fall of that year around the same time as *The Manchurian Candidate*. He starred in *Gigot*, based on his own story, and followed up with a large role in *Requiem for a Heavyweight*. Since both of these films came out within a month of each other, at the same time as *Manchurian*, it is likely that he simply wasn't available to take the Senator role.

Sinatra also suggested Lucille Ball to play Shaw's mother. Lucy had not had many opportunities to explore her ability to play drama. Since 1951 she had been concentrating on TV comedy, including the iconic *I Love Lucy* series, and she was currently the star of *The Lucy Show*. However, in between those projects, she took on a seriocomic co-starring role with Bob Hope in *The Facts of Life* (1960); based on that, Sinatra thought she'd be good for the role of Shaw's mother. John Frankenheimer wanted Lansbury, but Sinatra countered that she was too young (only three years older than Laurence Harvey playing her son). Frankenheimer arranged a screening of his film *All Fall Down* which featured Lansbury, and that convinced Frank she would be right for the part. And it is really no exaggeration to

The Manchurian Candidate (1962) 171

claim that her performance in this film makes her character one of the most chilling villains in screen history. On a side note, Janet Leigh was served with divorce papers from her actor-husband Tony Curtis the morning before she reported to the set to film her first scene.

The editing in this film is well done and contributes much to the telling of the story, particularly in the opening reel's brainwashing sequence: It presents the viewer with so many different perspectives of the situation. The stark black-and-white cinematography is stunning, and Frankenheimer sets up shots for maximum effectiveness. (The scene where Shaw kills the Senator and his daughter, the body of the Senator in the foreground, the daughter in the background, and Shaw standing between them, is especially effective.) This film remains very haunting and holds up exceptionally well.

Just as with the 1954 film *Suddenly*, about a presidential assassination, there have been rumors about *The Manchurian Candidate* being pulled from distribution after the November 1963 assassination of John F. Kennedy. According to Michael Schlesinger, who worked at MGM/UA when the movie was released on video:

> By late 1963, the film had simply played out. The original deal was for ten years, and it was, to put it charitably, not a very good one. When the time came to renew in 1972, Sinatra's attorneys opted to take the movie back and bury their "mistake" [of having accepted the original deal]. Frank's attorney thought it was such a bad idea that he literally crafted a *Producers*-type deal. It was so bad, in fact, that every time the picture played, Sinatra really did lose money. So you can see why he was so anxious to bury his mistake. (Frank, who never looked backward, didn't know or care.) And so it remained "lost" until 1987, when the New York Film Festival requested it for its 25th anniversary. By then, Sinatra had new attorneys with no ax to grind and they consented to release the film. The reaction was so overwhelming that MGM/UA immediately struck a new—and much fairer—deal to reacquire the rights. We opened the film in February 1988 to fabulous reviews and tremendous business, and it has stayed available for theaters, TV and home entertainment ever since. But it was never "withdrawn" prior to 1972.[172]

Sinatra does a great job conveying both subtle paranoia and abject terror. The closeup of his face at the start of the film, when he lunges out of bed screaming after a nightmare, is terrifying. His scenes with Janet Leigh are highlights, and he effectively conveys both desperation and determination in the scene toward the end when he tries to de-program Shaw. Also notice the look of shock and terror on his face when Shaw turns the gun on himself at the end. Sinatra's performance is proof that when he commits to heavy material like this (as opposed to the breezy Rat Pack comedies he'd recently done), he is willing and able to also commit to delivering a fantastic, emotional performance.

Janet Leigh was served with divorce papers from Tony Curtis the first day of filming *The Manchurian Candidate*. Pictured: Sinatra, Leigh.

The success of *The Manchurian Candidate* was quite welcome to Sinatra, whose album release at the time, "All Alone," turned out to be his first since 1950 to fail to make the Top 20. Among its tracks was the Turk-Hadman 1926 waltz "Are You Lonesome Tonight?" which had been a hit as a ballad for Elvis Presley in 1960. In 1962, none of Frank's singles cracked Top 40, not even a duet with Sammy Davis, Jr., "Me and My Shadow," which tanked at #64. Frank did, however, have some fun this year doing a cameo in *The Road to Hong Kong*, the last movie to feature Bing Crosby and Bob Hope as co-stars.

After completing *The Manchurian Candidate*, Sinatra did a heavily made-up cameo in John Huston's *The List of Adrian Messenger* before venturing onto his next project. Wanting to do lighter fare after so heavy a drama as *The Manchurian Candidate*, he chose for his next movie a comedy from a play by Neil Simon.

Come Blow Your Horn

Directed by Bud Yorkin
Screenplay: Norman Lear, from the play by Neil Simon

Producers: Bud Yorkin, Norman Lear and Howard W. Koch
Cinematography: William H. Daniels (Technicolor)
Editor: Frank Keller
Song:
"Come Blow Your Horn"; Music: Jimmy Van Heusen; Lyrics: Sammy Cahn
Cast: Frank Sinatra, Lee J. Cobb, Molly Picon, Barbara Rush, Jill St. John, Dan Blocker, Phyllis McGuire, Tony Bill, Carole Wells, Barbara Maggio, Herbie Faye, John Indrisano, Phil Arnold, Mary Grace Canfield, Shelby Grant, June Erickson, Charles Maier, R.G. Brown, Carole Evern, Frank Gardner, Warren Cathcart, Charlotte Fletcher, James Cavanaugh, Frank Hagney, Grady Sutton, Eddie Quillan, Norman Lear, Harvey Johnson, Hollis Morrison, Al Silvani, Jack Nestle, Greta Randall, Lisa Seagram, Fred Zendar, Romo Vincent, Elizabeth Thompson, George Sawaya, Dean Martin (cameo)
Released June 5, 1963
Essex Productions for Paramount
112 minutes

One would safely assume that a screenplay by Norman Lear based on a hit Broadway play by Neil Simon would be a lot of laughs. *Come Blow Your Horn* was Simon's first play. He had been writing for television, most notably Sid Caesar's *Your Show of Shows* along with such luminaries as Woody Allen and Mel Brooks. Lear—later responsible for such groundbreaking TV series as *All in the Family* and *Maude*—had already written, with Ed Simmons, some of Dean Martin and Jerry Lewis' best material, working closely with the comedians themselves. But despite this level of talent, *Come Blow Your Horn* is little more than a pleasant trifle.

Paramount offered Simon the job of adapting his play, but he turned it down—and "[t]here went $75,000," he later recalled. He continued:

> But I had about two inches of my foot in the door of the theater and was not about to give up my toehold to the beckoning finger of Hollywood. They went on without me to make the film of *Come Blow Your Horn* starring Frank Sinatra and I was anything but pleased with the results. Whatever charm the play might have had was lost in a ring-a-ding-ding pseudo-hip Hollywood comedy that had more glitz than wit. it was a profitable picture for Paramount, opening at Radio City Music Hall, and although I walked by it 20 times to see a title of mine on the marquee, I was up to more important things.[173]

The play *Come Blow Your Horn* had opened on Broadway in 1961 at the Brooks Atkinson Theatre and ran for 677 performances. Simon had moved on from television and was going full force as a playwright, but the experience of *Come Blow Your Horn* the movie stayed with him. Many of his plays were made into movies, and he would hereafter have some control over the screenplays.

The story deals with young, ambitious Buddy Baker (Tony Bill), who resides with his parents but seeks a greater, more exciting life. His swinging older brother Alan (Sinatra) works for their father's company—dealing in artificial fruit—but still manages to get out and enjoy life. Alan finds Buddy's interest endearing and ego-inflating, so he takes Alan under his wing. He picks out his wardrobe, introduces him to upstairs neighbor Peggy (Jill St John) and gives him some romantic tips. Alan's girl Connie (Barbara Rush) is becoming impatient with Alan's carefree lifestyle and wants him to settle down. Alan is beaten up by a man who thinks Alan has been seeing his wife; that, and the possibility of his own parents getting a divorce, prompts Alan to settle down. He lets Buddy have his bachelor pad.

It is interesting how this film presents the two brothers. Alan doesn't see anything bad about his carefree lifestyle or feel the effects of it until he starts to see the same traits mirrored in Buddy, and realizes that he doesn't like what he sees.

Neil Simon's writing was heavily watered down in *Come Blow Your Horn* with Sinatra (left) and Tony Bill.

In the trajectory of Sinatra's filmography, *Come Blow Your Horn* has at least some significance for presenting the actor's screen persona as one who understands the aging process. While Neil Simon responded negatively to what he called the "ring-a-ding-ding" presentation, the film does feature Sinatra as a singer who gets slapped with a dose of reality and the realization that he has become a bit too old for this sort of lifestyle. Sinatra was a middle-ager by this time, and his introspection would soon extend to his music with his quintessential 1965 album "September of My Years."

Despite this significance to Sinatra, *Come Blow Your Horn* is pretty accurately described by Simon's dismissive account. It seems that Sinatra's detached indifference to his screen work would pop up randomly, while in other projects, like *The Manchurian Candidate*, his real talent as an actor would be displayed.

Neil Simon's misgivings and a bad *New York Times* review notwithstanding, *Come Blow Your Horn* was a success—the 15th highest grossing film of 1963. Moviegoers wanted simple, relaxing fare as much as they wanted the heavy, complicated dramatic narrative offered by a film like *The Manchurian Candidate*. And they got it with this comedy.

About a month before the release of *Come Blow Your Horn*, Sinatra released the album "The Concert Sinatra" in which he sang show tunes while backed by Nelson Riddle's 76-piece orchestra. It reached #6 on the charts. But the title song from *Come Blow Your Horn* stiffed as a single, not even reaching the Top 100.

The success of *Come Blow Your Horn* told Sinatra that he could relax and have fun making a lightweight picture and still achieve some measure of success. So he took on a property that combined two of his favorite genres—Westerns and comedies—and teamed up with Rat Pack pal Dean Martin. But *4 for Texas* turned out to be a troubled production.

4 for Texas

Produced and Directed by Robert Aldrich
Screenplay: Robert Aldrich and Teddi Sherman
Cinematography: William H. Daniels (Technicolor)
Editor: Frank Keller
Cast: Frank Sinatra, Dean Martin, Anita Ekberg, Ursula Andress, Charles Bronson, Victor Buono, Edric Connor, Nick Dennis, Richard Jaeckel, Mike Mazurki, Wesley Addy, Marjorie Bennett, Virginia Christine, Ellen Corby, Jesslyn Fax, Jack Elam, Fritz Feld, Percy Helton, Jonathan Hole, Jack Lambert, Paul Langton,

Keith McConnell, Michele Montau, Maidie Norman, Bob Steele, Mario Siletti, Eva Six, Abraham Sofaer, Michael St. Angel, Grady Sutton, Ralph Volkie, Max Wagner, William Washington, Dave Willock, Caryl Lee Hill, Allyson Ames, Arthur Godfrey, Al Bain, Alex Ball, Al Beaudine, Nick Borgani, Joe Brooks, Alphonso DuBois, Eileen O'Neill, Bill Dyer, Fred Fisher, Charles Fogel, George Ford, Joe Garcio, Joseph Glick, Jack Gordon, Sam Harris, John Hudkins, Eugene Jackson, Mike Lally, Robert Locke Lorraine, John Marlin, William H. O'Brien, Monty O'Grady, John Pedrini, Charles Picerni, Fred Rapport, Norman Stevens, Hal Taggart, Harry Wilson, Herbert Winters, Danny Borzage, George Boyce, Dick Cherney, Kid Chissell, Michael Cirillo, Bud Cokes, Alphonso Dubois, Bill Dyer, Gene LeBell, Hal Needham, Robert Robinson, Sammy Shack, Ray Spiker, Paul Stader, Charles Sullivan, Carol Anderson, Gayle Baker, Brandon Beach, Byron Berry, Myron Berry, Calvin Brown, Mushy Callahan, Lesley-Marie Colburn, Steve Condit, Marcel De la Brosse, George DeNormand, Sandy Edmundson, Daniel Elam, Wesley Gale, Ralph Gambina, Bobby Gilbert, George Golden, Sol Gorss, Joe Gray, Duke Green, Chuck Hicks, George Holmes, Charles Horvath, Clyde Howdy, Idell James, Michael Jeffers, Chester Jones, Matty Jordan, Johnny Kern, Jim Michael, Gigi Michel, Mike Miranda, Hans Moebus, Enesto Molinari, Charles Morton, Manuel Padilla, Harvey Parry, Gil Perkins, Joe Ploski, Ray Purchot, Teddy Quinn, Mike Ragan, Harry Raven, Rodd Redwing, Greg Rhinelander, Jeffrey Sayre, Sandy Steffans, Bill Walker, Joe Yrigoyen, Teddy Buckner and His All Stars, The Three Stooges (Moe Howard, Larry Fine, Joe DeRita)
Released December 25, 1963
Warner Brothers
124 minutes

As early as November 1960, producer-director Robert Aldrich announced a Western comedy project entitled *Two for Texas* from a script by Teddi Sherman. This project was shelved, but resurrected for Dean Martin, who signed on in January 1963. By then, Aldrich had a major hit with *What Ever Happened to Baby Jane?* so Warner Brothers agreed to help finance the project along with Aldrich's company and Martin's company. When Sinatra signed on to co-star in March 1963, his Essex Productions became involved.

The female co-stars were going to be Anita Ekberg and Gina Lollobrigida. Ekberg signed on, Lollobrigida did not. That part was then offered to Sophia Loren but, despite being offered a million dollars for four weeks work, she also turned it down. Ursula Andress was hired shortly before shooting began in May 1963, and the title was changed to *4 for Texas*.

The cast was rounded out with top Western movie actors including Charles Bronson, Richard Jaeckel, Mike Mazurki, Jack Elam and Bob Steele. Aldrich added Victor Buono to the cast, having worked well with him in *Baby Jane*.

Aldrich was not satisfied with the script, nor with his own rewrites. Furthermore, Sinatra was becoming more and more lackadaisical, even in a case where he had his own money in the project. Aldrich later claimed that in the 37-day shooting schedule, Sinatra worked no more than 80 hours, despite being top-billed.[174]

4 for Texas opens with a stagecoach transporting $100,000 and pursued by both Zack Thomas (Sinatra) and Joe Jarrett (Martin) as well as an outlaw gang headed by a villain named Matson (Bronson). There is a standoff between Zack and Joe even though each man has for respect the other. Despite another conflict over a waterfront casino, Zack and Joe decide to join forces against Matson and his gang, who are involved with a corrupt banker (Victor Buono). Zack finds romance with Elya (Ekberg), Joe with Maxine (Andress).

Aldrich had some sound misgivings about the script. *4 for Texas* is something of a loosely episodic mess. What holds it together are the star performances. Even though he was becoming more casual and disinterested in his movie projects, Sinatra still comes off as interesting and amusing on screen. Martin's charisma exudes with little effort, and their camaraderie sustains the weak spots in the script. Martin being the calming influence on Sinatra extended to their real-life endeavors, including their popular Rat Pack performances in Las Vegas.

Bronson smartly plays it very straight as the chief villain, which offsets Buono's more bombastic portrayal. Bronson had already done *The Magnificent Seven* (1960) and that prepared him well. He went right into the western *Guns of Diablo* after this project.

Sinatra made several demands that producer-director Aldrich balked at, including ideas about what he would wear, that he would be given shaves and massages in most of his scenes, his wanting close-ups of his face looking toward the camera to show off his blue eyes, and other such things. Aldrich would stand up to him, but eventually would give in simply to keep the peace.

Sinatra also asked that Aldrich find room for the Three Stooges in the movie. This was at a time when the Stooges were enjoying a sudden resurgence in popularity. As discussed in the *Pal Joey* chapter, Sinatra, a longtime fan of the slapstick trio, had asked them to appear on his TV show

(Left to right): Anita Ekberg, Sinatra, Dean Martin and Ursula Andress in the lightweight Western comedy *4 for Texas*.

when Shemp Howard was a part of the act, and the comedians returned the favor by promoting *Pal Joey* in one of their short comedies featuring Joe Besser who took the late Shemp Howard's place and finished out the Stooges' contractual short comedies with Columbia. Once the contract was fulfilled, the Stooges all figured their time in show business had completed. Besser went on to other projects, Moe Howard had invested wisely and was a wealthy man, and Larry was planning to manage apartments.

4 for Texas (1963)

In 1958, Columbia released the older Stooges comedies, featuring Moe and Larry with Curly Howard, to TV and they became an overnight sensation with the kiddie market. The Stooges were contacted by Columbia and asked to re-form to make some feature-length movies for kiddie matinees. But Besser was contracted to other projects and couldn't return to the act. Moe and Larry hired burlesque comic Joe DeRita, who agreed to shave his head and be called Curly-Joe, capitalizing on the TV fame of Curly Howard, who had left the act in 1946 after suffering a stroke, and died in 1952.

Aldrich had no idea how to add the Stooges, but decided that a scene where a nude painting of Maxine is delivered could be expanded to have the Stooges make the delivery and perform one of their routines. When the Stooges arrived on the set, the resourceful Moe explained two of the act's longtime comedy bits that would work in the context of the scene. Their "point to the right" routine and "you just hit a man from Texas" fit perfectly in the proceedings. Oddly, it is not Sinatra but Dean Martin who gets involved in the trio's antics. Dino even gets to administer a triple face slap.

Sinatra was right about adding the comedians to the movie. When *4 For Texas* was released, the Stooges were still popular on TV with their old shorts, and they had starred in equally popular new feature films *The Three Stooges Meet Hercules* (1961) and *The Three Stooges in Orbit* (1962). Their presence in *4 for Texas*, a mere cameo, was not only promoted in the posters and newspaper ads, a snippet appeared in the movie's trailer. There were even newspaper reports when they were added to the *4 for Texas* cast:

> The Three Stooges Larry Fine, Moe Howard and Curly-Joe DeRita have been set for roles in *4 For Texas*.... The comedy team recently completed *The Three Stooges Go Around the World in a Daze* at Columbia and have just returned from a personal appearance at the Calgary Stampede in Calgary, Alberta, Canada.[175]

Advertising that the Three Stooges were in *4 for Texas* added to its success.

And *4 for Texas* really needed everything possible to ensure its box office. Its production budget ballooned to more than $4 million. Fortunately, the movie was popular enough to turn a small profit. Beautiful establishing shots are filled with striking Mojave scenery.

There are some who consider *4 for Texas* a Rat Pack movie. It really isn't. Sinatra and Martin are its only Rat Packers. Thus, it is no more a Rat Pack movie than *Some Came Running* had been. However, Sinatra's next movie project featured Martin and Sammy Davis, Jr., of the Rat Pack. *Robin and the 7 Hoods* turned out to be the quintessential Rat Pack movie.

Robin and the 7 Hoods

Directed by Gordon Douglas
Screenplay: David Schwartz
Producer: Frank Sinatra
Cinematography: William H. Daniels (Technicolor)
Editor: Sam O'Steen
Songs:
"My Kind of Town," "Mr. Booze," "All for One and One for All," "Don't Be a Do-Badder," "Any Man Who Loves His Mother," "Style," "Bang! Bang!"; Music: Jimmy Van Heusen; Lyrics: Sammy Cahn
Cast: Frank Sinatra, Dean Martin, Sammy Davis, Jr., Bing Crosby, Peter Falk, Barbara Rush, Victor Buono, Hank Henry, Robert Foulk, Allen Jenkins, Jack LaRue, Roger Carricart, Joseph Ruskin, Phil Arnold, Harry Swoger, Bernard Fein, Richard Bakalyan, Sonny King, Phillip Crosby, Al Silvani, Harry Wilson, Caryl Lee Hill, Mickey Finn, Richard Simmons, Hans Conried, Tony Randall, Edward G. Robinson, Manuel Padilla, Jr., Sig Ruman, Thom Conroy, Eugene Jackson, Barry Kelley, Chris Hughes, Al Bain, Chet Allen, James Casino, Jimmy Dime, Joseph Glick, John Delgado, Joe Gray, Jim Michael, John Pedrini, Al Wyatt, Walter Bacon, Toni Basil, Oscar Blank, George Boyce, Benjie Bancroft, Linda Brent, Michael Cirillo, Even Bernhardt, Robert Buckinham, Robert Cole, Roger Creed, Billy Curtis, Jerry Davis, Ann D'Aubray, Sayre Dearing, Joe Evans, Rudy Germane, George Golden, Jack Gordon, Herschel Graham, Buck Harrington, Ed Haskett, Chester Hayes, Lars Hensen, Chuck Hicks, Red Morgan, Francis McDonald, Milton Rudin, Myrna Ross, Carolyn Morin, Eddie Ness, Bill Zuckert, Mark Sherwood, Larri Thomas, Marc Winters, Charles Sherlock, Richard Sinatra, Bernard Sell, John Pedrini, Carolyn Morin, Clark Ross, Ray Pourchot
Released June 24, 1964
Warner Brothers
123 minutes

The last note Frank Sinatra ever sang in a movie was at the conclusion of *Robin and the 7 Hoods*. The man who rocketed to fame as the Voice, whose talent as an interpreter of song got him his close-up before he was ready for it, made his last musical in far different fashion than he made his first: on his terms. He not only starred and produced, he shared the screen and off-camera laughs with his closest show biz pals (Dean Martin and Sammy Davis, Jr.) and the fellow crooner he admired and whose accomplishments at the mike and on the mark rivaled his own (Bing Crosby). It all adds up to the best of the trilogy of Rat Pack films, a middle-aged swan song to the ring-a-ding-ding lifestyle the movies celebrated for as long as they could stave off the '60s counterculture.

The roster of Rats is trimmed of Peter Lawford and Joey Bishop this go-round—the former the result of the lingering and never-resolved feud over where President Kennedy slept on his visit to Palm Springs two years earlier, the latter for reasons never explained. Bishop was announced in a brief August 1963 press item as joining the cast,[176] but didn't wind up in the film, and no subsequent news item reported or even speculated why. Perhaps more curiously, Lawford—certainly no singer—was eyed before the JFK kerfuffle for the role that ended up going to Crosby.

But it was Sinatra's original co-producer who gobbled up the most headlines in the run-up to the filming of *Robin and the 7 Hoods*. Gene Kelly, the dancer-singer turned director-auteur who shared the screen three times with Sinatra as the latter served his big-screen apprenticeship in the 1940s, was announced as the film's producer in the summer of 1963. Sinatra tapped his old buddy with an eye on making it a four-film partnership, mindful that Kelly's phone wasn't ringing in the mid–60s the way it had the prior couple of decades. The announcement set industry tongues wagging, predicting tensions between the old friends because of Sinatra's loose work habits. Kelly was nonchalant. "I told Frank I don't care if he only works an hour a day. It's his money. And a guy has the right to do what he wants with his own money."[177]

Three months later, it was announced that Kelly had quit the film, citing the old Hollywood dodge of "artistic differences."[178] Sinatra biographer James Kaplan relayed the rest of the story: "'I wasn't making any decisions,' Kelly said later. 'I was taking orders.

Robin and the 7 Hoods is arguably the best of the Rat Pack films, given that it's a musical featuring accomplished musical stars.

Quietly, I like the boys, but friendship isn't always everything in this business."[179] (Bob Hope may have begged to differ, tossing off this gem at the end of an AP feature exploring Kelly's likely challenges at the helm of the film: "How about Sinatra giving Crosby a job," Ol' Ski Nose said of Ol' Blue Eyes casting Der Bingle. "That's like Joseph P. Kennedy asking J. Paul Getty to cut the grass."[180])

Sinatra's "I'm in charge here" style may have been more than an accomplished talent like Kelly cared to confront, but it served the film, its players and its audience well. He nabbed Gordon Douglas, who directed him in 1955's *Young at Heart,* to helm the movie. Douglas was a Sinatra favorite, directing him in three successive films in 1967 and '68 that required a similar sort of atmospheric action as *Robin and the 7 Hoods.* (Douglas is also the answer to a fun Hollywood trivia question: Who's the only man to direct films starring Sinatra and Elvis Presley—1962's feature *Follow That Dream?*) Sinatra's shrewdest production choice, though, was enlisting Sammy Cahn and Jimmy Van Heusen to craft the score. They delivered several catchy, entertaining songs that drove the narrative well— and one certifiable classic, Sinatra's "My Kind of Town (Chicago Is)." The musical moments make the film legitimate movie entertainment—nothing to stack alongside Sinatra's best work but still a fully formed film that aims at a loftier goal than just offering another glimpse into the private shenanigans of its stars.

Sinatra, to no one's surprise, assumes the Robin Hood role and imbues it with the laid-back, above-it-all charm that by now had become his signature embodiment of a film role, regardless of genre. His Robin is a suave mid-level hood, a loyal lieutenant to the gang's leader, Big Jim (Sinatra's beloved Edward G. Robinson, in a pleasant if limited cameo). Martin, as Little John, is once again Sinatra's second-in-command, while Davis slips comfortably into his familiar role as the unquestioning sidekick, in this case patterned and named after Will Scarlett.

When Big Jim is murdered by the ambitious Guy Gisbourne (a scene-stealing Peter Falk), Robin and his gang look to bring Gisbourne down. Much of the lampooning of the legend of Sherwood Forest that follows is clever: The Gisbourne character, instead of raising taxes on the poor, strong-arms a 50 percent cut of his fellow racketeers' spoils. The love-at-first-sight that blooms between Robin and Maid Marian is depicted here in prototypical Rat Pack fashion: When "Robbo" first sees Marian (Barbara Rush as Big Jim's more-than-meets-the-eye daughter), he leers to a henchman, "I think she's a good-lookin' dame." Proving that serviceable screenwriter David Schwartz gets the source material and what he's asked to do with it, the central conceit of Robin Hood robbing from the rich to give to the poor is presented as a PR stunt to make Robbo a hero and

(Left to right): Sinatra, Sammy Davis, Jr., and Dean Martin were the only Rat Packers in *Robin and the 7 Hoods* because of their song and dance skills.

therefore harder for Gisbourne to rub out. The richest moment, though, is the famous first meeting between Robbo and Little John. It's not played here as a battle of strength, but rather a battle of billiards skill and wit. Little John doesn't just run the table; Martin out-cools Sinatra while doing it.

These moments are fun trifles, but the real entertainment in *Robin and the 7 Hoods* is the musical elements. Here again, as producer, Sinatra shows savvy—and generosity. He gives the best production number to the most multitalented member of his cast. Davis' "Bang! Bang!" (as Will shoots up Gisbourne's casino) is a showstopper, allowing him to display his vocal chops, tap-dancing prowess, some nifty handgun tricks and his well-known gift for mimicry.

Crosby is the chief beneficiary of his producer's creative largesse. He is charming in "Don't Be a Do-Badder," a clever tune about the virtues of behaving oneself, which Crosby sings to a group of cute orphans benefitting from Robbo's philanthropy. He steals the show as the preacher in the "Mr. Booze" production number, an elaborate ruse in which Robbo's illegal casino is transformed through architectural wizardry into a mission–soup kitchen. Watching the widely known imbibers Crosby, Sinatra, Martin and Davis testifying to the evils of alcohol is good toe-tapping fun.

Sinatra's shining moment comes during "My Kind of Town," which Robbo sings to a crowd of supporters after he is exonerated from a set-up masterminded by the soon-to-be-gotten-rid-of Gisbourne. It's the star's only solo (though he shot a version of "I Like to Lead When I Dance" that got cut from the picture but turns up on the soundtrack album). It is a vintage Sinatra performance: His vocals are crisp and his phrasing immaculate, and he makes fine use of the crooner mannerisms that served him so well in the bobbysoxer years. For bonus points, he does it all in a suit and hat the same shade of green as the artificial turf of a miniature golf course. The song earned Cahn and Van Heusen an Oscar nomination (*Mary Poppins*' "Chim Chim-Cher-ee" won) and became a Sinatra concert staple for the next 30 years.

No number captured the Rat Pack ethos, or Sinatra's delight in sharing the screen and songbook with his comrades, better than "Style." Crosby's Allen A. Dale is given the spotlight again, as the dandier Robbo and Little John sing him through the transformation of his bland wardrobe and timid demeanor. By the time the song reaches its climax, with Dale bedecked and attitude-adjusted like the "swellest of swells," Sinatra and Martin thoroughly, joyously abandon any pretense of playing good-natured gangsters and bootleggers in the Roaring Twenties. They are just Frank and Dean, 48 and 46, respectively, smiling ear to ear like schoolboys as they clown around with their friend Bing. The effect on the audience is identical.

Not everything about the making of *Robin and the 7 Hoods* was cause for celebration, though. While at a cemetery on November 22, 1963, to film the comical scene in which Big Jim is buried, a crew member spotted a gravestone for a John F. Kennedy (1802–1884). It was an occasion for jokes until news broke that afternoon that President Kennedy had been assassinated. A few weeks later, on December 8, after Sinatra had rehearsed a kidnapping scene, word came from Lake Tahoe that his son Frank Jr. had been abducted. The kidnappers demanded $240,000 ransom, which Sinatra quickly gathered. The FBI oversaw the exchange, which the kidnappers bungled. Frank Jr. was freed, the money returned and the culprits caught. The kidnapping scene was deleted from the picture.

Robin and the 7 Hoods did modest box office; its $4.2 million take was the lowest of the trilogy of Rat Pack films. Critics were generally kind. The *Oakland Tribune* called it a "jolly romp dedicated to the proposition that adolescence begins at 40."[181] The *Fort Lauderdale News* found it "a terrific musical comedy" because "the stars are not just playing themselves."[182] James Powers of *The Hollywood Reporter* agreed: "*Robin and the 7 Hoods* is better than its predecessors because there are not so many inside jokes, because there is more story and with it, new jokes, and because the stars work harder."[183]

Sinatra's steady, generous hand as producer on *Robin and the 7 Hoods* led him to assume even more creative control on his next picture. The war drama *None But the Brave* would be the first and only film directed by the man who had opportunity to learn much while performing under the guiding hands of Oscar winners Joseph Mankiewicz, Vincente Minnelli, Fred Zinnemann, Lewis Milestone and Frank Capra.

None But the Brave

Produced and Directed by Frank Sinatra
Co-producer: Kikumaru Okuda
Screenplay: John Twist and Katsuya Susaki, from a story by Kikumaru Okuda
Cinematography: Harold Lipstein (Technicolor)
Editor: Sam O'Steen
Note: The first Japanese-American co-production, produced by Kikumaru Okuda for Toho Studios and by Frank Sinatra for Warner Brothers
Cast: Frank Sinatra, Clint Walker, Tommy Sands, Brad Dexter, Tony Bill, Sammy Jackson, Richard Bakalyan, Rafer Johnson, Jimmy Griffin, Christopher Dark, Don Dorrell, Phillip Crosby, John Howard Young, Roger Ewing, Richard Sinatra, Laraine Stephens, Joe Gray, Tatsuya Mihashi, Takeshi Katô, Homare Suguro, Kenji Sahara, Masahiko Tanimura, Tôru Ibuki, Ryûchô Shumpûtei, Hisao Dazai, Susumu Kurobe, Takashi Inagaki, Kenichi Hata
Released February 24, 1965
Warner Brothers, Tokyo Eiga Co. Ltd.
106 minutes

During the year he turned 50, Sinatra was once again choosing to explore interesting and challenging roles as well as introspective music choices. He starred in three features, all of which were among his better efforts in their various genres. He started out the year by choosing to take a shot at directing a movie, something for which he had exhibited no real previous interest. While the reputation of *None But the Brave* is much lower than the movie deserves, Sinatra's only film as a director is far better than one might assume.

A tandem production between the Japanese Toho Studios and Sinatra's company, *None But the Brave* isn't a simple film. It is one of complexities in both the narrative and the characters; a fairly daunting project for a first-time director, even one who had been acting in films for nearly 25 years.

The story deals with a Japanese platoon stranded on a Pacific island when an American plane crashes. The surviving American soldiers and the Japanese engage in a series of violent clashes. The Japanese had been building a boat, and one of their battles destroys it. Realizing their situation would improve if they joined forces, there is a truce among the remaining soldiers: They reside side by side but do not cross into each other's territory. When radio contact is established with American forces, and a U.S. vessel is headed to the island, the Japanese are asked to surrender. Refusing, they ambush the American soldiers, resulting in a final battle that kills the remaining eight Japanese and reduces the 11 Americans to five.

Sinatra plays a medic whose attitude towards the idea of war is rebellious. Because Sinatra also directed, his screen time is more limited than his usual starring films. Clint Walker as a solid, brave captain is the real lead here, with Tatsuya Mihashi leading the Japanese actors. Sinatra gathered several acquaintances to round out the cast including Tony Bill from *Come Blow Your Horn* and actor friends Richard Bakalyan (whom Frank affectionately called Dickie B) and Brad Dexter, along with daughter Nancy's husband Tommy Sands. He gets great performances out of all. Sands might be a bit over the top, but that is likely how Frank wanted him to portray the overzealous character.

Sinatra's approach to the material as a director shows the same level of talent in filmmaking that he had as an actor. His cinematic vision belies his novice status as a director from his opening scenes establishing the Japanese army's status on the island. For nearly ten minutes, the film introduces the characters and their situation, Sinatra wisely having them speak Japanese rather than the

Sinatra delivered another strong performance in *None But the Brave*.

broken English found in some films of the era. Throughout the film, we see the perspective between the Japanese forces and the Americans, noting that they are essentially the same despite being on opposing sides.

Sinatra keeps the film at a good pace, with the two factions engaging in several skirmishes, until gradually making contact and declaring a truce. During this, Sinatra never allows his film to become uneven, although its narrative exposition is randomly disrupted by battle scenes. There are little nuanced measures taken by Sinatra as a filmmaker, including the way he places his characters within the frame, how he utilizes tracking shots, and the way he cuts from closeups to wider and more encompassing visuals. He is not a stylist in the manner of a John Ford or Alfred Hitchcock, but for a first-timer he exhibits a real skill that might have been honed if he continued to pursue filmmaking.

None But the Brave predates the similar films John Boorman's *Hell in the Pacific* (1968) and Clint Eastwood's *Flags of Our Fathers* and *Letters from Iwo Jima* (both 2006). Eastwood received accolades for his films, which offered both the American and Japanese perspective of war. Sinatra's movie did it first and in one movie.

Tatsuya Mihashi narrates the film, in English, as the character he plays, in the form of a letter to his wife, helping to keep the narrative in perspective. Although it is effective, it is decidedly unnecessary. And the film does come to a halt during a quiet scene when Sinatra as the medic shares a flashback story about the captain played by Walker, while Mihashi's character shares his own backstory. This scene takes away from the proceedings and disrupts the pace.

One of the film's highlights is the battle where the Japanese boat is destroyed. Both sides are shown in anguish while watching their only means of escape go up in flames. The Japanese designer of the boat charges the wreckage and is shot dead by an American soldier. Another high point is a storm sequence where Sinatra uses quick edits and an effective series of shots, responding to the special effects of wind and rain with a keen visual sense that adds dramatic impact. Finally, there is a striking scene when a merry Japanese fisherman who has been supplying food to both sides, goes into the ocean to retrieve more fish, but is attacked by a shark. Both the American and Japanese commanders fire at the shark together, but are unable to save him. It shows the opposing forces working together, offering an underlying anti-war message that would have been popular with 1965 moviegoers.

One notable and rather frightening event that occurred during filming was when, during a break, Sinatra and the wife of executive producer Howard Koch were swimming in the ocean and got caught up by the waves. Actor Brad Dexter, a big, muscular guy, ran into the rough waters, risking his own life to save the two of them. Dexter claimed that Frank never outwardly thanked him for saving his life, but from that point on, Sinatra considered him a close friend and kept him in his tight-knit inner circle for the rest of his life.

Sinatra very much wanted this movie to be a success. But it didn't

None But the Brave was the only film Sinatra directed. His skills as a first-time filmmaker were impressive.

please critics nor make back its costs. This may be why Sinatra never bothered to direct another film. This is unfortunate because *None But the Brave* holds up as a strong action drama with excellent performances and solid direction. *New York Times* reviewer Bosley Crowther called it "a fake concoction"[184] which is inaccurate and unfair. Years later, Robert Horton of Washington's *The Herald* was far more accurate when he called it "much more interesting and compelling than its reputation would suggest."[185]

Sinatra was interested in doing another military movie after reading David Westheimer's novel *Von Ryan's Express*. He wanted to buy the movie rights, but discovered they had already been purchased by 20th Century–Fox. Sinatra offered to play the lead role, and his offer was accepted.

Von Ryan's Express

Directed by Mark Robson
Screenplay: Wendell Mayes and Joseph Landon, from the novel by David Westheimer
Producers: Saul David and Mark Robson
Cinematography: William H. Daniels (Color)
Editor: Dorothy Spencer
Cast: Frank Sinatra, Trevor Howard, Raffaella Carra, Brad Dexter, Sergio Fantoni, John Leyton, Edward Mulhare, Wolfgang Preiss, James Brolin, John Van Dreelen, Adolfo Celi, Vito Scotti, Richard Bakalyan, Michael Goodliffe, Michael St. Clair, Ivan Triesault, Jacques Stany, Paul Muller, John Mitory, Gino Gottarelli, Ian Abercrombie, Christopher Riordan, Joe Gray, Arthur Brauss, Peter Hellman, Domenick Delgarde, Benito Prezia, Buzz Henry, Barry Ford, Bob Rosen, Horst Ebersberg, Walter Linden, Eric Micklewood, Al Wyatt, James Sikking, Ron Veto, Michael Romanoff, Al Silvani, Brad Stevens, Lee Stanley
Released June 23, 1965
P-R Productions for 20th Century–Fox
117 minutes

Frank Sinatra's last war picture is filled with echoes of his first. It's based on a popular novel—in this instance one by former POW David Westheimer. Its action revolves around a cadre of characters trying to survive one of World War II's bookends—in this instance its chaotic final days. Sinatra again plays a character not universally beloved by those whose side of the conflict he shares. But *Von Ryan's Express* also spotlights the seismic shifts in Sinatra's screen persona and Hollywood clout since his Oscar-winning turn in *From Here to Eternity* 12 years earlier. His Col. Joseph Ryan is the calm and collected, somewhat reluctant leader of the men who earns their respect, while his Pvt. Angelo Maggio was the impulsive, quick-tempered mascot who desperately wanted to win their respect. Perhaps what the films share most vividly, though, are performances designed to prove a point: Maggio was the first role that allowed The Voice to demonstrate his acting prowess was Oscar-worthy. Ryan is the late-career role that allowed The Chairman to demonstrate that prowess still existed in greater measure than most of his '60s output demanded of him.

Sinatra wasn't so much enthused by the project as mindful it could resurrect his slumping box office status while offering a big payday. 20th Century–Fox chief Darryl F. Zanuck dangled gross-profit participation, an almost unheard-of deal. That financial generosity to hook Sinatra reveals how desperate Zanuck was to score a blockbuster for the studio after the critical and box office disaster that was *Cleopatra*. Putting a budget Band-Aid on the Elizabeth Taylor-Richard Burton historical drama, the cost of which ballooned to $44 million by its 1963 release against Fox's profit cut of just more than $40 million, was the reason Zanuck returned to the studio after a few years as an independent producer.

Zanuck saw *Von Ryan's Express* as an ideal vehicle to tap into the moviegoing public's affinity for the boy's-adventure take on the war popular at the time in the films *The Longest Day* (1962) and *The Great Escape* (1963). Its producer Saul David waxed excited when asked about the moneymaking potential of war-themed movies, particularly among the younger crowd increasingly filling cinemas. "Today's teenagers are fascinated by World War II and eagerly see any war movie," he said. "Even the girls love war. To the teenager, Hitler

Sinatra gives one of his last truly great performances in *Von Ryan's Express*.

is rapidly emerging as a sort of romantic arch-fiend, a modern-day Genghis Khan."[186]

Sinatra's Col. Ryan is an American pilot whose plane was shot down outside an Italian P.O.W. camp in 1943. The Nazis have seized Italy in what Ryan intuits from his battle briefings will be the last days of the war; his first impulse is to "knuckle under" since the Allies are no more than a couple of weeks away from ending the conflict. But that thought doesn't sit well with most of the 600-plus prisoners, British captives who have been behind wire for more than two years. Their senior officer, Major Eric Fincham (Trevor Howard), is so obsessed with escape, even with liberation in sight, that he is withholding malaria drugs needed by the prisoners. He's saving them to be used if and when one of his escape attempts succeeds.

Ryan's desire to stay out of the camp's affairs is undone by his station: As a colonel, he outranks Fincham and becomes camp C.O. Ryan orders Fincham to distribute the medicine to ill prisoners, then infuriates the Brit by revealing details of an escape plan to the camp's buffoonish commandant in exchange for better treatment of those prisoners (living on limited rations and clothed in dirty rags for months). Ryan's motives mean little to Fincham & Co., even after the senior officer slyly finagles new clothes for them by ordering all prisoners to strip naked and burn their rags. Ryan is punished for that stunt (a trip to the camp sweat box) and gets the nickname "Von Ryan" for what Fincham and his men view as aiding the Axis.

Sinatra imbues Ryan with a confidence that is not cocksure but contained. It's a stark, welcome contrast to most of his 1960s work. Sinatra's eyes were always his most striking physical asset, and they continue to be his greatest acting strength when he brings his "A" game to a movie set, as he does here. A scene almost incidental to the narrative, when Ryan describes a key battle the Allies won while he was still on the outside, is lit by his matter-of-fact magnetism: The men erupt exultantly at good news from the front. Ryan looks away as they exchange huzzahs and embraces, narrowing his gaze in bewilderment, not at the men's understandable joy, but in trying to read—outside the camera's scope—how his captors will respond. It cements Ryan's status as a careful man, one who says little but observes all. (Howard goes the opposite direction—his Fincham always seems in the middle of or on the verge of apoplexy. While it's a solid performance, perhaps that's why Sinatra "offered everything under the sun and moon" to lure Sean Connery to the cast. The It boy of the moment for his cheeky but "chill" work as the British spy James Bond turned down the offer because the film didn't have another "role as important as Frankie's."[187])

Sinatra is also served by the physical changes that being almost 50 had wrought in him. He was not fat, but thicker of face and frame, a nod to the aging process he acknowledged to Ed Sullivan months before shooting started. He told Sullivan he needed to drop about 15 pounds before stepping in front of director Mark Robson's cameras. "I never thought the day would come," he mused, "when I'd have to go on a diet."[188] His appearance on screen indicates he postponed his weight-loss plans.

The stouter frame adds verisimilitude to the action that follows—the "guts and glory, arrogance and fury" the movie's trailer promises and which comprises most of the film. All is set in motion when Italy surrenders. The guards flee and the British try the commandant as a war criminal. He claims to have repudiated fascism, but the men, thirsty for revenge, don't buy a syllable of it. Ryan orders him put in the sweat box. Sinatra does more superb and subtle acting as he watches the men carry out the sentence by hoisting the commandant to his punishment: He conveys pity, concern, justice and ultimately softness in his wordless reactions. The commandant's contrition was indeed fake, however. He is rescued from the box by German soldiers and directs his liberators to the prisoners. The healthy Allies are captured and piled into a train to be taken across Italy to Austria; the injured are shot to death. Though Fincham remains unsure about Ryan's loyalties, the two plot with the now-united men to overtake the train and divert it to neutral Switzerland.

The suspense is taut and the action as staged by Robson thrilling as the prisoners try to stay a step ahead of their pursuers—who for most of the rest of the picture don't know they're pursuing anyone. That's because the Allies overtake the prison train's crew unbeknownst to the Nazi troop train trailing it. Ryan and Fincham work together ever more closely to devise acts of derring-do to keep the Nazis in the dark. Sinatra is convincing as the prototypical World War II everyman, who has to muster physical strength and flexibility not practiced in years to combat the enemy. But the most entertaining transformation is that of Captain Costanzo (Edward Mulhare), the Allies' German-speaking chaplain. He goes from a man of the cloth to a commander of the swastika with seamless perfection. Mulhare steals every scene he's in.

The biggest trouble the Allies encounter as they race to freedom involves the escape of two prisoners they took when commandeering the train. One of them, the commander's secretary (Italian model Raffaella Carra, in her English-speaking film debut), had earlier tried to seduce Ryan. Sinatra gives his finest extended performance of the film in that scene: There is sad sympathy in those blue eyes as she clumsily tries to entice Ryan by slipping on nylons. The discomfited twitches of Sinatra's face as the dance plays out are the reaction of a man of conscience and character contemplating what war does to the innocent. This earlier interplay adds pathos to the escape scene during one of the train's station stops.

Ryan calls after her to stop running so he doesn't have to shoot her. She doesn't listen—so he empties his rifle into her back. Sinatra flashes abject emptiness in his newly jowly face, then steals an ashamed look at one of the local children who witnessed the killing. Ryan's so shocked and devastated that when the more seasoned soldier Fincham tries to hurry him onto the departing train, the colonel swings his gun in the major's direction and snaps, "Get your hands off me or I'll blow your head off."

The Nazis learn of the escaped prisoners aboard the train. They chase it down as it nears the Swiss border; there are also Luftwaffe bombings. The P.O.W.s not in the boxcars hop out to stave off the Nazis. Fincham shoots his way back aboard with several men. Ryan is the last in the line scrambling toward the train. Mere yards from his rail ride to freedom, he is first staggered, then felled, by a fusillade of bullets. Sinatra plays Ryan's death as he played his life: close to the emotional vest. It is a quick and quiet demise, punctuated by Ryan falling silently out of Robson's frame. The viewer's last glimpse of him is a look of resigned agony reminiscent of Sinatra's brilliant cold-turkey scene in *The Man with the Golden Arm*. The moment also offers another parallel with *From Here to Eternity*: the only other war picture in which Sinatra's character is killed (and only the third, *Suddenly* being the second, in which his character dies).

Sinatra earned solid notices for *Von Ryan's Express*. *The San Francisco Examiner* said the movie was "at its best when running scared—speeding crazily from the Nazis in a fantastic railway escape," and hailed Sinatra for bringing "a commendable, nerves-of-steel vitality to his role as Ryan."[189]

It was also the hit Fox needed, raking in $17.1 million—more than any other film Sinatra made in the '60s and more than all three Rat Pack pictures combined. That it turned out so well surely pleased, and probably surprised, Zanuck. The production was almost as fraught with peril as the train chase that producer David said would make it "the most dangerous film ever made."[190] For starters, Sinatra did not appreciate Robson's painstaking shooting style, demanding it be altered so his scenes could be filmed consecutively, with minimum waiting time between set-ups. Robson said that was technically possible but would require major extra effort and expense. When Sinatra didn't get what he wanted, Fox gave him the use of a yacht during his off hours as appeasement. He immediately took it for a cruise and stopped reporting for work for a few days—and Fox took his side. Later, when he balked at staying in Rome with the rest of the cast and crew, the studio rented him an 18-room villa outside the city, complete with indoor and outdoor pools and a helipad. Each day a chartered helicopter whisked him to the location in Cortino d'Ampezzo, in the Dolomite Alps, while everybody else in front of and behind the camera made the long drive by car. Yet even the posh accommodations weren't quite enough to please the man who would be Von Ryan: Sinatra tossed $10,000 of his own money at making improvements to his temporary mountain home.[191]

Von Ryan's Express also marked a milestone in Sinatra's personal life when on the Fox lot (where the impressive and expensive prison camp set was erected to give the movie a grander scale), he met Mia Farrow, who was filming the nighttime TV soap opera *Peyton Place* on one of the stages.

Actor Christopher Riordan, who played one of the *Von Ryan's Express* soldiers, observed the beginning of the relationship that soon made Hollywood headlines:

> Sinatra was very aloof, very distant from everyone. The only person he really spoke to was Brad Dexter. He didn't even communicate much with the director. However, I had just finished shooting my scene with him when [actor] John Leyton brought Mia Farrow over to him. So I happened to be standing next to Frank Sinatra when he was introduced to Mia.[192]

Intrigued by the charismatic man old enough to be her father, Farrow began wandering over to the *Von Ryan's Express* set daily. In a matter of days, the star just shy of 50 was flying the ingenue just shy of 20 to his Palm Springs compound. They married in 1966 and divorced two years later.

Sinatra, while taking flack for his May–December affair, would pair up for his next film with his favorite pally from the Rat Pack. He and Dean Martin topped their sixth marquee together in *Marriage on the Rocks*, a comedy that trafficked in romantic subject matter more suitable for their age and stage of life than Sinatra's off-screen domestic situation.

Marriage on the Rocks

Directed by Jack Donohue
Screenplay: Cy Howard, from his story "Community Property"
Producer: William H. Daniels
Cinematography: William H. Daniels (Technicolor)
Editor: Sam O'Steen
Cast: Frank Sinatra, Dean Martin, Deborah Kerr, Cesar Romero, Hermione Baddeley, Tony Bill, John McGiver, Nancy Sinatra, Davey Davison, Michel Petit, Trini Lopez, Joi Lansing, Darlene Lucht, Kathleen Freeman, Flip Mark, DeForest Kelley, Sigrid Valdis, Parley Baer, Byron Foulger, Billi Adare, Linda Foster, Carol Anderson, George Ford, Jean Bartel, Stanley Farrar, Nick Borgani, Douglas Dean, Roberto Contreras, Jacqueline D'Avril,

John Fox, Daniel Nunez, Nacho Galindo, Karen Norris, Frank Gerstle, Marie Gomez, Jorge Moreno, Louis Nicoletti, Gay Gordon, Tina Mongasing, Maria Haro, Ethelreda Leopold, Mario Magana, William Meader, Hedley Mattingly, Rony Nyman, Alex Tinne, Emma Palmese, Theresa Testa, Ron Stein, Al Silvani, Reta Shaw, Christopher Riordan, Maria Pons, Joe Raciti, Linda Rivera, Concepcion Sandoval, Jesus Sandoval
Released June 23, 1965
A-C Productions and Sinatra Enterprises for Warner Brothers
109 minutes

There are a lot of impressive elements to *Marriage on the Rocks*, a romantic comedy that is witty, funny and engaging. Sinatra casts himself against type, he sought out Deborah Kerr to co-star (and she also played against type), Dean Martin could have easily walked through his part but he gives it his all. Toss in real-life Sinatra daughter Nancy, another appearance by Tony Bill in a supporting role, and the welcome contributions of Cesar Romero, Hermione Baddeley, John McGiver, Joi Lansing, Kathleen Freeman, Byron Foulger and Parley Baer, and *Marriage on the Rocks* stands out as one of Sinatra's most enjoyable lightweight comedies.

Another factor that is worth considering is that Sinatra and Martin make no attempts to be younger than their ages. The entire point of this film is how middle-agers are making their way through life, attempting to understand and adapt to the culture that has changed drastically since they were young.

Sinatra plays Dan Edwards, a sober, hard-working business owner. He has been married to Valerie (Deborah Kerr) for 19 years and has two children. His business partner is Ernie Brewer (Dean Martin), a confirmed bachelor whose wealth nets him a sports car and beach house that make him attractive to much younger women. Handsome, carefree and amusing, "Uncle Ernie" is beloved by Dan's kids, because he usually accepts their often wrongheaded choices. The film opens on Dan's anniversary. He dictates a card to go along with a bracelet that he has Ernie pick out for her. He then invites Ernie over to watch a prizefight on television. Ernie indicates that Dan should perhaps do something romantic with his wife on their anniversary, whereupon Dan indicates that it is no longer necessary as he is married and settled into a comfortable, undemanding lifestyle where romance is superfluous. Meanwhile, Valerie is in the office of a lawyer (John McGiver) demanding a divorce from her dull husband, wishing she had instead married the carefree Ernie.

This sets up a series of sequences where Dan and Valerie go to Mexico

(Left to right): Sinatra, Deborah Kerr and Dean Martin on the *Marriage on the Rocks* set.

on a second honeymoon, but are accosted by enterprising Miguel Santos (Cesar Romero) and end up accidentally divorced. When they plan to re-marry there to set things right, Dan is taken away by business. Ernie attempts to smooth things over and, due to the language barrier, he ends up married to Valerie. Valerie could sign the papers to divorce Ernie while they are still in Mexico (as Ernie wants) but chooses to use the situation to get back at Dan for never paying attention to her. They return home and Dan decides to teach them both a lesson by refusing to cooperate. He moves into Ernie's beach house-bachelor pad, while Ernie must now try to cope with life as a responsible husband and father.

The comic dynamic among Sinatra, Martin and Kerr is enhanced by the punctuating work of several supporting characters. Hermione Baddeley is Dan's live-in Irish mother-in-law who walks about the house playing bagpipes, drinking and insisting that Dan and Valerie aren't married because their wedding did not occur in a church. Nancy Sinatra is Dan and Valerie's teenage daughter, who wants to live in an apartment with her go-go–dancing girlfriend. Their son David (Michel Petit) gets ideas from his buddy Rollo (Flip Mark), whose parents are divorced, which nets him new bikes and other guilt-based luxuries. Meanwhile, Ernie is enjoying the consistent company of Lola (Joi Lansing), a semi-skilled secretary whose beauty and pampering are what keeps her comfortably employed. Cesar Romero delightfully cuts up in a comic manner as the pushy Mexican official in charge of divorces, marriages and the village's only hotel.

While Martin settles easily into a very typical role for him, he adds a great deal of comic nuance, some reactions dating back to his days teamed up with Jerry Lewis. He offers a committed comic performance, exhibiting his real skills as a comedy actor. Kerr was noted for playing rather prim, proper women so to see her offer a boisterous performance complete with a couple of dance club scenes is delightful. Kerr told the press:

> This is my first real comedy role. I thought it would be wonderful to do. I was thrilled when Frank called and asked me to do it. Trembling in my boots, I said I will. It was nice of them to remember me for the role. But it was shrewd of them to do it. When I tell people I'm with Frank Sinatra and Dean Martin, they say: WHAT! ...I'm terribly interested to see how the chemistry is going to work out. Of course, too, with this sort of film, things develop as you're working on it. I must say I look forward to it. I'm only wondering how I'll manage to do the Watusi.[193]

There is a dance scene in a go-go club in which an uninhibited Valerie cuts it up with Ernie while staid Dan watches from a table. Clad in a tuxedo, Dan obviously disdains the music, the dancing and the general atmosphere of a youth culture that is crowding out that with which he feels comfortable.

Actor Christopher Riordan appeared in that scene, but his part was eventually cut out due to his costume:

> Walter Plunkett, the costume designer, went to specialty shops to check out the "mod" clothes of the day and put me in an electric blue suit that was so tight it appeared to be painted on. When I arrived on the set in that suit, the first person I saw was Deborah Kerr. I was nervous, thinking she'd be cold and uppity, but she was warm, delightful, sweet and quite bawdy. She took one look at me and said, "In that thing you are wearing, I can tell what you had

for breakfast!" Frank Sinatra was once again distant as he had been when I worked with him on *Von Ryan's Express*. There was no sense of camaraderie. Dean Martin was exactly the opposite; joking and funny. Everyone liked him. I didn't talk to Nancy Sinatra on this film, but a year later I worked with her on some dance numbers for *The Ghost in the Invisible Bikini*. I expected her to be aloof like Frank, but she was sweet and cooperative.[194]

Although Sinatra had somewhat made his peace with rock'n'roll since dismissing it as being performed by "cretinous goons," in 1965 he was turning 50, and the British groups like the Beatles and the Rolling Stones had pushed his style of music further into being preferred by older "squares" who couldn't adapt to the changing culture. In an attempt to connect at least somewhat with a younger audience, Sinatra does have a song number in the film performed by Trini Lopez, who plays himself. Trini does a number at the go-go club, getting an enthusiastic response from the young crowd. In fact, Lopez was a recording artist on Frank's record label Reprise, and had two hits, "If I Had a Hammer" in 1963 and "Lemon Tree" in 1965.

It is the change in dynamic that brings around the characters' various perspectives. Valerie, now stuck married to Ernie, realizes the security that Dan offered her and the family is a thing of the past; Ernie cannot run a household. The children realize Uncle Ernie is hardly the cool guy he had once seemed when he is now responsible for their welfare. Suddenly he is against the daughter living with her friend, and against the boy having a motorcycle—two things that bachelor Dan now allows. It is definitely a situation where they all wanted what the others had (especially in the instance of Valerie often dreaming of what it would have been like had she married Ernie instead of Dan), but once they had it, they didn't find it to be that great. It is all played for laughs and each actor rises to the occasion nicely.

Nancy Sinatra was a last-minute replacement for current Sinatra girlfriend Mia Farrow, who was going to play the daughter role. This was a result of a combination of Mia's busy schedule on TV's *Peyton Place* and the unsettling idea of Frank's girlfriend playing his daughter. Nancy was going through a divorce from husband Tommy Sands at the time, so playing in a movie about divorce was often uncomfortable for her. She is appealing and amusing.

Tony Bill, a favorite of Sinatra's since his appearance in *Come Blow Your Horn*, plays a stuffy psychology student who is dating Dan's daughter. Bill's wife gave birth to a daughter during production of this film. She gave birth to their son during the filming of *None But the Brave*. Tony told the press, "I can't afford to be in any more Sinatra pictures." Frank was very moved when Tony and his wife named their daughter Francesca.

Davey Davison plays the go-go dancer with whom Dan's daughter wants to live. In one revealing scene, she tells Dan how she came from a broken home and neglectful parents so she has decided to live under her own terms. She ends up spending a lot of time with Dan once he becomes a bachelor and, in a confrontation with Valerie, claims that they might consider getting married. Valerie icily responds, "For your wedding, I'll buy a crib for you and an oxygen tent for Dan!" Davison plays the role with a comic edge when required, and with a dramatic edge when needed to better define the character. She does an excellent job.

There was at least one casting choice that ended up in conflict. Frank wanted Sonny Tufts to play a role in the movie, and Tufts, whose career was at low ebb, coveted the role. However, according to the trades, Sonny's agent demanded $2000 per week with a three-week minimum guaranteed work, and full script approval. As a result of these demands, Tufts did not get the role.

Cy Howard's original script (titled *Divorce American Style*) was considered a bit too risque, so it was rewritten as *Community Property*. Director Jack Donahue had directed both Sinatra and Martin in their TV appearances and handles this feature film effectively enough. It was his first of only two theatrical features. He had directed a TV movie a year earlier.

Marriage on the Rocks was not exactly a flop as has been indicated in some studies, but it wasn't as big a hit as it should have been and, because of the salaries involved, it lost money. It also wasn't well received in Mexico where part of the movie was set. In fact, Mexico was so upset with how its people were portrayed, they banned Frank Sinatra from the country, even though he owned property there.

The press offered some curious announcements about upcoming Sinatra projects including a serious Western he planned to produce, direct and star in, but that never came to fruition. It was also announced in the trades that he would star opposite Sandy Dennis in a movie version of Muriel Resnick's play *Any Wednesday*, but the 1966 film version stars Jason Robards and Jane Fonda.

Sinatra turning 50 in 1965 was dealt with more directly by his recording career where he became introspective about it via the album "September of My Years," which remains one of his finest. This concept album included such tracks as "Last Night When We Were Young," "It Gets Lonely Early" and "September Song," all of which confront the aging process. The most expressive track, "It Was a Very Good Year," has lived on as a perennial classic of middle-aged angst.

There was a 50th birthday salute to Sinatra on Walter Cronkite's popular news show, and he was awarded the Man of the Year award and

Entertainer of the Year award from the Conference of Personal Managers West. It was the first time both awards were given to the same person.

So, despite being considered out of touch and from another era by the youth culture, Sinatra had achieved a level of stardom that surpassed any necessary popularity in the immediate culture. "September of My Years" resonated strongly with another demographic entirely, and that same contingent of moviegoers enjoyed *Marriage on the Rocks*. Unfortunately, they weren't enough to make the expensive movie a success.

Sinatra switched to action-adventure for his next movie, which had a Rod Serling screenplay from a novel by Jack Finney. *Assault on a Queen* was to be directed by Ken Hughes but since Sinatra's company was one of the producers, Sinatra put Jack Donohue at the helm.

Assault on a Queen

Directed by Jack Donohue
Screenplay: Rod Serling, from the novel by Jack Finney
Producer: William Goetz
Cinematography: William H. Daniels (Technicolor)
Editor: Archie Marshek
Cast: Frank Sinatra, Virna Lisi, Tony Franciosa, Richard Conte, Alf Kjellin, Errol John, Murray Matheson, Reginald Denny, John Warburton, Lester Matthews, Val Avery, Gilchrist Stuart, Ronald Long, Leslie Bradley, Arthur Gould-Porter, Alan Baxter, Ray Kellogg, Frank Baker, Donald Lawton, Barbara Morrison, Jack Raine, Robert Shawley, Lawrence Conroy, Bob Hoy, Douglas Deane, Noel Drayton
Released June 15, 1966
Seven Arts Productions and Sinatra Enterprises for Paramount
106 minutes

"A role that fit him like a glove in a property that creaked like an old shoe"—that's how Sinatra biographer James Kaplan described *Assault on a Queen*.[195] It's a fitting, if incomplete, encapsulation. It's fitting because the story was conceived seven years earlier, in 1959, as a *Saturday Evening Post* serial that was repackaged into a novel. It sat on a few Hollywood shelves in the years since, in large part because its trifle of a story was considered too ridiculous for the morphing tastes of 1960s movie audiences. The plot focused on a ragtag collection of treasure-hunters who get the farfetched idea to use an old German U-boat to stick up the storied ocean liner the RMS *Queen Mary* in the middle of the Atlantic Ocean. Producer Ray Stark snatched up the rights in 1960, and almost immediately came to believe the plot was too unbelievable to attract filmgoers of the era.

What a difference a year makes. In 1961, headlines were blaring about how terrorists had brazenly hijacked a Portuguese cruise liner with 900 passengers and crew aboard. The attack occurred on January 22 and lasted until February 2, when the Portuguese and Spanish rebels who seized the *Santa Maria* to effect political change in Portugal were granted political asylum in Brazil. The gossip columnists said that Stark had the last laugh, because now his project with the too-silly-to-believe plot had actually happened—at least the overtaking-a-ship-in-mid-ocean part. Stark wasted no time in hatching a production plan, signing Mel Ferrer to produce and likely direct the picture—but not star. "It's not for me," Ferrer said. "Peter Sellers or Alec Guinness would be our man."[196]

Nothing would come of that iteration of the film, but in 1964 it was reported that Stark was still grinding away, this time securing an agreement with the *Queen Mary*'s owners to film on board the ship—with Sean Connery's name attached to the project "because everything is offered to Sean first."[197] It appears the role was indeed put before the Scottish star—dangled along with a $500,000 payday.[198] He didn't take it.

A year later, Sinatra did. The rights to *Assault on a Queen* had passed from Stark to producer William Goetz, an old Sinatra pal who would serve as his friend's best man when he married Mia Farrow in July 1966. Sinatra was, as Kaplan noted, a precise fit for the role of Mark Brittain (certainly better than Connery, 15 years his junior, would have been). Brittain is a World War II vet, a lieutenant who served aboard a submarine in the Pacific. A bit fuller of face and slower of step than during his wartime heyday, he's living a laid-back life as a fishing-charter captain in the Bahamas, an undertaking he shares with his war buddy Linc (Errol John).

Sinatra expressed belief in the film's potential in an on-set interview with the Associated Press—while at the same time signaling the problems the production would face: "It's a good story and a forerunner in the field of far-out plots. The book has been laying around for ten years. But listen, you can get away with these stories if you hook the audience in the first eight to twelve minutes. And if you keep moving fast. And we move fast in this one, believe me."

A few lines later in the story, Sinatra proves his point—but not in the way he likely meant to. Reporter Bob Thomas quotes him as saying as a scene experiences some delay, "What are we waiting for? Let's get moving." For good measure, several additional lines later, the star lets loose an exasperated "Incredible!" after the chattering of workers on an adjoining stage momentarily slows production again.[199]

Production may have moved fast—a favorite pace for on-set Sinatra—but the film's narrative did not. While Sinatra the actor has the look and manner for the part, he gives not merely a passing-through performance, but one missing the spark that colored other roles even when he didn't break much of a performance sweat, like in the Rat Pack films. Adding to the general listlessness of the endeavor is that Sinatra the co-producer doesn't appear to put forth the kind of focused effort he had in earlier films in which he wore multiple hats. Case in point: He wanted the legendary Duke Ellington to do the score, but due to scheduling conflicts and poor production planning, the jazzman only had about three weeks to complete the work. Although he is screen-credited as the music's sole composer (the first African American to be so recognized on a studio picture), only five of Ellington's original recordings are in the final movie.[200] The result of the star-producer's less-than-thoroughly-engaged effort is a bit of a mishmash.

At the macro level, it's the fault of the script penned by an off-his-game Rod Serling. It's full of flat characters, weak dialogue and illogical set-ups—while also being devoid of rousing action set-pieces one would expect from a film about robbing the world's most famous ocean liner. Consider how Brittain winds up in on the heist plan in the first place: He agrees to dive in search of Spanish galleons for treasure-hunters Rosa Lucchesi (Virna Lisi), Vic Rossiter (Anthony Franciosa) and Eric Lauffnauer (Alf Kjellin) only after the man from whom he rents his fishing boat demands the $641 he's owed before he'll let Brittain re-board it. Rosa (the financier of the outfit) pays him his $700 diver's fee up front. So, when on his first descent he swims across the U-boat, he has no reason to agree to be part of the scheme the ex–Nazi Lauffnauer and the greedy Rossiter dream up about liberating the *Queen Mary* of its bank holdings and gold bullion. He could just saunter away with Linc to resume his quiet life, which it seems natural he would do since he's not flashed a single felonious impulse since being introduced.

There is also a distinct backlot-and-rear-projection feel to all but the couple of unimpressive interiors shot aboard the *Queen Mary*. Director Jack Donohue, who worked exclusively in TV (including on Sinatra's late–'50s variety show) before Sinatra hired him to direct his previous film *Marriage on the Rocks*, helms here like a TV director—right down to ending several scenes with fades to black, as if making room for sponsors' commercials. The small-scale, low-budget feel is augmented by Donohue's decision to shoot the refurbishment of the U-boat as a series of quick-cut solo scenes in which individual cast members scrub and hammer off barnacles and rust, rewire propulsion systems, solder pipes, replace batteries and paint the exterior. Even the character-driven scenes, whether by sunlight or moonlight, play like moments from *The Love Boat*, staged in front of either rear-projected water or tank water on a stage. The fact that the bold plan of oceanway robbery is hatched in a tiny seaside motel room speaks to the movie's smallness amid the large stakes in which its plot traffics.

It does not help that Sinatra's performance bears none of the depth and nuance he so often demonstrated. He appears tired and disinterested most every time he is on screen. When Brittain first meets Rosa, Sinatra seems as if he's talking through Lisi, not even at her, and certainly not to her. His eyes, where the soul of his best acting lives, are wide and unchanged throughout the exchange, never withdrawn and refocused as if Brittain is having a conversation in which he is interested in the information he's receiving. The performances don't improve much in the pair of flirtatious scenes the duo shares prior to the heist, which are most notable for the distracting number of cigarettes each smokes. That lack

Sinatra appears bored throughout much of *Assault on a Queen*, in which he starred with Virna Lisi.

of dynamism didn't stop Paramount's publicity department from planting a cheeky item in the gossip columns that the pair "should win at least the du Pont Award—as the Best Chemistry of the Year."[201] Neither did it still Serling's typewriter from tapping out this line of dialogue, hard to imagine Sinatra uttering even as one of his man-child characters from his days as Gene Kelly's sidekick: "She's so deep in my gut, we breathe together."

Most indicative of Sinatra not seeking, let alone seizing, opportunities to inject his performance with subtle shades of meaning is the scene in which Brittain asks Lauffnauer to go over everybody's roles and the timing of their execution one last time. Lauffnauer does so, running through the precise duties of every member of the team from a sheet he has distributed to them. As Kjellin looks at each fellow actor, engaging them with gestures and eye contact, Sinatra sits bent forward, the paper in front of him, not looking up once or even moving his head to indicate he's reading the piece of paper. His motionlessness lasts for 26 seconds, even though Kjellin points at him three times to emphasize aspects of Brittain's responsibilities.

The heist fails, but the romance between Brittain and Rosa succeeds, as they lifeboat away with Linc. They are the robbery's only survivors as the credits roll.

Assault on a Queen was a critical and box-office disappointment. It made just $2.7 million and earned such brickbats from critics: "leaky vessel"[202] and "too deep in foam."[203] The final injury to Sinatra came a week after release, when a *Daily News* columnist noted that the production booklet for the film, in an attempt to play up the hipness of the goings-on, listed the lead as "Frank Sinatra Esq."—but tacked on a more-hip-than-they-intended typo: "Chairman of the Broad."[204]

While he did not generate heat in theaters, Sinatra was on fire in record stores and on radio in 1966. "*Strangers in the Night*," released a few weeks before *Assault on a Queen*, reached #1 on the pop album charts—his first top showing of the decade. The title track also landed atop the pop singles chart—and "Summer Wind" charted as well. "Strangers in the Night" went on to win Record of the Year and earn Sinatra Top Male Vocal Performance honors at the Grammys the following Spring. Its appeal wasn't just American, either: Sinatra launched a British Invasion of his own with "Strangers in the Night" to knock the Rolling Stones from the top spot on England's Big Three hit-parade charts: New Musical Express, Melody Maker and Disc. It marked the first time he had reached that pinnacle since 1954 with "Three Coins in the Fountain."

The Naked Runner

Directed by Sidney J. Furie
Screenplay: Stanley Mann, from the novel by Francis Clifford
Producer: Brad Dexter
Cinematography: Otto Heller (Technicolor)
Editor: Barrie Vince
Cast: Frank Sinatra, Peter Vaughan, Derren Nesbitt, Nadia Gray, Toby Robins, Inger Stratton, Cyril Luckham, Edward Fox, J.A.B. Dubin-Bhermann, Michael Newport, Robert Wisepart, Stanley Meadows, James Payne, Victor Beaumont, Roy Hanlon, Joscik Barbarossa
Released September 11, 1967
Sinatra Enterprises for Warner Brothers
101 minutes

As indicated in our chapter on *None But the Brave,* actor Brad Dexter once saved Sinatra from drowning. Sinatra returned the favor, at least partially, by agreeing to star in Dexter's first film as a producer. When the title role in the the movie *Harper* went to Paul Newman, Sinatra asked new producer Dexter to find him a vehicle. *Harper* was released even before Frank's previous film *Assault on a Queen,* so if he indeed sought to play Harper, as some have indicated, he had to be inquiring about it while filming *Marriage on the Rocks.*

Sinatra badly needed a successful movie since his previous two, *Marriage on the Rocks* and *Assault on a Queen* performed poorly. Unfortunately for him, *The Naked Runner* was not it.

Sam Laker (Sinatra), an O.S.S. operative during World War II, is now a furniture designer preparing to attend a business conference in Leipzig, East Germany, with his teenage son. Laker is contacted by his former commander (now a British Intelligence officer) and asked to deliver a message in East Germany. Laker is reluctant until he is informed that the message could mean life or death to a young female European agent to whom he Laker is indebted. Sam's son is kidnapped and Sam is told that, to ensure the youngster's safe return, he must perform an assassination. Laker agrees to the mission out of desperation, but his victim never shows up. As a result, he is told that his son was killed. Sam becomes obsessed with revenge.

The Naked Runner was produced by Sinatra's company. He hired Sidney J. Furie to direct after admiring Furie's work on *The Ipcress File* (1965). And unlike his lackluster work in *Assault on a Queen*, Sinatra drew upon his acting talents for some of the more emotional *Naked Runner* scenes.

Sinatra gets caught up in espionage in *The Naked Runner*.

However, this does not mean he was any more responsible. During filming, he took time off to campaign for California Governor Pat Brown, who was running against Republican challenger Ronald Reagan. After the campaign, Sinatra decided he didn't want to return to location filming in Europe and chose to film all of his remaining scenes separately in California, while the actors on location had to work with his stand-in, James Payne. (Pat Brown ended up losing the gubernatorial election in a landslide.)

The Naked Runner premiered in New York on July 19, 1967, and went into release the following September. *The New York Times* stated:

> I couldn't get involved by this picture, no matter how tricky and wild is Sidney J. Furie's direction, nor how diligently Mr. Sinatra plays the sadistically recruited assassin, nor how elaborately others play their phony roles. Furthermore, I was offended by this presumption of projecting murder as a solution with such complete nonchalance.[205]

The Naked Runner's box office number were helped a bit by the fact that at some venues it was on the bottom half of a double-bill with *Bonnie and Clyde*, a major hit. But exhibitors indicated that many moviegoers came for *Bonnie and Clyde* and did not stay for *The Naked Runner*.

The problem with the film is that the script is poor and the direction is leaden. It is a very lifeless, dull espionage thriller and Sinatra's character is very cold and dull. This is not a factor in his performance. Sinatra's acting is really not bad, overall, but his decision to shoot all of his scenes in California may have made the movie less cohesive. The abrupt ending is what is perhaps most unsettling. It never gives Sam the opportunity to grapple with, or even realize, what just happened to him. We don't see any sort of emotional moment or reunion with his son, who is actually still alive. The movie as a whole is rather dull and the ending made everything seem inconsequential. The story's kidnapping element is interesting in that Sinatra's own son was kidnapped in December 1963. Sinatra paid a ransom, which was almost fully recovered when his son was found, unharmed, and the kidnappers arrested. There were rumors that Sinatra Jr. staged the event as a publicity stunt, but the FBI indicated that this was not the case.

A few critics professing to like *The Naked Runner* wrote good reviews, but it has been claimed in other studies that these reviewers were shills who were essentially writing press releases and not assessments based on an objective critical approach. Critics, and columnists, were unimpressed with the film's convoluted plot, filled with phony kidnappings and calculated, emotionless murders. Herb Kelly stated in his column:

> Frank Sinatra has put on some weight and he's no longer the skinny, delicate fellow of years past. Even so, the script writer and director of the movie *The Naked Runner* have given him a burden too heavy to carry. There's a limit to what a man can do. Sinatra must be given credit for going beyond the call of duty to make *The Naked Runner* a good picture. It's not his fault that it fails.[206]

Sinatra's music career continued to flourish. A year after his massive hit "Strangers in the Night," he came out with the album "The World We Knew" around the time of *The Naked Runner*, and it performed well. Containing such diverse songs as Charlie Chaplin's "This Is My Song" and Rodgers and Hammerstein's "Some Enchanted Evening," the LP's big success was his duet with daughter Nancy, "Somethin' Stupid." Another chart topper, it was #1 for four weeks. It was Frank's second gold record and Nancy's third.

Tony Rome

Directed by Gordon Douglas
Screenplay: Richard Breen, from the novel by Marvin H. Albert

Producer: Aaron Rosenberg
Cinematography: Joseph Biroc (Color)
Editor: Robert Simpson
Cast: Frank Sinatra, Jill St John, Richard Conte, Gena Rowlands, Simon Oakland, Jeffrey Lynn, Lloyd Bochner, Robert J. Wilke, Virginia Vincent, Joan Shawlee, Richard Krisher, Lloyd Gough, Babe Hart, Templeton Fox, Rocky Graziano, Elisabeth Fraser, Shecky Greene, Jeanne Cooper, Harry Davis, Stanley Ross, Sue Lyon, Buzz Henry, Deanna Lund, Michael Romanoff, Tiffany Bolling, Joe E. Ross, Linda Dano, Beau Jack, Sean Bursell, Carl Starling, Levi Forte, Norman Marlow, Jilly Rizzo
Released November 10, 1967
20th Century–Fox
110 minutes

Sinatra had brought an impressively varied assortment of characters to life by 1967, his 24th year in motion pictures. He started out literally playing himself, then moved on to sailors, soldiers, scoundrels and singers—not to mention what could make up the opening words of a good barroom joke: a priest, a lawyer and a mobster. He had received rave reviews, international success that rivaled (and in some years surpassed) the lofty heights he'd achieved as a singer—and an Academy Award. And yet, it was not until *Tony Rome* that Sinatra found not so much a *role*, but a *part*, that he felt suited him so well that he played it twice. It was not the title character in *Tony Rome* that made Sinatra feel so at home as much as that title character's profession: law enforcement.

In 1964, on the *Von Ryan's Express* set, Sinatra hinted at the trajectory his career would take in the September of his acting years. "I want to play a tongue-in-cheek private eye," he told a visiting reporter. "One of those guys who always gets the stuffings kicked out of him. I think that would be fun to do."[207] A year after the interview, the opportunity presented itself. Brad Dexter, who parlayed rescuing Sinatra from drowning during filming of *None But the Brave* into a co-starring role in *Von Ryan's Express*, wound up vice-president in charge of all film activities for Sinatra Enterprises.[208] When he spied the script for *Harper*, a private-eye story with noir notes that producers hoped would revive the genre, Dexter tried to convince the boss to take the part. After all, Humphrey Bogart—who owned the noir genre two decades earlier—was one of Sinatra's idols; what a great opportunity to pay homage to him. But Sinatra passed, despite being the first choice of producer Elliott Kastner.[209]

Paul Newman wound up with the role. His performance and the film were near-universally applauded for the reasons Dexter cited in his pitch to Sinatra: It was a tough, cool, cynical story revolving around a flawed but likable hero.

But thanks to Hollywood's tradition of copycatting film genres that demonstrate a box office pulse, Sinatra still got his chance to step into a gumshoe's shoes. In fact, when he first became attached to *Tony Rome*, the project was called *Gumshoe*, based on a novel that had received little notice. The role netted him a $1 million payday—at $50,000 a week[210]—and afforded him the opportunity to catch the film industry's newest trend by the tail:

> The persona of the private investigator fit Frank Sinatra perfectly. ...Audiences expect detectives to resemble their idealized version of Frank Sinatra: the man in question has been around the block more than once, is bruised, tough, cynical yet still possesses a small private reservoir of hope. Tough with men, wary with women, the chivalrous knight who has seen it all but still fights the daily fight. ...A hero with the touch of a loser about him.[211]

And he gets the stuffings kicked out of him. A lot.

Tony Rome's base of operations is Miami Beach, where he's equally comfortable and quip-equipped in a seedy seaside motel or a tony mansion. The story alternates between the two worlds, with the occasional scene-setting stop aboard Rome's powerboat, well-stocked with beer (Sinatra was a Budweiser spokesman at the time) and occasionally hosting two of the film's three leading ladies. Jill St. John has the most robust role, playing Ann Archer, an out-of-town swinger who catches Tony's eye and flirts with him without conceding the relational upper hand. She is neither femme fatale nor damsel in distress—and director Gordon Douglas makes excellent use of her scenes with Sinatra as they drive or share a meal to both establish

The title role as the private eye in *Tony Rome* fit the latter-day Sinatra.

Tony's character and his backstory. Sue Lyon has a less interesting role as Diana Pines, the spoiled little rich girl whose "mommy issues" set the plot in motion because she keeps winding up passed out drunk in places other than Daddy's house. She also loses a piece of heirloom jewelry—and Tony is hired to find the pin. (The gossip mavens reported that Mrs. Sinatra, Mia Farrow, was briefly eyed for the part, which was said to have been retrofitted to suit her, with producers willing to wait until she finished shooting *Dandy in Aspic* in London to make it happen.[212])

Gena Rowlands plays Rita Kosterman, Diana's plucked-from-a-shady-life stepmother. Rowlands shares the screen with Sinatra in the movie's best-acted scene, when Rome first meets Rita at her well-appointed home. She is sitting at a table with an ornate chess set; Tony asks her questions to determine what she might know about the missing jewelry, passing the initial moments by never even looking at her, but holding and studying a couple of the chess pieces. It's a brilliant choice by Sinatra, not to make eye contact. At the outset, Rome is not trying to interrogate Rita, but gain her trust, and holding her gaze might prevent her from opening up. That's the way a detective with Rome's experience would handle the interplay. Sinatra knew that he didn't have to turn on his acting highbeams—those piercing blue eyes—in order to create tension and meaning in the scene.

Tony Rome's plot is a bit hard to follow as the movie wears on—and it does wear on, clocking in at almost two hours and feeling even longer. But plot is never really the point here. The film is designed as a showcase for Sinatra's charm in a role he was not born to play, but had aged into playing pitch-perfectly. The movie's entertainment value rides on the series of vignettes the audience knows will add up to the bad guys (including comedian Shecky Greene) being brought to justice—so there's no need or even much inclination to check the math it takes to get there. Sinatra is fully present and dialed in at every moment. In scenes with Rome's disgraced former partner, Turpin (Robert J. Wilke), Sinatra lets the viewer see Rome's distaste for having to take a job from him. Yet later, after Turpin is murdered and Rome gambles his way into some money, Sinatra flashes just the right touch of respect for the man Turpin used to be in paying for his funeral. The scenes between Sinatra and Richard Conte (as Lt. Dave Santini, Rome's friend and Police Department contact) either amuse with well-paced banter or crackle with tension. The standout in the latter case is Sinatra conveying equal parts anger and betrayal when Santini brings up the suicide of Rome's father, a police officer who killed himself after he accused the wrong rich man, and that rich man ruined his career. The exchange adds a layer of insight into why Rome left the force, and why he's so quick to play things light: so he doesn't have to experience things heavy.

Not every vignette lands—particularly those that try too hard to be bawdy. The scene of an elderly woman showing up at Rome's disheveled one-room office to ask if he will "meet my pussy" because she thinks someone is trying to poison the animal is silly and sophomoric and tonally all wrong even for such a generally light-hearted picture. It's more interesting and rewarding for audiences to see shades of Rome's personality revealed in brief interludes, like when he's driving Ann Archer to town and she suggests they stop off for a drink. He reaches across her into his glove box, retrieves a bottle and hands it to her. One vignette that would likely have been fun never got beyond Sinatra's wish list: He asked Jackie Gleason, who famously called Miami home, if he'd consider making a cameo appearance. The Great One was open to it, but only for $250,000.[213] Sinatra settled for a walk-on from boxing champ Rocky Graziano.

Director Douglas is owed a great deal of the credit for what makes *Tony Rome* such a rollicking ride despite its dead spots. His take on Miami is writ large, making ample use of the film's 65 locations. His strategic use of hand-held photography injects dynamism into not just the action sequences, but also key bits of exposition. His tracking shot when Rome is escorted through the grand room of the Kosterman mansion hints at the bigness of the case the detective is taking on even before he knows how many tentacles it has. One writer enthused about Douglas' camerawork, "[R]arely has a metropolitan area been used so thoroughly by a motion picture production ... ranging all the way from flophouses to luxury hotels and from trailer parks to palatial estates."[214]

Tony Rome was not a blockbuster, even by 1960s standards, but its $4 million take was enough for 20th Century–Fox to greenlight a sequel—the only follow-up franchise installment of Sinatra's career. The reviews were mixed, but critics who liked it appreciated what Sinatra appreciated about playing a private eye. As the *Los Angeles Times*' Charles Champlin put it, "What gives the movie its strength and interest is that in *Tony Rome*, Sinatra is able to play a character much like himself, or part of himself: wisecracking, tough, mobile, romantic, world-bruised but idealistic."[215]

The Detective

Directed by Gordon Douglas
Screenplay: Abby Mann, from the novel by Roderick Thorp
Producer: Aaron Rosenberg
Cinematography: Joseph Biroc (Color)
Editor: Robert Simpson

Cast: Frank Sinatra, Lee Remick, Ralph Meeker, Jack Klugman, Horace McMahon, Lloyd Bochner, William Windom, Tony Musante, Al Freeman, Jr., Robert Duvall, Pat Henry, Patrick McVey, Dixie Marquis, Sugar Ray Robinson, Renee Taylor, James Inman, Tom Atkins, Jacqueline Bisset, Sharon Henesy, Richard Kirshner, Ted Beniades, Don Fellows, Lou Krugman, Paul Larson, Alan Manson, George Plimpton, Joe Santos, Arnold Soboloff, Philip Sterling, Mark Dawson, Earl Montgomery, Mikel Angel, James Dukas, Tom Gorman, Peg Murray, Lou Nelson, Frank Raiter, Jose Rodriguez, Diane Sayer, Stephen Wright, Peter York, Jilly Rizzo
Released May 28, 1968
20th Century–Fox
114 minutes

By the time *Tony Rome* was playing in theaters, Sinatra was already active on a serious neo-noir with the same producer, director and cinematographer. Having felt comfortable in the role of a detective, Sinatra was interested in extending beyond the approach used in *Tony Rome* and accepted a script by Abby Mann, who had won a Best Adapted Screenplay Oscar for Stanley Kramer's *Judgment at Nuremberg*. Sinatra was drawn to the central character, who was darker and more brutally realistic than the cinematic norm of the time, as well as the edgy story. Cinema was in transition, and filmmakers began making movies with content that had been taboo. *The Detective* dealt with homosexuality much more graphically and seriously, while the dialogue contained more profanity than was usually allowed. Sinatra liked the idea that *The Detective* was so

Sinatra enjoyed playing detectives at this stage of his career, and found success with *The Detective*.

progressive and it attracted him to the property. It was a smart move. *The Detective* was his biggest box office hit since *Von Ryan's Express*.

Robert Evans first owned the rights to Roderick Thorp's 1966 book, but was soon hired to run Paramount. To get out of his contract, he gave the property to 20th Century–Fox. Mark Robson was attached to the project as a director, but Sinatra preferred to work with Gordon Douglas, with whom he had worked often, including the recent *Tony Rome*. Frank had worked with Douglas on many projects and was comfortable with his approach.

There was a bit of tumult in Sinatra's marriage to the much younger Mia Farrow, chiefly because he realized that she had ambitions as an actress more so than as a wife. Mia would later recall incidents in their marriage where Frank "for the first time felt like a square."[216] In an effort to combine their relationship and Mia's ambitions, Frank arranged that she play opposite him in *The Detective*, which went into production in the fall of 1967. However, Mia was working on Roman Polanski's *Rosemary's Baby* for Paramount and, as that film's lead, had at least a month of shooting left. Frank delayed the production, but when the Polanski film continued to roll on, the irate Sinatra ordered Mia to walk off the project and join his. She didn't want to do that, so Frank called new Paramount head Robert Evans and complained. Evans let Sinatra know that they hired Mia Farrow the actress, not Mrs. Sinatra. Frank then had divorce papers sent by messenger to the set of *Rosemary's Baby*, and Jacqueline Bisset was cast in the *Detective* role intended for Mia.

New York City police detective Joe Leland (Sinatra) investigates the murder of a man who was beaten and his genitals removed. Other policemen on the case are appalled and don't know how to react to something so grisly and extreme; Joe is grounded and focused. He remains so as further snooping uncovers the victim's sordid gay lifestyle. A friend of the victim tells of the victim's mysterious roommate (Tony Musante). When that man is found, he confesses and is put to death. This haunts Leland, who believes the man was insane.

A man (William Windom) jumps to his death and his much younger wife (Bisset) asks Leland to look into it. Leland discovers that the suicide is connected to the gay man's murder. He and his partner (Jack Klugman) get little cooperation from a psychiatrist (Lloyd Bochner). They eventually discover that the man who committed suicide went to a gay club in an attempt to "get it out of his system," and ended up going home with the murder victim, killing him out of a maddening guilt over his homosexual feelings.

As a subplot to the central narrative, Leland is shown as having a great deal of difficulty with his much younger wife (Lee Remick), an element

Jacqueline Bisset played a role originally slated for Mia Farrow in *The Detective*.

that paralleled Sinatra's relationship with the much younger Mia Farrow. While the attraction remains, as does some level of caring and affection, the incompatibility issues between a free-spirited progressive and a staid detective, often haunted by the cases he's trying to unravel, are brought to the surface an add further tension to Leland's work.

The Detective was billed as "the first adult detective drama," and while the dialogue seems tame today, the "hell," "damn," and "full of crap" statements were challenging in 1968. At that time, there wasn't even an MPAA ratings system in place. That didn't happen until November 1968, several months after the release of *The Detective*. At the time of this film's release in May, the tag line "Suggested for mature audiences" was the only hint that perhaps youngsters should not attend the film.

The Detective shows how homosexuality was looked upon by some as a decadent lifestyle filled with swishy stereotypes, serious bodybuilders and dark proclivities that drive people to murder and suicide. When the roommate is interrogated, he is repeatedly called "faggot" by the officers. While unsettling in more enlightened times, it gives a serious and accurate look at how gay people were then perceived by some, and shows a cultural advancement for even acknowledging what certain members of society would consider to be its seamy underbelly during these times. However, even though the way the film portrays homosexuality is frequently problematic, it does not endorse the way the gay men in the movie are treated; in fact, it's occasionally a very interesting exploration of the discrimination they faced. When the officers call them faggots, it's not in a situation where we're rooting for the officers (who are obviously very over-aggressive). The way Sinatra portrays Joe as being a bit disapproving of these cops' behavior is telling.

Having his own personal problems during the filming of *The Detective*, Sinatra was able to bring all of that tension into the character he was portraying. Joe Leland is very stern, serious and no-nonsense. Even when the case becomes complicated, he exudes a confidence and an understanding as he perseveres. Director Douglas often lets the shot rest on Sinatra's pensive expression, his piercing blue eyes, as Jerry Goldsmith's effective lazy jazz plays in the background. It is all quite well done.

The Detective got uniformly good reviews from the critics and was a financial success—two things that Sinatra hadn't been getting with his last few films. Mia Farrow's *Rosemary's Baby* was another movie that challenged cinema's past restrictions—and was a far greater success.

One amusing bit of trivia regarding *The Detective*: In 1979, the novel's author Roderick Thorp wrote a follow-up, *Nothing Lasts Forever*; set on Christmas Eve, it featured Detective Leland trapped in the 40-story oil corporation office building where his daughter works. As Leland waits for a Christmas party to end, the building is attacked by terrorists. Thorp had allegedly been inspired to write this book after watching *The Towering Inferno* (1974). The movie rights were acquired and a film project was in development in 1987. Because Sinatra's contract stipulated that he would star in any sequels, the lead role was offered to him. Sinatra realized that, now in his early 70s, he wouldn't be appropriate for the part. He suggested that a younger man play the role, and that it should be his wife who works in the building. It eventually turned out to be the film *Die*

Hard (1988), with Bruce Willis starring as Detective John McClane, who gets trapped in the Nakatomi Corporation building where his estranged wife works.

Lady in Cement

Directed by Gordon Douglas
Screenplay: Marvin Albert, from his novel
Producer: Aaron Rosenberg
Cinematography: Joseph Biroc (Color)
Editor: Robert Simpson
Cast: Frank Sinatra, Raquel Welch, Richard Conte, Martin Gabel, Lainie Kazan, Pat Henry, Steve Peck, Virginia Wood, Richard Deacon, Frank Raiter, Peter Hock, Alex Stevens, Christine Todd, Mac Robbins, Tommy Uhlar, Rey Baumel, Pauly Dash, Andy Jarrell, Dan Blocker, Bunny Yeager, Lanita Kent, Dick Sterling, Coz Serapere, Shirley Parker, Chris Robinson, Joe E. Lewis, B.S. Pully, Al Algiro
Released November 20, 1968
20th Century–Fox
93 minutes

Sinatra had such a grand time making *Tony Rome* that he reprised the title role a year later in the only sequel of his acting career. A prototypical Hollywood Part II, *Lady in Cement* sets familiar characters in new but similar situations and revisits the most winning narrative and performance beats while seeking to expand the universe of the original. What is lost in production and tonal freshness the second time around is here offset by the leading man's contagious *joie de vivre* in playing the small-time private eye with a big-time heart against all occupational odds. It also helps that the plot is more accessible this time around, if once again mostly incidental to the audience enjoying the experience. The line on the ledger where *Lady in Cement* most surpasses its predecessor is in its new supporting performances.

Miami private eye Tony Rome is once again angling to stave off his bookie—only as this film opens, he's not looking to do so for his professional fee of $100 a day plus expenses. He's launched a get-rich-quick scheme with a pal who works for the police vice squad. (The role is played by comedian Pat Henry, who had long opened for Sinatra on tour and who made his film debut earlier in the year in *The Detective*. The part was

Lady in Cement (1968) 217

initially reserved for Sinatra's old Rat Pack buddy Sammy Davis, Jr., but a delay in shooting caused by a Sinatra illness left Davis unavailable.)[217] Rome and his vice squad colleague are searching for storied Spanish galleons in the waters off the coast (Sinatra's second time in two years chasing sunken treasure as a diver, following 1966's *Assault on a Queen*). But Rome doesn't find long-submerged doubloons; he finds a recently submerged dame—her feet encased in a block of cement, Mafia-style. After fighting off a few circling sharks, Tony dutifully reports the murder to his friend Lt. Dave Santini (Richard Conte back for another go-round). As in the first film, the P.I. quickly finds himself in the middle of a complicated case in which a cadre of Miami's rich and dangerous are the chief suspects.

The lady of the title, the audience will come to learn, is Sandra Lomax. We first hear her name when Waldo Gronsky (Dan Blocker of TV's *Bonanza*), a brutish mountain of a man, hires Rome to find her. The scene in which he does so is one of the best in the picture, one of the vignettes that once again supersede the plot as the film's chief source of entertainment. Blocker brings a benevolent affability to the role. Gronsky is clearly a heavy, but a likable and witty one. His dual nature—the good bad guy—is evident from the start: He compliments Rome for his pluck and sense of humor even as he tosses him around the apartment. Sinatra gets off one of Rome's best witticisms in the midst of the beatdown, responding to Gronsky's polite but pointed question about whether he has any other smart-aleck comments to offer: "Yeah, what sells best, the frozen peas or the corn?"[218]

The follow-up to *Tony Rome*, *Lady in Cement* was the only sequel in Sinatra's film career.

As in the first film, Rome's efforts to solve the murder have him bouncing between low- and high-class establishments and suspects. His first lead takes him to a waterfront strip bar named Jilly's (after his longtime friend of the same name, Jilly Rizzo, who pops up in a cameo as a customer). There he meets Maria (Lainie Kazan), Sandra's fellow stripper and roommate. Rome and the dancer share some flirtatious banter, until Danny Yale (Frank Raiter), the club's gay manager, shows up to threaten Tony with a beating from his bouncer-boyfriend. A few more scenes follow with Yale and his protector-paramour, much of them intending to capture the free-wheeling humor Rome flashed in the first film. They miss the mark, because the jokes aren't weathered observations about life on the business side of a badge. They're mean-spirited and unfunny mockery of the characters' sexuality. It's wince-worthy to see and hear Sinatra toss out such swishy stereotypes for laughs, so much so that it's a relief—not just to the plot because it removes one suspect from the pool of possibilities—when Yale is killed.

On the non-seedy side of town, Rome encounters Kit Forrest (Raquel Welch), a party girl and heiress. Her first words to him as she climbs out of her posh pool are, "Well, shall I scream 'rape' now or wait and phone in a complaint?" Sinatra's at-rest acting is his best work in the Tony Rome films—and he has a quiet moment that adds important shading to the character as the conversation with Kit continues inside her house. She's still wearing the robe she put on over her bikini as she lounges on the couch, and Rome studies her as he asks her about Sandra Lomax. Sinatra conveys the sense that Rome is checking her out, but not lecherously. The softness and inquisitiveness in his eyes and voice illustrate that Rome isn't sizing her up to get her out of her robe, but to see what information for his case he might get out of her. The exchange also reinforces that for all his world-weary shoulder-shrugging, Tony has the nobility to keep rooting around until he gets to the bottom of a case. Not to get paid. But to get justice.

Welch is a weaker presence here than Jill St. John was in a similar role in the original. She does not hold her own with Sinatra as a performer, so her character can't hold her own with his. When it comes to light at the film's denouement that Kit, an alcoholic, believes she stabbed Sandra to death in a fight over a man who played the two against each other, it doesn't ring true. Welch so straddles the fence between damsel in distress and femme fatale that she offers insufficient weight to produce dramatic tension over which one Kit Forrest really is. Welch acquits herself far better in the lighter moments—such as when she and Rome drop into a floating crap game as he investigates on the other side of the tracks. Welch is charming playing Kit as the dice sharp who takes all the undertakers' money—and Sinatra embodies the hang-loose essence of Rome by spending the entire game nearly taking a nap atop a casket that is soon to be pressed into service.

Kit turns out not to be the killer. Neither does Gronsky. (Neither does Rome, who like in the original film gets framed momentarily and has to ditch the half-hearted pursuit of Santini.) But they both know the killer well: Kit fought for his affection with Sandra, and Gronsky got outfoxed by him in a mob deal with Sandra as an accomplice. The bad guy Rome's after turns out to be Paul Mungar (Steven Peck), the son of Al Mungar (Martin Gabel). Al is a former mobster looking to live life on the straight and narrow after getting out of the rackets. Gabel is excellent, his interplay with Sinatra a smorgasbord of two old pros playing old rivals who have grown disinterested in opposing each other any more in anything other than passive-aggressive banter. Gabel brings an avuncular charm to his scenes with Welch: Mungar offers her the one thing her multimillion-dollar inheritance *doesn't*, protection from the underbelly of life in Miami. That his own son tried to frame her for Sandra's murder after killing her himself surprises the old man as much as it surprises the audience. Paul is such a small fish in screen time before his reveal as the killer that he couldn't even have been considered a red herring if he had turned out innocent. As hard-to-swallow as he is as the mastermind trying to reestablish the Mungar family in the Miami underworld, it does make for some fast-talking fun at the climax as Rome pretends to toss him Gronsky as a patsy—without the big man's advance knowledge.

Lady in Cement director Gordon Douglas, helming his third Sinatra starrer in a row, doesn't get quite the canvas to paint on as he did in *Tony Rome*. While there is again ample location work throughout Miami, the sequel doesn't call for the same amount of action set-pieces. The most energetic one is not a fight but a flight: Rome running through streets, hotels and sand to stay beyond the reach of Santini and his men. What Douglas does allow in good measure here is ad-libbing by his star. When the script called on Sinatra, at 155 pounds, to help Blocker, at 290, stagger across a stretch of sand after Gronsky is injured, the smaller man tossed out the line, "Haven't you ever heard of diet food?"[219] An even more personal quip, at least from Sinatra's vantage point, comes after Rome questions Kit's relationship with Al Mungar. "Maybe you're the kind of dame that collects hoods," he says. "I used to know a broad who collected bullfighters." It's an unexpected bit of self-deprecation from the man who lost Ava Gardner to a couple of toreadors.

Lady in Cement was less successful than *Tony Rome*, so Fox's plans for a trilogy never materialized. (The third film was to be called *My Kind of Love*.[220]) Blocker was singled out by reviewers for delivering an image-erasing performance. "Blocker, that docile 'Hoss' of TV's *Bonanza*, puts on a one-man show," one reviewer wrote. "Shattering his TV image, Blocker takes on hoods and cops alike."[221] Another critic added: "There's no horsing around with Blocker, he's a violent, rough guy and he steals the picture."[222] Despite Blocker's theft, *The Los Angeles Times* felt he left enough of the picture around for Sinatra to shine:

> Sinatra projects this ex-cop-turned-private-shamus with a time-tested fictional blend of insouciance, cynicism, battered but surviving idealism, wise-crackery, courage, libido, thirst and all the more interesting hungers.[223]

Dirty Dingus Magee

Produced and Directed by Burt Kennedy
Screenplay: Tom Waldman, Frank Waldman and Joseph Heller, from the book by David Markson
Cinematography: Harry Stradling (Metrocolor)
Editor: William Gulick
Cast: Frank Sinatra, George Kennedy, Anne Jackson, Lois Nettleton, Jack Elam, Michele Carey, John Dehner, Henry Jones, Harry Carey, Jr., Paul Fix, Marya Thomas, Terry Wilson, Willis Bouchey, Don "Red" Barry, Tom Fadden, Mina Martinez, Sheila Foster, Irene Kelly, Diane Sayer, Jean London, Gayle Rogers, Timothy Blake, Lisa Todd, Maray Ayres, Carol Anderson, Mae Old Coyote, Lillian Hogan, Florence Real Bird, Ina Bad Bear, David Burke, Mike Wagner, Duncan Inches, Grady Sutton, Morgan Justin, David Cass
Released November 18, 1970
MGM
91 minutes

Sinatra was off movie screens for all of 1969, and his recording career had him struggling through attempts to be hip with versions of "Yesterday," "Mrs. Robinson," and "Both Sides Now"—all popular hits by youthful singers and songwriters including John Lennon-Paul McCartney, Paul Simon and Joni Mitchell. Ironically, the most noted song he recorded that year was "My Way," which became a staple. A flourishing storyteller ballad with lyrics written by Paul Anka, it also was a hit for Elvis Presley, who sang it at his 1973 "Aloha from Hawaii" concert. Not a success for Sinatra at first, the song's status grew over time. Along with its success in America, "My Way" topped the U.K. charts for a record 75 weeks. According to daughter Tina: "He didn't like ['My Way']. That song stuck and he couldn't get it off his shoe. He always thought that song was self-serving and self-indulgent."[224]

The year 1969 opened tragically for Sinatra when his father suffered a fatal heart attack on January 24. While Frank's connection with his mother is far more noted, he was deeply affected by his father's passing. It was also a year of deep introspection. The entire 1960s had been a challenge, with several ups and downs. With successes like *The Manchurian Candidate* and *Von Ryan's Express*, there was an attempt by Brad Dexter to have Sinatra expand his roles in movies and respond to the changing trends in filmmaking. He even gave Frank a copy of the Anthony Burgess novel *A Clockwork Orange* to discuss its cinematic potential, but Sinatra found it completely unacceptable. (It was famously made into a 1971 film by Stanley Kubrick.)

Sinatra felt much more comfortable with the detective dramas he settled into at decade's end. But after *Lady in Cement* performed disappointingly, he lost interest in movies almost completely. Then for some reason he was attracted to David Markson's comical Western novel *The Ballad of Dingus Magee*, about a 19-year-old petty criminal and the various offbeat characters surrounding him. The screenplay adaptation reworked the book so that the 54-year-old Sinatra could play the role.

While some have opined that the film version *Dirty Dingus Magee* is a quirky, ahead-of-its-time anti–Western, others claim it is just another one of Frank's comedy Westerns like *4 for Texas*. Our take on it: *Dirty Dingus Magee* is a mess, the worst movie of Sinatra's career. It is the quintessential example of a Sinatra movie in which he walks through his part with a bored indifference. His limited enthusiasm permeates the entire movie. Despite a veteran Western director in Burt Kennedy and a script by the Waldman brothers who had written such comedies as *The Party* (1968) and contributed to the Pink Panther series, *Dirty Dingus Magee* is a total misfire.

Hoke Birdsill (George Kennedy) complains to the mayor (Anne Jackson) of a lawless town that he was robbed by his old friend-foe Dingus Magee (Sinatra). Dingus robbed a stagecoach of its strongbox, which contained Hoke's loot. Ironically, it turns out that Dingus can't open the strongbox. The mayor also runs the bordello. The town has no sheriff, so she gives the job to Hoke. Dingus continues with his criminal activity with help from his Indian companion (Michele Carey). Meanwhile, Hoke helps the mayor-madam keep soldiers from going to Little Big Horn by riling up the Indians there; Belle doesn't want to lose the soldiers' business. Dingus ends up in trouble with the Indians due to his sexually charged female friend, as well as Sheriff Hoke, who wants his loot back.

Sinatra and Michele Carey wasted their time in *Dirty Dingus Magee*.

The characters essayed by Sinatra and Kennedy do not have as amusing a rapport as Sinatra had with, say, Dean Martin. This movie's characters frustratingly fluctuate between being rivals and partners, with each taking turns being on either side of the law. And while the cast is rounded out with old cowboy movie veterans (including Jack Elam and Don "Red" Barry), this dollop of Western film authenticity doesn't help at all. Critic Roger Ebert blamed Sinatra for its failure:

Dirty Dingus Magee (1970)

> *Dirty Dingus Magee* is supposed to be a comedy, and it was directed by Burt Kennedy, who is supposed to be a director of Western comedies, but its failure is just about complete. I lean toward blaming Frank Sinatra, who in recent years has become notorious for not really caring about his movies. If a shot doesn't work, he doesn't like to try it again; he might be late getting back to Vegas. What's more, the ideal Sinatra role requires him to be in no more than a fourth of the scenes, getting him lots of loot and top billing while his supporting cast does the work.[225]

Ebert wasn't the only critic disappointed with *Dirty Dingus Magee,* and the moviegoing audience generally agreed. Surprisingly, the critic for *Variety* was quite pleased:

> *Dirty Dingus Magee* emerges as a good period Western comedy, covering the spectrum from satire through double entendre to low slapstick.... Sinatra plays an amiable roustabout, always eager but never quite able to satisfy the unending passions of Indian maiden Michele Carey. ...The gag subplots move along at a good pace.[226]

While the trade paper's reaction was in the minority, it does indicate that the film was well-received in some quarters.

Dirty Dingus Magee gives substantial roles to female characters, something that some of Sinatra's earlier movies failed to do. It is particularly gratifying that Anne Jackson plays the mayor. The downside is that basically all of the female characters' motivations and actions revolve around seeking the male characters' attentions.

For a while, it looked like *Dirty Dingus Magee* would conclude Sinatra's movie career. After proving himself early on as a good actor with ability and turning in performances that should define his screen career as an actor, his filmography almost ended with what is probably his worst movie.

The year 1970 was another challenging one for Sinatra. It included a dust-up at a Las Vegas casino that resulted in his having to testify regarding alleged mob ties in New Jersey, and concluded with his decision to retire from show business, which he publicly announced in March 1971. The one bright spot in 1970 was his daughter Nancy's December marriage to Hugh Lambert; a union that produced two daughters. The two remained married until Hugh's passing in 1985.

Fortunately, Frank Sinatra would only be "retired" for two years. *Dirty Dingus Magee* was not his final film. And while he wouldn't make another theatrical movie for ten years, remaining off theater screens for all of the 1970s, Sinatra's actual final film, *The First Deadly Sin,* might be his best since *Von Ryan's Express.*

Sinatra in the '70s

The disappointment of *Dirty Dingus Magee* was Sinatra's motion picture nadir of the decade. His recording career was doing no better. March's release of the concept album "Watertown" was the least successful major release of his career, the only album not to chart in the top 100 of the Billboard *200*. The album, written and co-produced by Bob Gaudio of the Four Seasons, is a collection of soliloquies—Sinatra called them "saloon songs" throughout his career—in which the narrator tells of his personal tragedies. The heartache is the result of his wife running away from their small-town life in Watertown, New York, for the big city, leaving him to raise their two sons alone. It's the only album Sinatra ever voiced over pre-recorded orchestral tracks, and the intimacy required of the personal emotions the songs are intended to convey suffers for it. It would be the last time Sinatra cut an album in this fashion.

The year ended on an expectant note: Sinatra signed on to play the title role in *Dirty Harry*, yet another detective, but this one with a twist keyed to its time. Warner Brothers, in announcing the deal, described the "contemporary suspense drama" as pitting the star's "violent and brutalized police detective" against "a psychopathic mass-murderer."[227] As pre-production ramped up, the title was changed to *Dead Right* so Sinatra wouldn't appear in two *Dirty*-titled films back to back. Alas, bringing Harry Callahan to life on the big screen was not to be for Sinatra. He dropped out of the film in November because the role required too much physical action for him (his right hand was healing from surgery to correct Dupuytren's contracture, a shortening of the muscular tissue in the palm and fingers[228]). The film got its original name back and made Clint Eastwood a superstar.

A few months later, Sinatra announced he was stepping away from more than just Harry Callahan's .44 Magnum. On March 24, 1971, he placed an item in the New York *Daily News* that he was retiring from show business at age 55:

> I wish to announce, effective immediately, my retirement from the entertainment world and public life. For over three decades I have had the great and good fortune to enjoy a rich, rewarding, and deeply satisfying career as an entertainer and public figure. Through the years people have been wonderfully warm and generous in their acceptance of my efforts.
>
> My work has taken me to almost every corner of the world and privileged me to learn by direct experience how alike all people really are—the common bonds that tie all men and women of whatever color, creed, religion, age, or

social status to one another; the things mankind has in common that the language of music, perhaps more than any other, communicates and evokes.

It has been a fruitful, busy, uptight, loose, sometimes boisterous, occasionally sad, but always exciting three decades. There has been little time for reflection, reading, self-explanation, and that need every man has for a fallow period, a long pause in which to seek better understanding of the vast transforming changes now taking place everywhere in the world. This seems a proper time to take that breather.[229]

Three weeks later, Sinatra accepted the Jean Hersholt Humanitarian Award at the 43rd Academy Awards. Presenter Gregory Peck heralded him for "keeping his humanitarianism out of the public view" before listing his efforts to raise money and build facilities to help ill and needy children across the globe. In accepting the Oscar, Sinatra pointed out the extra time he had as "what is known in the vernacular as a retired man" had led him to ponder "why you have to get famous to get an award for helping others." He added a poignant postscript: "If your name is John Doe, what you get is tired." Talking to the press after the ceremony, he swatted away suggestions he might un-retire, then laid out his immediate plans: "I want to take a whole year and just do nothing. After that, I'm going to stay in Palm Springs and try to write a little bit. Maybe a book on music."[230]

Before he could hunker down in the desert, though, there was the matter of saying a proper performance goodbye. He had already been booked to appear at a benefit concert for the Motion Picture and Television Relief Fund arranged by Peck, so when the June 13, 1971, date rolled around, his appearance was billed as his musical farewell. Sinatra took the stage waving a finger at the audience and scolding them, "Don't you cry," then performed seven songs. He began at the beginning, his Harry James era hit "All or Nothing at All"; got a standing ovation with his usual show-closer "My Way," and ended the set with "Angel Eyes." The crowd, some of whom had spent $5000 a ticket to be there, watched him miming the barroom drunk he always played while performing the song as he sauntered off stage crooning the final line: "'Scuse me while I disappear."[231]

It would be a brief disappearing act. Sinatra unretired in 1973, returning to the album charts with "Ol' Blue Eyes Is Back," a rather treacly album that nonetheless nestled just outside the Billboard Top 10 en route to gold-record status. A live concert collection ("The Main Event") and TV special (also titled *Ol' Blue Eyes Is Back*) quickly followed—the latter featuring a splendid song-and-dance routine in which old friends Sinatra and Gene Kelly bemoaned the limitations brought on by the aging process while reliving their onscreen days as they crooned "We Can't Do That Anymore." The next year brought box office success for *That's Entertainment!*, which not only spotlighted the days when Sinatra and Kelly could do that just fine, but also got Sinatra some contemporary camera time as one of the film's roster of hosts.

Sinatra did not appear in another film until 1977. When he did, it was for the small screen: *Contract on Cherry Street*. He owned the rights to the novel it was based on, because it was one of his mother Dolly's favorites, and she urged him to make the movie someday.[232] "Someday" came when Dolly Sinatra died in a private plane crash while flying from her home near his in Palm Springs to Las Vegas. Sinatra's production company brought on two-time Oscar-winning scribe Edward Anhalt (*Panic in the Streets*, 1950, and *Becket*, 1964) to write the teleplay; he produced a three-hour adaptation that NBC spread out over its entire primetime on November 19. Sinatra stars as Detective Inspector Frank Hovannes, the boots-on-the-ground head of New York's elite Organized Crime Unit. He's a good cop at a bad time: Crime is rampant in the city (the opening credits do a nice job of setting the sordid scene), and the department brass are more interested in looking like they're doing something about it than actually doing something about it. Frustration mounts for Hovannes and his team, especially his right-hand man and best friend Ernie Weinberg (an excellent Martin Balsam), who feel increasingly impotent. When Weinberg is killed during a by-the-book raid that ends up with no prime suspects apprehended, Hovannes throws the book away. He unloads a shotgun into his friend's killer, then launches an ambush on one of two mob factions they're after, hoping suspicion falls on the other faction and the criminals rid the city of each other.

Sinatra returned to acting after a seven-year absence in the made-for-TV film *Contract on Cherry Street*, based on a favorite novel of his mother's.

Contract on Cherry Street is overlong (two hours would have sufficed) and its middle section, where the gang members try to figure out who carried out the contract, keeps Sinatra off-screen for a third of the film. But it offers an honest, unflinching look at the changing nature of policing in the '70s, as the cops adopted the tactics of robbers to create a reasonable facsimile of justice. Sinatra may have never gotten to play Dirty Harry, but he gets to play by Dirty Harry's rules here. He delivers a solid if not particularly noteworthy performance as an honest cop pushed beyond his breaking point. How Hovannes deals with the fallout of his actions offers Sinatra some nice opportunities to play a man wrestling with internal conflicts—spotlighting the resignation and weariness he still conveys with a glance, a nod, a wave of his hand. Hovannes' more light-hearted moments are Sinatra's best: swapping war stories with Weinberg in their favorite bar, smirking and barely holding in a laugh when a punk 30 years his junior tries to insult and intimidate him. The TV movie's ratings were solid and its reviews mixed. One critic wrote, "[I]t bristles with excitement and proves that Sinatra the actor is as good or better than Sinatra the singer."[233]

Sinatra the actor would have one more chance to prove his talents. *The First Deadly Sin* was to be his motion-picture starring role swan song, and it would remind audiences how he could command the screen in quiet ways.

The First Deadly Sin

Directed by Brian G. Hutton
Screenplay: Mann Rubin, from the novel by Lawrence Sanders
Producers: George Pappas and Mark Shanker
Cinematography: Jack Priestly (Color)
Editor: Eric Albertson
Cast: Frank Sinatra, Faye Dunaway, David Dukes, George Coe, Brenda Vaccaro, Martin Gabel, Anthony Zerbe, James Whitmore, Joe Spinell, Anna Navarro, Jeffrey DeMunn, John Devaney, Robert Weil, Hugh Hurd, Jon DeVries, Eddie Jones, Victor Arnold, Frank Bongiorno, Reuben Green, Tom Signorelli, Richard Backus, Fredrick Rolf, Carol Gustafson, Michael Ingrahm, Bill Couch, Larry Loonin, Denise Lute, Robert Cendello, Sherman Jones, Nick Cairis, Bruce McLane, Scott Palmer, David Vaszuez, Ramon Franco, Leila Danette, Rosalyin Braverman, Ramona Brooks, Sophia Sopher, Bill Vitale, Nan Whitehead, Chico Kasindir, Paul Hunt, Dadi Pinero, Riki Colon, Nick DeMarinis, Henry Bradley, Jay Hargroce, Don Jay, James Hayden, Deborah Howell, Ludea Melendez, Iliana Barsann, Pearl Franklin, Ellen Whyte, Theta Tucker, David Gideon, Floyd Katske, Venessa Pesce, Vivian Oswald, Gloria Sauve, Robert Dadah, Tony Rugnetta, Dennis O'Neill, Bruce Willis

Released October 3, 1980
Artanis Productions and Cinema VII for Filmways Pictures
112 minutes

Producer Elliott Kastner wanted Sinatra as his leading man in the second film he ever produced, 1966's *Harper*. In 1980, he finally got his man. *The First Deadly Sin* was nowhere near the same kind of movie; *Harper* called for a rakish title character with insouciant charm and vitality. Sinatra during his Tony Rome years could have pulled it off, but Paul Newman, who took the role after Sinatra passed, was sublimely cast. Similarly, 65-year-old Sinatra was the pitch-perfect choice to play New York City police detective Edward X. Delaney, a cop weeks from retirement. Delaney has never been his squad's superstar, never a favorite of or a thorn in the side of his superiors. Nothing about him is flashy, nothing is sharp or particularly witty. He's what appears to be a solid cop in an ever-more-squalid city, a man his colleagues not only expect, but encourage to slide into retirement without expending too much energy or ingenuity. There are just a couple of complicating circumstances. The murder everyone wants him to go through the motions investigating increasingly looks to be the work of a serial killer, and the mysterious illness his wife is battling may steal her away just as he's ready to really settle down and spend the rest of his life with her.

The First Deadly Sin, adapted from the novel by Lawrence Sanders and altered significantly in the process, affords Sinatra an opportunity at the end of his film career that he was denied at its beginning and resisted in its middle: to act his age. His early roles, especially those opposite Gene Kelly, required him to play an overgrown adolescent—shy and uncertain around women he could never muster the maturity to regard with romantic interest. While that was a persona thrust on him by the studios, Sinatra himself had, as he aged, been gun-shy about completely embracing his advancing years. Arrested adolescence was the order of the day in much of his 1960s output. That's when he began to take acting more cavalierly, as less an opportunity to breathe life into a three-dimensional character and more of an opportunity to put on a show with his pals. But here, as Delaney, Sinatra allows himself to embody, and convey, the physicality and the reserve of a man halfway through his seventh decade. Delaney is not world-weary in the glib, above-it-all sense that Tony Rome was. He's just weary. It's the quietest performance of Sinatra's career—in emotion and mannerism alike.

It is fitting, given how many roles he and Marlon Brando fought over throughout their careers, that Sinatra got the part only after his *Guys and Dolls* co-star turned it down—and the $4 million salary that came with it. Brando was about to go into a nearly decade-long sabbatical from films, and Sinatra was ending his own. `Speculation ran rampant during pre-production that rock star David Bowie was in line for the role of the serial killer, but he demurred.[234] Bowie's reps said it was because he didn't like the script. Kastner cried foul, saying the role was never offered to Bowie, and adding, "Bowie seems to be making a career out of publicizing this."[235] Even Johnny Carson's *Tonight Show* sidekick Ed McMahon was said to be in line for "a role as Frank Sinatra's sidekick"—an odd rumor since Delaney doesn't *have* a sidekick.[236]

The First Deadly Sin opens with the first example of what turns out to be director Brian G. Hutton's signature approach to action: intercutting between two disparate scenes. The first here is a murder in which a man is attacked, seemingly at random, as he walks near a church. The assailant delivers what looks to be a hammer blow to his victim's head before fleeing. That scene is juxtaposed with a surgery inside a hospital operating room. All we know immediately is that both scenes are bloody; we come to learn both also involve Delaney. He's the cop assigned to the murder case, and the surgery is being performed on his wife, whose kidney is removed in an attempt to rid her body of the infection she's battling after a bout with kidney stones. Both scenes play out independently, setting the film's rhythm of Delaney engaging in detective work, then visiting his wife in the hospital. He spends the rest of the film chasing clues to solve the mysteries behind both bloody scenes.

At the murder site, Delaney learns from the coroner (a typically and effectively flinty James Whitmore) that the victim's wound was inflicted with a round object. Before Delaney can do much thinking about that information, he is contacted by the precinct with notice of his wife's surgery. He rushes away from the scene to check on her. He is refused access by her doctor because she's still in recovery, so he goes to the office to continue investigating the murder. While Delaney's motivation may be to simply take his mind off his wife's condition, the way Sinatra plays the scene of him alone at his desk going through the victim's wallet for clues is powerful in its subtlety and nuance. Delaney gingerly removes and examines each item in such a way as to make clear he truly cares—not just about solving the case, but that a man is dead and has left loved ones behind. Hutton adds a minimalist exclamation point with the next scene, in which Delaney walks slowly down the now-empty street in front of the church. Sinatra's physicality has never been more restrained. His pace is slow, purposely so. Viewers can see in his expressionless face that Delaney does not relish getting to his destination: the victim's chalk outline.

When Delaney finally sees his wife the next day, Sinatra is gentler and

Sinatra stars opposite Faye Dunaway in the underrated *The First Deadly Sin*.

more tender than he's ever been on screen. Faye Dunaway, as wife Barbara, is wasted in the role. This is in large part because she is usually wasted—i.e., under sedation—in the role. Despite the fact that she spends the entire picture in a hospital bed in either medical coverings or nightgowns partially obscured by sheets, the opening credits see fit to announce: "Ms. Dunaway's Costumes by Theoni V. Aldridge." Yet Sinatra rises above the weak situations screenwriter Mann Rubin gives him and his fellow Oscar winner Dunaway. Whether he is softly calling her "Kiddo" almost every time he addresses her or buying and reading to her from a favorite childhood book she brings up in one of her near-hallucinogenic states, Sinatra plays Delaney as trying to reassure himself his wife will be okay as much as he's trying to reassure *her* of that fact.

Unfortunately, from a narrative standpoint, each subsequent stop at the hospital only serves to thwart the momentum that builds during the investigation scenes. More satisfying, and additionally indicative of the full array of acting prowess Sinatra brings to the role, is a scene he plays silently after Delaney's follow-up visit to the coroner. When he returns to his and Barbara's empty apartment and goes through the mail, every move is compact, careful, slow. Sinatra then walks through the place like he worked the stage while performing a saloon song: deliberately but with no particular destination in mind. Buying time. The pause becomes his most arresting acting move, meaning everything and nothing depending on the viewer. Delaney finally enters the bedroom—whether it's by happenstance or intent is unclear. He sits for a few beats, then briefly rubs his forehead before turning in for the night because he has determined, without a word or a single outsized move, that there is no better alternative.

From this moment on, the investigation plot builds satisfyingly. The first layer folded in has Delaney enlisting the aid of the arms and armaments curator at the Metropolitan Museum of Art to help him identify what weapon could have left a circular hole in the victim's skull. Martin Gabel is a delight as the curator, playing him as a lonely, bored academic thrilled at the chance to do more than talk about weapons used to kill in antiquity. His citywide search for the weapon—which turns out to be a small ice axe used in climbing—gives the movie a much-needed comic-relief valve.

The curator's find sheds light on more than one murder, because Delaney does some citywide searching of his own—through unsolved murder records with similar m.o.s and wounds to the victim. He realizes he's hunting a serial killer—and is further assisted by the curator and the wife of the first victim (Brenda Vaccaro) to narrow the suspect pool through the client records of the sporting goods shop where the exact model of ice axe was found. Delaney does some more leg work that leads him to Daniel Blank (a suitably creepy David Dukes), who the audience already knows to be the killer.

Delaney does some deft detective work—nothing showy, but effective. He bribes the doorman at Blank's swanky apartment building to get a look inside—and discovers the murder weapon hidden pretty much in plain sight. But rather than celebrating, he emotionlessly leaves it where he found it. He closes in on Blank in another of Hutton's quick-cut connection scenes: Delaney and Blank getting ready for their nights out—the cop to catch the killer, the killer to claim another victim. The scene ends in a rush of adrenaline, as the two men see each other across an empty street. Blank begins to walk toward Delaney—who doesn't flinch. Again, the pause is a powerful, even chilling move for Sinatra. Blank spooks and runs back to his apartment, where he has a breakdown. Delaney sneaks in and confronts him, only to have Blank snap out of it and brag about his friends in high places getting him off. Delaney listens passively, saying nothing—once again Sinatra acting by not reacting. The cop takes aim and assassinates the killer, a conclusion popular during the crime dramas of the time: the law taking the law into its own hands.

All that is left to wrap up is the fate of Barbara. Fresh from turning in his retirement papers, Delaney returns to her hospital room to read to her. In mid-sentence, she dies. It's a beautiful scene. Shot by Hutton with

Sinatra (left) and David Dukes share a laugh on the set of *The First Deadly Sin*.

Sinatra at the center of the frame and Dunaway at its front edge, it doesn't fade to black until Delaney reads a few more sentences. Sinatra cries—not aggressively, but with slight sniffles and quavering voice. A reaction true to the quietness of his portrayal from the opening scene.

The film took some hits from critics for its deviations from Sanders' novel—including eliminating Blank's backstory that helps explain his actions—but Sinatra earned significant praise for his work. Gene Siskel, after celebrating that *Dirty Dingus Magee* would no longer be Sinatra's last film, said that the star "remains as glaringly charismatic as ever. Few actors are as compelling as Sinatra in scenes where all he does is silently stare out of a hospital or walk around in an empty apartment."[237]

Author Tom Santopietro placed Sinatra's performance in its deserved context as the coda to his movie career.

The First Deadly Sin (1980)

When it is mentioned at all, [*The First Deadly Sin*] it is referred to simply as Sinatra's last starring role in a motion picture. It may be his last starring role, but it is also a helluva good performance, one that puts to use all the craft he had absorbed in his forty years in Hollywood. As a valedictory performance, it's one of the all-time greats.[238]

Sinatra After the Movies

The First Deadly Sin concluded Sinatra's screen career proper, but it was not his last theatrical movie appearance, nor was it his final acting role. In 1984, Sinatra did a cameo as himself in *Cannonball Run II,* director and ex-stuntman Hal Needham's sequel to his wildly popular feature *The Cannonball Run* (1981). *Cannonball Run II* starred Burt Reynolds and also featured Rat Packers Dean Martin and Sammy Davis, Jr., plus Shirley MacLaine. This connection was the likely reason why Sinatra agreed to the cameo. According to Needham, Frank showed up very early to shoot his two brief sequences and left the set before the other actors showed up. Thus, he never appears on screen with the other actors; Frank's double, with his back to the camera, did. It was Sinatra's final appearance in a theatrical movie.

Sinatra's final acting role was on television's *Magnum P.I.* Sinatra plays a retired detective whose granddaughter is murdered. He goes after them with the help of Magnum (Tom Selleck). Sinatra, acting in a role for the first time in about seven years, really threw himself into his performance, improvising during some scenes, and exhibiting full commitment to the project. Once again playing a detective, he is truly in his element and offers an impressive performance. Sinatra told *TV Guide* about the character he plays: "I believe he's really unhappy because he's retired. He hasn't got the job any more. He was put out to pasture. I understand that phase."[1]

Sinatra's presence resulted in the episode being the most watched in the show's history, and this led to the series being renewed for another season. Selleck, who thought the current season would be the last, had committed to three movies, so he had to work on the series in between films. Sinatra enjoyed the *Magnum P.I.* experience so much, he agreed to return during the final season in the same role. Sadly, conflicting schedules didn't allow that to happen. About Selleck, he stated: "We could do a wonderful romantic comedy. We could be here or in New York or Monte Carlo, and the two of us would go out looking for girls together. I haven't had so much fun since *Eternity*."[2]

Two more cameo appearances, playing himself, followed. This included a 1989 cameo on TV's *Who's the Boss*, which starred his friend Tony Danza, and a 1993 cameo for friend Don Rickles' failed sitcom *Daddy Dearest*. These were his final TV series appearances.

Beset by a myriad of health problems as the 1990s continued, Sinatra suffered a heart attack in 1997. After that, he made no more public appearances. His wife Barbara, whom he married in 1976, was by his side when he died on May 14, 1998. His last words were reportedly, "I'm losing." Frank Sinatra was eulogized in papers throughout the world, most calling him the greatest American singer of the 20th century, indicating his only rivals were Bing Crosby and Elvis Presley. The lights of Las Vegas dimmed in his honor. The casinos went silent for one minute.

Sinatra's funeral was held six days after his death at the Church of the Good Shepherd in Beverly Hills. It was attended by many show biz luminaries among its nearly 700 mourners, including Joey Bishop, the last living member of the Rat Pack, ex-wives Mia Farrow and Nancy, Don Rickles, Nancy Reagan, Jack Nicholson, Gregory Peck, Kirk Douglas, Sidney Poitier, Sophia Loren and fellow singers Paul Anka, Vic Damone and Tony Bennett. Bennett and Frank Sinatra, Jr., gave eulogies, and Sidney Poitier read from the Bible. On Sinatra's gravestone, it states: "The Best Is Yet to Come."

Because Sinatra's status as an icon comes from his magnificent contribution to popular music, his work in movies has frequently been overlooked. As this text has indicated, Sinatra was a naturally talented actor with an sense of timing that sustained him over many films and netted him an Oscar and other awards. His best work in movies will live as long as his finest recordings.

Chapter Notes

Frank Sinatra Before the Movies

1. Lahr, John. *Show and Tell: New Yorker Profiles.* Berkeley: University of California Press, 2000.

The Films

1. As quoted in Kelly, Kitty. *His Way: The Unauthorized Biography of Frank Sinatra.* New York: Bantam Books, 1986.
2. Crowther, Bosley. "THE SCREEN: Lower and Lower." *New York Times.* January 22, 1944.
3. Wilson, Earl. *Sinatra: An Unauthorized Biography.* New York: Macmillan, 1976.
4. "'Step Lively' review." *Tampa Bay Times.* November 13, 1944.
5. Paredes, Nora. "Pictures Stink! Sinatra Says He's Quitting Films." Syndicated: United Press Syndicate. September 9, 1944.
6. "Anchors Aweigh" review. *Los Angeles Times.* August 1, 1945.
7. Reviews as found in *The Films of Frank Sinatra.* New York: Citadel, 1971.
8. "Ruark Is Puzzled Over Sinatra's Pals in Havana." Syndicated: Scripps-Howard. February 20, 1947.
9. "Sinatra Denies He's Lucky's Pal." *Pittsburgh Press.* February 23, 1947.
10. Johnson, Erskine. "In Hollywood." Syndicated: Newspaper Enterprise Association. May 4, 1948.
11. "'The Miracle of the Bells' review." *Rochester Democrat and Chronicle.* May 7, 1948.
12. Cameron, Kate. "Kissing Bandit review." *New York Daily News.* November 19, 1948.
13. Kathryn Grayson was originally slated for the role.
14. Kelly, Kitty. *His Way: The Unauthorized Biography of Frank Sinatra.* New York: Bantam Books, 1986.
15. Not the song that Sinatra would popularize in the 1980s, which is actually titled "(Theme from) New York, New York."
16. "'On the Town' review." *Vancouver Sun.* December 31, 1949.
17. "Sinatra in New Dramatic Role." *Valley Times.* April 24, 1954.
18. "Russell-Sinatra-Marx Film at N.Y. Paramount." *Brooklyn Daily Eagle.* December 26, 1951.
19. "Star Trio on Stanley." *Pittsburgh Sun-Telegraph.* December 27, 1951.
20. Parsons, Louella. "Sinatra Sings for New U.I. Musical." *Los Angeles Times.* February 18, 1951.
21. Winters, Shelley. *Shelley, Sometimes Known as Shirley.* New York: Ballantine, 1981.
22. Schneeberger, Gary. Interview with the author. 1991.
23. Santopietro, Tom. *Sinatra in Hollywood.* New York: St. Martin's Press, 2008.
24. Thomas, Bob. "Hollywood Highlights." Syndicated: Associated Press. October 23, 1952.
25. Sinatra, Nancy. *Frank Sinatra, My Father.* New York: Doubleday, 1985.
26. Borgnine, Ernest. *Ernie: The Autobiography.* New York: Citadel, 2008.
27. Brogdon, William. "From Here to Eternity." *Variety.* July 29, 1953.

28. McCarten, John. "The Current Cinema." *New Yorker.* August 8, 1953.
29. "'Young at Heart' Rated Appealing." *Spokane Chronicle.* January 1, 1955.
30. Locklair, Winston. "Sinatra and Doris Day Playing in New Movie." *Charlotte Observer.* December 28, 1954.
31. Amador, Victoria. *Olivia de Havilland: Lady Triumphant.* Lexington: University Press of Kentucky, 2019.
32. Thomas, Bob. "'Not Mitchum!' Cry Critics as Producer Casts Movie." *Los Angeles Times.* October 4, 1954.
33. Thomas, Bob. "Sinatra in New Dramatic Roles." *Valley Times.* April 24, 1954.
34. Mosby, Aline. "Singer in Serious Film Role." *Press Democrat.* April 23, 1954.
35. "Goldwyn Buys 'Guys, Dolls,' for a Million." *Times.* March 5, 1954.
36. Nixon, Rob. "Guys and Dolls." TCM.com.
37. Wilson, Earl. "The Midnight Earl." *New York Post.* June 2, 1955.
38. Kilgallen, Dorothy. "The Voice of Broadway." Syndicated: Hearst. October 11, 1955.
39. Schneeberger, Gary. "Jean Simmons Interview: Hollywood Hotline." *Journal Times.* May 11, 1990.
40. O'Haire, Patricia. "A Star Over Detroit." *New York Daily News.* August 20, 1976.
41. "Old Vic Plans 'Guys and Dolls'— Sir Larry as Nathan Detroit." Syndicated: Associated Press, June 11, 1970.
42. "Frank Sinatra in 'Guys and Dolls' Movie Version." Syndicated: *New York Herald Tribune* News Service. September 22, 1954.
43. Beck, Meyer. "Sinatra Heads for New Glory." Syndicated: *New York Herald Tribune* News Service. June 19, 1955.
44. Bacon, James. "Goldwyn Plunges Deep into Off-Beat Musical." Syndicated: Associated Press, May 25, 1955.
45. *Ibid.*
46. Brando, Marlon. *Songs My Mother Taught Me.* New York: Random House, 1994.
47. Adams, Marjory. "Brando Best Since Barrymore, Says Producer Goldwyn." *Boston Globe*, November 13, 1955.
48. Ross, Don. "Sinatra's on Top of the World Again." *New York Herald Tribune* News Service. November 5, 1955.
49. "'Guys and Dolls' review." *Variety.* November 3, 1955.
50. "'Guys and Dolls' review." *Motion Picture Herald.* November 5, 1955.
51. "'Guys and Dolls' review." *Labor's Daily.* November 23, 1955.
52. Johnson, Erskine. "Johnson in Hollywood." Syndicated: Newspaper Enterprise Association. November 18, 1955.
53. Sinatra, Frank. "New York." Rhino ASIN: B002L2ALEU. 2009. Compact disc.
54. Marx, Arthur. *Everybody Loves Somebody Sometime—Especially Himself.* New York: Hawthorn, 1974.
55. Parsons, Louella. "Tender Trap Bought For Debbie." Syndicated: Hearst. January 31, 1955.
56. Hopper, Hedda. "Sinatra's Next For Metro Is Tender Trap." *Los Angeles Times.* April 13, 1955.
57. *Ibid.*
58. Guilfoil, Kelsey. "Novel of Damned Puts Chicagoan in First Rank." *Chicago Tribune.* September 11, 1949.
59. Parsons, Louella. "Louella Parsons in Hollywood." Syndicated: Hearst. November 12, 1949.
60. Lee, Charles. "Spotlight on Books." *News-Journal.* November 27, 1950.
61. Parsons, Louella. "Louella Parsons in Hollywood." Syndicated: Hearst. March 15, 1950.
62. Fujiwara, Chris. *The World and Its Double: The Life and Work of Otto Preminger.* New York: Macmillan, 2009.
63. Parsons, Louella. "Louella Parsons on Hollywood." Syndicated: Hearst. March 25, 1955.
64. Schallert, Edwin. "Preminger Sets 'Golden Arm' Deal with Sinatra." *Los Angeles Times.* May 3, 1955.
65. Wilson, Earl. "On the Town." Syndicated: June 1, 1975.
66. Scheuer, Phillip K. "Frank Sinatra Wants to Be His Own Boss So He's Adding Producer Headaches." *Los Angeles Times.* November 6, 1955.
67. Asher, Colin. *Never a Lovely So Real: The Life and Work of Nelson Algren.* New York: W.W. Norton, 2019.
68. Curran, Elmer L. "Hollywood News." *News Leader.* December 15, 1955.
69. Bacon, James. "Frank Sinatra Plays, Works Hard." Syndicated: Associated Press. January 17, 1961.
70. Cronin, Steve. "Sitting on Top of the World." *Modern Screen.* February 1956.

71. Cantarini, Martha Crawford, and Chrystopher J. Spicer. *Fall Girl: My Life as a Western Stunt Double*. Jefferson, NC: McFarland, 2010.
72. Bacon, Syndicated: Associated Press.
73. Pearson, Drew. "Washington Merry-Go-Round." Syndicated: U.S. News Syndicate. November 11, 1955.
74. "Otto the Bold." *Independent Film Journal*. March 2, 1959.
75. Thomas, Bob. "Movie on Drugs Causing Battle." Syndicated: Associated Press. September 22, 1955.
76. "UA Quits MPAA After Code Seal Denied to Arm." *Independent Film Journal*. December 10, 1955.
77. Powers, Dorothy R. "Skillful Acting by Sinatra Gives Power to Dope Drama." *Spokesman-Review*. February 8, 1956.
78. Parsons, Louella. "Louella Parsons on Hollywood." Syndicated: Hearst. December 30, 1955.
79. Scheuer, Philip K. "Sordid Film on Drugs." *Los Angeles Times*. December 28, 1955.
80. Parsons, Louella. "Louella Parsons on Hollywood." Syndicated: Hearst. November 23, 1955.
81. Parsons, Louella. "Louella Parsons in Hollywood." Syndicated: Hearst. February 1956.
82. Sperber, A.M., and Eric Lax. *Bogart*. New York: William Morrow, 1997.
83. "'High Society' review." *Time* magazine. August 6, 1956.
84. Sinatra Interview. *Western World*. October 27, 1957.
85. "Dateline Hollywood." Syndicated: INS News Service. October 30, 1957.
86. "Dick Kleiner," Syndicated: January 12, 1956.
87. "Sinatra and Sammy Davis Making Film." *Los Angeles Times*. December 31, 1955.
88. http://guidetomusicaltheatre.com/shows_j/jazztrain.html
89. Johnson, Erskine. "He Says He's Never Been Away." Syndicated: Newspaper Enterprise Association. January 19, 1956.
90. No relation to Martha Stewart, the more contemporary businesswoman.
91. Nollen, Scott Allen. "'Pal Joey': The Quintessential Sinatra Film Musical." Liner notes to *Frank Sinatra in Hollywood (1940–1964)*. Reprise/Warner Bros. ASIN: B000066BN9. 2002. Compact discs.

92. Barlow, Robert. "Pittsburgh's Gene Kelly Musical Comedy Sensation." *Pittsburgh Post-Gazette*. January 7, 1941.
93. Price, Edgar. "Review of 'Pal Joey.'" *Brooklyn Citizen*. December 26, 1940.
94. Nollen, "Pal Joey."
95. Graham, Sheila. "In Hollywood." Syndicated: North American Newspaper Alliance. February 13, 1941.
96. Kilgallen, Dorothy. "Voice of Broadway." Syndicated: Hearst. May 28, 1949.
97. Thomas, Bob. "Hollywood Highlights." Syndicated: Associated Press. February 26, 1953.
98. Bacon, James. "More Women Than Men Come to See Mae." Syndicated: Associated Press. December 6, 1954.
99. Schallert, Edwin. "Kazan Likely to Direct 'Pal Joey' and 'Picnic'; Dramatist's Wife Signs." *Los Angeles Times*. September 20, 1954.
100. Lyons, Leonard. "Kirk Gets Thanks, Frankie Gets Job." Syndicated: McKnaught. May 1, 1956.
101. Nollen, "Pal Joey."
102. Hopper, Hedda. "Hollywood by Hedda Hopper." Syndicated: April 14, 1956.
103. Hopper, Hedda. "Hollywood by Hedda Hopper." Syndicated: June 10, 1956.
104. Thomas, Bob. "Sinatra Starts 'Pal Joey,' Lewis Story; No More TV." Syndicated: Associated Press. October 24, 1956.
105. Nollen, "Pal Joey."
106. "Job Open for Kosher Loving Dog." Syndicated: Associated Press. February 19, 1957.
107. "Spectacular Comeback by an Unkosher Dog." Syndicated: Associated Press. March 12, 1957.
108. "35 Changes." *The Evening St.*
109. Schallert, Edwin. "'Pal Joey' Sophisticated and Ingenious Musical." *Los Angeles Times*. October 26, 1957.
110. "Review of 'Pal Joey.'" *New York Times*. October 28, 1957.
111. Lindeman, Edith. "'Pal Joey' Movie Version Retains Much Bite, Wit." *Times-Dispatch*. December 23, 1957.
112. "'Pal Joey' Called Sinatra's Finest." *Abilene Reporter-News*. December 22, 1957.
113. Maltin, Leonard. Preface. Liner notes to *Frank Sinatra in Hollywood (1940–1964)*. Reprise/Warner Bros. ASIN: B000066BN9. 2002. Compact discs.

114. "Sinatra Firm to Make 'Kings Go Forth' Film." *Los Angeles Times*. February 3, 1957.
115. "Kings and Producer Wait to Go Forth." *Los Angeles Times*. October 13, 1957.
116. Thomas, Bob. "Sinatra Tells What Changed Him." Syndicated: Associated Press. December 4, 1957.
117. "Sinatra: Controversy Necessary For Films." Syndicated: Retrieved from the *Journal Times*. February 16, 1958.
118. Neibaur, James L. Jerry Lewis. Interview with author. 1993.
119. Graham, Sheila. "Hollywood Sidelights." Syndicated: North American Newspaper Alliance. May 18, 1958.
120. Hopper, Hedda."Hedda Hopper's Hollywood." Syndicated. July 29, 1958.
121. Bacon, James. "Frank Sinatra is Most In Demand Actor." Syndicated: Associated Press. September 10, 1958.
122. Crowther, Bosley. "Capra's 'A Hole in the Head'; Sinatra Is Starred in Story by Schulman." *New York Times*. July 16, 1959.
123. "Movie Chatter." Syndicated: Associated Press. January 13, 1959.
124. Mangan, Pat. "Author Sells First Novel for $300,000." *Miami Herald*. January 25, 1957.
125. Mauzy, Ruth. "McFadden Says…" *Muncie Evening Press*. March 23, 1957.
126. Parsons, Louella. "Louella's Movie-Go-Round." Syndicated: Hearst. January 14, 1957.
127. Parsons, Louella. "MGM Chief Lauds Sinatra Acting." Syndicated: Hearst. October 21, 1958.
128. Cameron, Kate. "Sinatra and Gina Star in Can Music Hall Picture." *New York Daily News*. January 3, 1960.
129. Carroll, Harrison. "Behind the Scenes in Hollywood." Syndicated: Central Press Association. January 5, 1959.
130. Duckett, Alfred. "Showbiz." *New York Age*. December 27, 1958.
131. Heffernan, Harold. "I Heard Today in Hollywood." Syndicated: North American Newspaper Alliance. January 19, 1959.
132. Kaplan, James. *Sinatra: The Chairman*. New York: Doubleday, 2015.
133. *Ibid*.
134. Allen, Tom. "The Clan: A Growing Power in Show Business." *Miami News*. December 18, 1960.
135. Kaplan, James. *Sinatra: The Chairman*. New York: Doubleday, 2015.
136. Scott, Vernon. "McQueen, Beatnik Without Portfolio, Takes Movie Role." Syndicated: United Press International. April 30, 1959.
137. Johnson, Erskine. "Hollywood Today!" Syndicated: Newspaper Enterprise Association. October 25, 1959.
138. "'Never So Few' review." *Variety*. December 31, 1959.
139. Costello, Ed. "Never So Few Called 'Great.'" *Spokesman-Review*. January 15, 1960.
140. *Ibid*.
141. Scott, John L. "Sinatra Thrives on Killer Pace." *Los Angeles Times*. January 25, 1959.
142. Hopper, Hedda. "Hollywood by Hedda Hopper." Syndicated: March 23, 1959.
143. Hopper, Hedda. "Hedda Hopper in Hollywood." Syndicated: May 29, 1959.
144. Santopietro, Tom. *Sinatra in Hollywood*. New York: St. Martin's Press, 2008.
145. "'Can-Can' Colorfully Lavish, Lively, Naughty." *Tampa Bay Times*. July 2, 1960.
146. "'Can-Can' Ooh La La Musical." *Film Bulletin*. March 14, 1960.
147. "'Can-Can' review." *Variety*. March 18, 1960.
148. "Rental Potentials of 1960." *Variety*. January 4, 1961.
149. Carlson, Peter. "Nikita Khrushchev Goes to Hollywood." *Smithsonian Magazine*. July 2009.
150. "Film Colony Is Appalled by K.'s Slap." Syndicated: Associated Press. September 22, 1959.
151. Du Brow, Rick. "Frank Sinatra Plans to Welcome Elvis Home." Syndicated: United Press International. November 1, 1959.
152. Neibaur, James L. *The Elvis Movies*. Lanham, MD: Rowman and Littlefield, 2014.
153. Nash, Alanna. *Elvis Aaron Presley: Revelations from the Memphis Mafia*. New York: HarperCollins, 1995.
154. Kaplan, James. *Sinatra: The Chairman*. New York: Doubleday, 2015.
155. Connolly, Mike. "Mr. Hollywood." Syndicated: *Hollywood Reporter*. September 9, 1958.

156. Hopper, Hedda. "Hedda Hopper in Hollywood." Syndicated: December 28, 1959.
157. Connolly, Mike. "Mr. Hollywood." Syndicated: *Hollywood Reporter*. December 4, 1959.
158. Hopper, Hedda. "Hedda Hopper in Hollywood." Syndicated: September 17, 1959.
159. Bacon, James. "Wild Script Is Prepared For Films." Syndicated: Associated Press. November 23, 1958.
160. Graham, Sheila. "Hollywood Sidelights." Syndicated: North American Newspaper Alliance. May 6, 1959.
161. Johnson, Erskine. "Hollywood Notes." Syndicated: Newspaper Enterprise Association. October 18, 1958.
162. Hopper, Hedda. "Hedda Hopper in Hollywood." Syndicated: July 18, 1958.
163. "'Ocean's 11' review." *Variety*. August 10, 1960.
164. Curtis, James. *Spencer Tracy: A Biography*. New York: Knopf, 2011.
165. LeRoy, Mervyn, and Dick Kleiner. *Mervyn LeRoy: Take One*. New York: Hawthorn, 1974.
166. Lighting Hits Twice. *Miami Herald* January 2, 1961.
167. "Sinatra and Tracy Star in Columbia's 'The Devil at 4 O'Clock.'" *New York Times*. October 19, 1961.
168. "Sinatra and Pals." *New York Daily News*. January 28, 1962.
169. "Sinatra to Play Host to Children." *New York Daily News*. January 30, 1962.
170. "Sergeants 3 review." *Variety*. February 10, 1962.
171. Hopper, Hedda. "Hedda Hopper in Hollywood." Syndicated: *Los Angeles Times*. January 2, 1962.
172. "A Manchurian Myth: Letter to the Editor." *Los Angeles Times*. January 9, 2010; interview with the authors July 2020.
173. Simon, Neil. *Rewrites: A Memoir*. New York: Simon & Schuster, 1996.
174. Silver, Alain, and James Ursini. *Whatever Happened to Robert Aldrich: His Life and Films*. New York: Limelight, 1995.
175. "Three Stooges Join Sinatra Film." *Oakland Tribune*. August 7, 1963.
176. "Joey Bishop Joins Cast of '7 Hoods.'" Syndicated: United Press International. August 9, 1963.
177. Bacon, James. "Sinatra's Unusual Work Habits Won't Give Gene Kelly Ulcers." Syndicated: Associated Press. September 8, 1963.
178. "Kelly Quits." Syndicated: United Press International. December 8, 1963.
179. Kaplan, James. *Sinatra: The Chairman*. New York: Doubleday, 2015.
180. Bacon, James. "Dancer is Producer—Singers Are Stars." Syndicated: Associated Press. September 7, 1963.
181. MacKenzie, Bob. "Sinatra Clan Stages Jolly Gangster Romp." *Oakland Tribune*. July 25, 1964.
182. Freund, Bob. "'Robin and the 7 Hoods' Terrific Musical Comedy." *Fort Lauderdale News*. June 25, 1964.
183. Powers, James. "'Robin and the 7 Hoods' review." *Hollywood Reporter*. June 25, 1964.
184. Crowther, Bosley. "'None But the Brave' review." *New York Times*. February 25, 1965.
185. Horton, Robert. "'None But the Brave' review." Amazon Editorial. May 13, 2008.
186. Bart, Peter. "Battle Fatigue Faces Audiences." Syndicated: *New York Times* News Service. November 1, 1964.
187. Graham, Sheila. "In Hollywood." Syndicated: North American Newspaper Alliance. May 31, 1964.
188. Sullivan, Ed. "Little Old New York." Syndicated: *Chicago Tribune-New York News*. July 3, 1964.
189. Eichelman, Stanley. "A Fiery 'Von Ryan's Express.'" *San Francisco Examiner*. June 24, 1965.
190. "Producer Inspects Dangerous Film Location in Italy." *Fort Lauderdale News*. September 18, 1964.
191. Wilson, Earl. "The Midnight Earl." Syndicated: *New York Post*. August 18, 1964.
192. Neibaur, James L. Christopher Riordan. Interview with author. 2020.
193. Albert, Don. "Town's Changed but Deborah Still Loves It." *Los Angeles Times*. March 21, 1965.
194. Neibaur, James L. Christopher Riordan. Interview with author. 2020.
195. Kaplan, James. *Sinatra: The Chairman*. New York: Doubleday, 2015.
196. Parsons, Louella. "Sought-After Judy Intrigued By Offer." Syndicated: United Press International. April 28, 1961.
197. Graham, Sheila. "Hollywood

Sidelights." Syndicated: North American Newspaper Alliance. October 22, 1964.
198. Wilson, Earl. "Last Night With Earl Wilson." Syndicated: October 13, 1964.
199. Thomas, Bob. "Piracy on Ocean Liner Theme of Sinatra Film." Syndicated: Associated Press. October 18, 1965.
200. Burlingame, Jon. Liner notes for *Assault on a Queen: Music from the Motion Picture*. Dragon's Den Records. 2016.
201. Lyons, Leonard. "The Lyons Den." Syndicated: McKnaught. September 20, 1965.
202. Carroll, Kathleen. "'Queen' Gives Viewers That Sinking Feeling." *Daily News*. July 28, 1966.
203. Funke, Phyllis. "Sub's 'Assault on Queen' Is Too Deep in Foam." *Courier-Journal*. June 17, 1966.
204. McHarry, Charles. "On the Town." *Daily News*. June 25, 1966.
205. "'Naked Runner' review." *New York Times*. July 19, 1967.
206. Kelly, Herb. "Sinatra Gives 'The Naked Runner' That Old Try." *Miami News*. July 29, 1967.
207. Kleiner, Dick. "'New' Sinatra is Docile as a Lamb." Syndicated: Newspaper Enterprise Association. December 2, 1964.
208. Martin, Betty. "Movie Call Sheet." *Los Angeles Times*. April 7, 1966.
209. Goldman, William. *Adventures in the Screen Trade: A Personal View of Hollywood and Screenwriting*. New York: Warner Books, 1983.
210. Bradford, Jack. "Sinatra Climbs into Million Dollar Class." Syndicated: April 5, 1967.
211. Santopietro, Tom. *Sinatra in Hollywood*. New York: St. Martin's Press, 2008.
212. Hopper, Hedda. "Hollywood by Hedda Hopper." Syndicated: February 17, 1967.
213. Graham, Sheila. "In Hollywood." Syndicated: North American Newspaper Alliance. May 2, 1967.
214. "'Tony Rome' Movie Review." *Progress-Index*. November 19, 1967.
215. Champlin, Charles. "Sinatra Turns into a Private Eye." *Los Angeles Times*. November 22, 1967.
216. Kelly, Kitty. *His Way: The Unauthorized Biography of Frank Sinatra*. New York: Bantam Books, 1986.
217. Muir, Florabel. "In Hollywood." Syndicated: *New York Daily News*. February 28, 1968.
218. Interestingly, Dan Blocker made his movie debut as. a space monster in the Three Stooges comedy "Outer Space Jitters" in which they plug Sinatra's movie *Pal Joey*.
219. "Sinatra Lugs Dan Blocker." *Express and News*. November 24, 1968.
220. Rourke, George. "Night Life: New Sinatra Film Slated Here in Fall." *Miami Herald*. June 8, 1967.
221. "Sinatra, Dan Blocker Star in Action Movie." *Ogden Examiner-Standard*. December 3, 1968.
222. Kelly, Herb. "Dan Blocker Steals 'Lady in Cement' Film." *Miami News*. November 23, 1968.
223. Champlin, Charles. "'Lady in Cement' at Chinese Theater." *Los Angeles Times*. November 8, 1968.
224. "Sinatra loathed 'My Way.'" BBC. October 30, 2000.
225. Ebert, Roger. "'Dirty Dingus Magee' review." *Chicago Sun Times*. November 23, 1970.
226. "'Dirty Dingus Magee' review." *Variety*. November 25, 1970.
227. "Frank Sinatra to Play 'Dirty Harry' Title Role." *Calgary Herald*. September 2, 1970.
228. Browning, Norma Lee. "Hollywood Today: Frank Drops Out." *Chicago Tribune*. November 12, 1970.
229. "Sinatra Is Going to Do It His Way; Retiring at 55." *Daily News*. March 24, 1971.
230. "Award to Sinatra." Syndicated: Associated Press. April 16, 1971.
231. Haber, Joyce. Frank Sinatra's Swan Song—His Way." *Los Angeles Times*. June 15, 1971.
232. Lofaro, Tony. "That's Showbiz." *Ottawa Citizen*. May 14, 1977.
233. Jankowski, Jack. "Police Drama Proves Superior Fare." *Albuquerque Journal*. November 19, 1977.
234. Leogrande, Ernest. "David Bowie Turns Down Film with Frank Sinatra." Syndicated: United Features. March 15, 1980.
235. "Rolling Stone." Syndicated: *Rolling Stone* magazine. April 27, 1980.
236. Fields, Larry. "Fussin' and Fightin' Over for Donna." *Philadelphia Daily News*. January 28, 1980.

237. Siskel, Gene. "Sinatra Shines in 'Sin.'" Syndicated: *Chicago Tribune* News Service. November 2, 1980.

238. Santopietro, Tom. *Sinatra in Hollywood*. New York: St. Martin's Press, 2008.

Sinatra After the Movies

1. "Frank Sinatra and Tom Selleck: They're Partners in Crime Solving." *TV Guide*. February 21–27, 1987.

2. *Ibid.*

Bibliography

Books

Amador, Victoria. *Olivia de Havilland: Lady Triumphant*. Lexington: University Press of Kentucky, 2019.
Asher, Colin. *Never a Lovely So Real: Life and Work of Nelson Algren*. New York: W.W. Norton, 2019.
Bacall, Lauren. *Lauren Bacall Now*. New York: Ballantine, 1994.
Borgnine, Ernest. *Ernie the Autobiography*. New York: Citadel, 2008.
Brando, Marlon. *Songs My Mother Taught Me*. New York: Random House, 1994.
Cantarini, Martha Crawford, and Chrystopher J. Spicer. *Fall Girl: My Life as a Western Stunt Double*. Jefferson, NC: McFarland, 2010.
Curtis, James. *Spencer Tracy: A Biography*. New York: Knopf, 2011.
Fujiwara, Chris. *World and Its Double: Life and Work of Otto Preminger*. New York: Macmillan, 2009.
Goldman, William. *Adventures in the Screen Trade: A Personal View of Hollywood and Screenwriting*. New York: Warner Books, 1983.
Kaplan, James. *Sinatra: Chairman*. New York: Doubleday, 2015.
Kaplan, James, and Jerry Lewis. *Dean and Me: A Love Story*. New York: Broadway Books, 2005.
Kelly, Kitty. *His Way: Unauthorized Biography of Frank Sinatra*. New York: Bantam Books, 1986.
Lahr, John. *Show and Tell: New Yorker Profiles*. Berkeley: University of California Press, 2000.
LeRoy, Mervyn, and Dick Kleiner. *Mervyn LeRoy: Take One*. New York: Hawthorn, 1974.
Lovell, Glenn. *Escape Artist: Life and Films of John Sturges*. Madison: University of Wisconsin Press, 2008.
Malone, Aubrey. *Defiant One: A Biography of Tony Curtis*. Jefferson, NC: McFarland, 2013.
Marx, Arthur. *Everybody Loves Somebody Sometime—Especially Himself*. New York: Hawthorn, 1974.
Nash, Alanna. *Elvis Aaron Presley: Revelations from the Memphis Mafia*. New York: HarperCollins, 1995.
Neibaur, James L. *Elvis Movies*. Lanham, MD: Rowman and Littlefield, 2014.
Ringold, Gene, and Clifford McCarty. *Films of Frank Sinatra*. New York: Citadel, 1971.
Santopietro, Tom. *Sinatra in Hollywood*. New York: St. Martin's Press, 2008.
Schoell, William. *Martini Man: Life of Dean Martin*. Dallas: Taylor, 1999.
Silver, Alain, and James Ursini. *Whatever Happened to Robert Aldrich: His Life and Films*. New York: Limelight, 1995.
Simon, Neil. *Rewrites: A Memoir*. New York: Simon & Schuster, 1996.
Sperber, A.M., and Eric Lax. *Bogart*. New York: William Morrow, 1997.
Wilson, Earl. *Sinatra: An Unauthorized Biography*. New York: Macmillan, 1976.

Bibliography

Articles and Reviews

Adams, Marjory. "Brando Best Since Barrymore, Says Producer Goldwyn." *Boston Globe*. November 13, 1955.
Albert, Don. "Town's Changed but Deborah Still Loves It." *Los Angeles Times*. March 21, 1965.
Allen, Tom. "The Clan: A Growing Power in Show Business." *Miami News*. December 18, 1960.
"Asphalt Street Put Down for 'Guys and Dolls.'" *Los Angeles Times*. December 3, 1955.
"Award to Sinatra." Syndicated: Associated Press. April 16, 1971.
Bacon, James. "Frank Sinatra Most In-Demand Actor." Syndicated: Associated Press. September 10, 1958.
Bacon, James. "Frank Sinatra Plays, Works Hard." Syndicated: Associated Press. January 17, 1961.
Bacon, James. "Goldwyn Plunges Deep into Off-Beat Musical." Syndicated: Associated Press, May 25, 1955.
Bacon, James. "More Women Than Men Come to See Mae." Syndicated: Associated Press. December 6, 1954.
Bacon, James. "Sinatra's Unusual Work Habits Won't Give Gene Kelly Ulcers." Syndicated: Associated Press. September 8, 1963.
Bacon, James. "Wild Script Is Prepared for Films." Syndicated: Associated Press. November 23, 1958.
Barlow, Robert. "Pittsburgh's Gene Kelly Musical Comedy Sensation." *Pittsburgh Post-Gazette*. January 7, 1941.
Bart, Peter. "Battle Fatigue Faces Audiences." Syndicated: *New York Times* News Service. November 1, 1964.
Beck, Meyer. "Sinatra Heads for New Glory." Syndicated: *New York Herald Tribune* News Service. June 19, 1955.
Bradford, Jack. "Sinatra Climbs Into Million Dollar Class." Syndicated: April 5, 1967.
Browning, Norma Lee. "Hollywood Today: Frank Drops Out." *Chicago Tribune*. November 12, 1970.
Cameron, Kate. "'Kissing Bandit' review." *New York Daily News*. November 19, 1948.
Cameron, Kate. "Sinatra and Gina Star in Music Hall Picture." *New York Daily News*. January 3, 1960.
"'Can-Can' Colorfully Lavish, Lively, Naughty." *Tampa Bay Times*. July 2, 1960.
"'Can-Can' Ooh La La Musical." *Film Bulletin*. March 14, 1960.
"'Can-Can' review." *Variety*. March 18, 1960.
Carlson, Peter. "Nikita Khrushchev Goes to Hollywood." *Smithsonian Magazine*. July 2009.
Carroll, Harrison. "Behind the Scenes in Hollywood." Syndicated: Central Press Association. January 5, 1959.
Carroll, Kathleen. "'Queen' Gives Viewers That Sinking Feeling." *Daily News*. July 28, 1966.
Champlin, Charles. "'Lady in Cement' at Chinese Theater." *Los Angeles Times*. November 8, 1968.
Champlin, Charles. "Sinatra Turns into a Private Eye." *Los Angeles Times*. November 22, 1967.
Connolly, Mike. "Mr. Hollywood." Syndicated: *Hollywood Reporter*. September 9, 1958; December 4, 1959.
Costello, Ed. "Never So Few Called 'Great.'" *Spokesman-Review*. January 15, 1960.
Cronin, Steve. "Sitting on Top of the World." *Modern Screen*. February 1956.
Crowther, Bosley. "Capra's 'A Hole in the Head'; Sinatra is Starred in Story by Schulman." *New York Times*. July 16, 1959.
Crowther, Bosley. "'None but the Brave' review." *New York Times*. February 25, 1965.
Crowther, Bosley. "THE SCREEN: Lower and Lower." *New York Times*. January 22, 1944.
Curran, Elmer L. "Hollywood News." *News Leader*. December 15, 1955.
"Dateline Hollywood." Syndicated: INS News Service. October 30, 1957.
"Dick Kleiner." Syndicated: January 12, 1956.

"'Dirty Dingus Magee' review." *Variety.* November 25, 1970.
Du Brow, Rick. "Frank Sinatra Plans to Welcome Elvis Home." Syndicated: United Press International. November 1, 1959.
Duckett, Alfred. "Showbiz." *New York Age.* December 27, 1958.
Ebert, Roger. "'Dirty Dingus Magee' review." *Chicago Sun Times.* November 23, 1970.
Eichelman, Stanley. "A Fiery 'Von Ryan's Express.'" *San Francisco Examiner.* June 24, 1965.
"Film Colony is Appalled by K.'s Slap." Syndicated: Associated Press. September 22, 1959.
"Frank Sinatra in 'Guys and Dolls' Movie Version." Syndicated: *New York Herald Tribune* News Service. September 22, 1954.
"Frank Sinatra to Play 'Dirty Harry' Title Role." *Calgary Herald.* September 2, 1970.
Freund, Bob. "'Robin and the 7 Hoods' Terrific Musical Comedy." *Fort Lauderdale News.* June 25, 1964.
"Goldwyn Buys 'Guys, Dolls' for a Million." *Times.* March 5, 1954.
Graham, Sheila. "Hollywood Sidelights" ("In Hollywood"). Syndicated: North American Newspaper Alliance. February 13, 1941; May 19, 1958; May 6, 1959; May 31, 1964; May 2, 1967.
Guilfoil, Kelsey. "Novel of Damned Puts Chicagoan in First Rank." *Chicago Tribune.* September 11, 1949.
"'Guys and Dolls' review." *Labor's Daily.* November 23, 1955
"'Guys and Dolls' review." *Motion Picture Herald.* November 5, 1955.
"'Guys and Dolls' review." *Variety.* November 3, 1955.
Heffernan, Harold. "I Heard Today in Hollywood." Syndicated: North American Newspaper Alliance. January 19, 1959.
Hopper, Hedda. "Hollywood by Hedda Hopper" ("Hedda Hopper's Hollywood"). Syndicated: April 14, 1956; July 18, 1958; July 29, 1958; March 23, 1959; May 29, 1959; September 17, 1959; December 28, 1959; January 2, 1962; February 28, 1965; February 17, 1967.
Hopper, Hedda. "Sinatra's Next for Metro Is Tender Trap." *Los Angeles Times.* April 13, 1955.
"Inside Hollywood." *Long Beach Independent.* February 5, 1943.
"Job Open for Kosher Loving Dog." Syndicated: Associated Press. February 19, 1957.
"Joey Bishop Joins Cast of '7 Hoods.'" Syndicated: United Press International. August 9, 1963.
Johnson, Erskine. "He Says He's Never Been Away." Newspaper Enterprise Association. January 19, 1956.
Johnson, Erskine. "Hollywood Today!" ("In Hollywood"). Syndicated: Newspaper Enterprise Association. November 18, 1955; October 18, 1958; October 25, 1959
Johnson, Erskine. "Johnson in Hollywood." Syndicated, Newspaper Enterprise Association. November 18, 1955.
Kelly, Herb. "Dan Blocker Steals 'Lady in Cement' Film." *Miami News.* November 23, 1968.
Kelly, Herb. "Sinatra Gives 'The Naked Runner' That Old Try." *Miami News.* July 29, 1967.
"Kelly Quits." Syndicated: United Press International. December 8, 1963.
Kilgallen, Dorothy. "The Voice of Broadway." Syndicated: Hearst. July 10, 1944; May 28, 1949; October 11, 1955.
"Kings and Producer Wait to Go Forth." *Los Angeles Times.* October 13, 1957.
Kleiner, Dick. "'New' Sinatra Is Docile as a Lamb." Syndicated: Newspaper Enterprise Association. December 2, 1964.
Lee, Charles. "Spotlight on Books." *News-Journal.* November 27, 1950.
"Lighting Hits Twice." *Miami Herald.* January 2, 1961.
Lindeman, Edith. "'Pal Joey' Movie Version Retains Much Bite, Wit." *Times-Dispatch.* December 23, 1957.
Locklair, Winston. "Sinatra and Doris Day Playing in New Movie." *Charlotte Observer.* December 28, 1954.
Lyons, Leonard. "Kirk Gets Thanks, Frankie Gets Job." Syndicated: McKnaught. May 1, 1956.
Lyons, Leonard. "The Lyons Den." Syndicated: McKnaught. September 3, 1943.
MacKenzie, Bob. "Sinatra Clan Stages Jolly Gangster Romp." *Oakland Tribune.* July 25, 1964.

"Manchurian Myth: Letter to the Editor." *Los Angeles Times*. January 9, 2010; interview with the authors July 2020.
Mangan, Pat. "Author Sells First Novel for $300,000." *Miami Herald*. January 25, 1957.
Manners, Dorothy. "Frank Sinatra to Co-Star in 'It Happened in Brooklyn.'" Syndicated: King Features. April 26, 1946.
Martin, Betty. "Movie Call Sheet." *Los Angeles Times*. April 7, 1966.
Mauzy, Ruth. "McFadden Says …" *Muncie Evening Press*. March 23, 1957.
Mosby, Aline. "Singer in Serious Film Role." *Press Democrat*. April 23, 1954.
"Movie Chatter." Syndicated: Associated Press. January 13, 1959.
Muir, Florabel. "In Hollywood." Syndicated: *New York Daily News*. February 28, 1968.
"'Naked Runner' review." *New York Times*. July 19, 1967.
"'Never So Few' review." *Variety*. December 31, 1959.
Nixon, Rob. "Guys and Dolls." TCM.com.
"'Ocean's 11' review." Variety. August 10, 1960.
O'Haire, Patricia. "A Star Over Detroit." *New York Daily News*. August 20, 1976.
"Old Vic Plans 'Guys and Dolls'—Sir Larry as Nathan Detroit." Syndicated: Associated Press, June 11, 1970.
"'On the Town' review." *Vancouver Sun*. December 31, 1949.
"Otto the Bold." *Independent Film Journal*. March 2, 1959.
"'Pal Joey' Called Sinatra's Finest." *Abilene Reporter-News*. December 22, 1957.
Parsons, Louella. "Lasky Backs Sinatra." Syndicated: Hearst. April 15, 1947.
Parsons, Louella. "Louella Parsons in Hollywood." Syndicated: Hearst. November 12, 1949; March 15, 1950; March 25, 1955; December 30, 1955.
Parsons, Louella. "MGM Chief Lauds Sinatra Acting." Syndicated: Hearst. October 21, 1958.
Parsons, Louella. "Sinatra Sings for New U.I. Musical." *Los Angeles Times*. February 18, 1951.
Parsons, Louella. "Tender Trap Bought for Debbie." Syndicated: Hearst. January 31, 1955.
Pearson, Drew. "Washington Merry-Go-Round." Syndicated: U.S. News Syndicate. November 11, 1955.
Powers, Dorothy R. "Skillful Acting by Sinatra Gives Power to Dope Drama." *Spokesman-Review*. February 8, 1956.
Powers, James. "'Robin and the 7 Hoods' review." *Hollywood Reporter*. June 25, 1964.
Price, Edgar. "Review of 'Pal Joey.'" *Brooklyn Citizen*. December 26, 1940.
"Producer Inspects Dangerous Film Location in Italy." *Fort Lauderdale News*. September 18, 1964.
Radcliffe, E.B. "Out in Front." *Cincinnati Enquirer*. July 29, 1944.
"Rental Potentials of 1960." *Variety*. January 4, 1961.
"Review of 'Pal Joey.'" *New York Times*. October 28, 1957.
Ross, Don. "Sinatra's on Top of the World Again." *New York Herald Tribune* News Service. November 5, 1955.
Rourke, George. "Night Life: New Sinatra Film Slated Here in Fall." *Miami Herald*. June 8, 1967.
"Ruark Is Puzzled Over Sinatra's Pals in Havana." Syndicated: Scripps-Howard. February 20, 1947.
"Russell-Sinatra-Marx Film at N.Y. Paramount." *Brooklyn Daily Eagle*. December 26, 1951.
Schallert, Edwin. "Kazan Likely to Direct 'Pal Joey' and 'Picnic'; Dramatist's Wife Signs." *Los Angeles Times*. September 20, 1954.
Schallert, Edwin. "'Pal Joey' Sophisticated and Ingenious Musical." *Los Angeles Times*. October 26, 1957.
Schallert, Edwin. "Preminger Sets 'Golden Arm' Deal with Sinatra." *Los Angeles Times*. May 3, 1955.
Scheuer, Philip K. "Sordid Film on Drugs." *Los Angeles Times*. December 28, 1955.
Schneeberger, Gary. "Jean Simmons Interview: Hollywood Hotline." *Journal Times*. May 11, 1990.
Scott, John L. "Sinatra Thrives on Killer Pace." *Los Angeles Times*. January 25, 1959
Scott, Vernon. "McQueen, Beatnik Without Portfolio, Takes Movie Role." Syndicated: United Press International. April 30, 1959.

"'Sergeants 3' review." *Variety*. February 10, 1962.
"Sinatra and Pals." *New York Daily News*. January 28, 1962.
"Sinatra and Sammy Davis Making Film." *Los Angeles Times*. December 31, 1955.
"Sinatra and Tracy Star in Columbia's 'The Devil at 4 O'Clock." *New York Times*. October 19, 1961.
"Sinatra: Controversy Necessary for Films." Syndicated: Retrieved from the *Journal Times*. February 16, 1958.
"Sinatra, Dan Blocker Star in Action Movie." *Ogden Examiner-Standard*. December 3, 1968.
"Sinatra Denies He's Lucky's Pal." *Pittsburgh Press*. February 23, 1947.
"Sinatra Firm to Make 'Kings Go Forth' Film." *Los Angeles Times*. February 3, 1957.
"Sinatra in New Dramatic Role." *Valley Times*. April 24, 1954.
Sinatra Interview. *Western World*. October 27, 1957.
"Sinatra Is Going to Do It His Way; Retiring at 55." *Daily News*. March 24, 1971.
"Sinatra Lugs Dan Blocker." *Express and News*. November 24, 1968.
"Sinatra May Part Company with MGM, Louella Says." Syndicated: Hearst. November 19, 1946.
"Sinatra to Play Host to Children." *New York Daily News*. January 30, 1962.
Sobel, Louis. "Hollywood Cavalcade." *San Francisco Examiner*. August 11, 1948.
"Spectacular Comeback by an Unkosher Dog." Syndicated: Associated Press. March 12, 1957.
"Star Trio on Stanley." *Pittsburgh Sun-Telegraph*. December 27, 1951.
"'Step Lively' review." *Tampa Bay Times*. November 13, 1944.
Sullivan, Ed. "Little Old New York." Syndicated: *Chicago Tribune-New York News* Syndicate. July 3, 1964.
"Theater and Its People." *Windsor Daily Star*. May 11, 1944.
Thomas, Bob. "Hollywood Highlights." ("Hollywood Column", "Hollywood Report"). Syndicated: Associated Press. July 3, 1946; August 4, 1948; October 23, 1952; February 26, 1953.
Thomas, Bob. "Movie on Drugs Causing Battle." Syndicated: Associated Press. September 22, 1955.
Thomas, Bob. "Not Mitchum!" Cry Critics as Producer Casts Movie. Los Angeles Times. October 4, 1954
Thomas, Bob. "Sinatra in New Dramatic Roles." *Valley Times*. April 24, 1954.
Thomas, Bob. "Sinatra Starts Pal Joey, Lewis Story; No More TV." Syndicated: Associated Press. Oct. 24, 1956.
Thomas, Bob. "Sinatra Tells What Changed Him." Syndicated: Associated Press. December 4, 1957.
"Three Stooges Join Sinatra Film." *Oakland Tribune*. August 7, 1963.
Todd, John. "'The Voice' Turns Hoofer for 'Anchors Aweigh' Role." Syndicated: International News Service. August 1, 1944.
"'Tony Rome' Movie Review." *Progress-Index*. November 19, 1967.
"UA Quits MPAA After Code Seal Denied to Arm." *Independent Film Journal*. December 10, 1955.
Ulanov, Barry. "Is Sinatra Finished?" *Modern Television and Radio*. December 1948.
"Walter Winchell on Broadway." Syndicated: King Features. April 28, 1943.
Weisman, Al. "Hard-Boiled Novelist of Chicago School." *St. Louis Post-Dispatch*. December 20, 1949.
Wilson, Earl. "The Midnight Earl." *New York Post*. June 2, 1955; August 18, 1964
Wilson, Earl. "On the Town." Syndicated: June 1, 1975.
"'Young at Heart' Rated Appealing." Spokane Chronicle. January 1, 1955.

Interviews

Neibaur, James L. Christopher Riordan. Interview with author. 2020.
Neibaur, James L. Jerry Lewis. Interview with author. 1993.

Neibaur, James L. Michael Schlesinger. Interview with author. 2020.
Schneeberger, Gary. Raymond Burr. Interview with author. 1991.
Schneeberger, Gary. Celeste Holm. Interview with author. 1991.

Other Media

Maltin, Leonard. "Preface." Liner notes to *Frank Sinatra in Hollywood (1940–1964)*. Reprise/Warner Bros. ASIN: B000066BN9. 2002. Compact disc.
Nollen, Scott Allen. "'Pal Joey': The Quintessential Sinatra Film Musical." Liner notes to *Frank Sinatra in Hollywood (1940–1964)*. Reprise/Warner Bros. ASIN: B000066BN9. 2002. Compact disc.
"Sinatra Loathed 'My Way.'" BBC. October 30, 2000.

Index

Abbott, George 37
Abbott and Costello 13, 100
Adamson, Harold 9, 46
The Adventures of Huckleberry Finn 138
Advise and Consent 138
The Affairs of Dobie Gillis 80
Albert, Eddie 111
Aldrich, Robert 176
Aldridge, Theoni V. 230
Algren, Nelson 85
All Fall Down 170
All Quiet on the Western Front 157
All Star Bond Rally 22
Allen, Lewis 57
Anchors Aweigh 2, 16–21, 22, 23, 24, 26, 32, 33, 34, 35, 38, 39, 64, 73, 88, 116
Anhalt, Edward 226
Anka, Paul 220, 235
Anderson, G.M. (Broncho Billy) 166
Andress, Ursula 177
The Andy Griffith Show 12
Armstrong, Louis 95
Ash Wednesday 199
Assault on a Queen 200–205, 217
Axelrod, George 168

Bacall, Lauren 95
Baddely, Hermione 195
The Badlanders 164
Baer, Parley 195
Bakalyan, Richard 186
Ball, Lucille 13, 170
Balsam, Martin 226
Barry, Don "Red" 222
Barry, Phillip 95
Bass, Saul 87
Becket 226
Bela Lugosi Meets a Brooklyn Gorilla 102
Bennett, Tony 235
Benny, Jack 152
Berkeley, Busby 17

Bernds, Edward 97
Bernstein, Elmer 87
Bickford, Charles 67
Bill, Tony 174, 195
Bill Haley and the Comets 99
Bishop, Joey 154, 156, 165, 191, 235
Bisset, Jacqueline 213
The Blackboard Jungle 99
Blaine, Vivian 74, 78
Blocker, Dan 217, 219–220
Bochner, Lloyd 213
Bogart, Humphrey 51, 52, 94, 95, 155, 159, 208
Bonnie and Clyde 206
Boorman, John 187
Bored of Education 62
Borgnine, Ernest 54, 93
Bowery Boys 97, 98
Bowie, David 229
Boy on a Dolphin 105
Brando, Marlon 52, 70–79, 84, 97, 115, 116, 176, 228, 229
Breakfast at Tiffany's 169
Broder, Jack 102
Bronson, Charles 145, 147, 177
Brown, Harry 157
Brown, Pat 206
Brown and Carney 13, 14
Buono, Victor 177
Burgess, Anthony 221
Burnett, W.R. 164
Burr, Raymond 47, 50
Burton, Richard 190

Cagney, James 62, 109, 115, 162
Cahn, Sammy 192, 184
Calhern, Louis 95–96, 97
Cannonball Run 159, 234
Cannonball Run II 234
Capone, Al 108
Capra, Frank 135, 137, 139, 140, 185

Carey, Michele 221, 223
Carmichael, Hoagy 81
Carson, Johnny 229
Casablanca 83
Chamales, Tom T. 141, 142, 144
Chaplin, Charlie 95, 207
Chaplin, Saul 97
Charney, Kim 57, 60
Chevalier, Maurice 148, 150, 152
Clark & McCullough 110
Cleopatra 190
Clift, Montgomery 52, 55, 69
A Clockwork Orange 221
Cohn, Art 108
Cohn, Harry 51, 52, 109, 115
Columbo, Russ 5
Come Blow Your Horn 172–175, 186, 198
Come Fill the Cup 62
Condon, Richard 168
Connery, Sean 201
Conrad, William 100
Conte, Richard 210, 217
Contract on Cherry Street 226–227
Coogan, Jackie 111, 113
Cooper, Gary 152
Cover Girl 109, 115, 116
Crain, Jeanne 111
Crawford, Broderick 67
Crawford, Joan 52, 89
Cronkite, Walter 200
Crosby, Bing 5, 6, 9, 11, 29, 71, 79, 93–97, 105, 108, 113, 135, 164, 168, 172, 190, 181
Curtis, Tony 122, 123, 124, 125, 126, 152, 157, 171, 172

Daddy Dearest 235
Damone, Vic 235
Dandridge, Dorothy 124
Danza, Tony 235
Dark, Christopher 57
Dark Command 164
Daves, Delmer 124
David, Saul 190
Davis, Sammy, Jr. 79, 102, 128, 143, 148, 153, 154, 156, 165, 172, 179, 183, 217, 234
Davison, Davey 199
Day, Doris 41, 62–65, 109
The Defiant Ones 107
DeHaven, Gloria 14, 15
De Havilland Olivia 67
The Delicate Delinquent 129
Dennis, John 54
Dennis, Sandy 199
The Detective 211–216, 221
The Devil at 4 O'Clock 159–163, 241, 249
Dexter, Brad 187–188, 205, 221
Dickinson, Angie 159

Die Hard 215–216
Dirty Dingus Magee 220–224, 232
Dirty Harry 224
Disney, Roy 20
Disney, Walt 20, 137, 139, 148
Donahue, Jack 199, 202
Donen, Stanley 32, 36, 37, 38, 42, 80
Don't Bother To Knock 51
Dorsey, Tommy 5, 6, 163
Double Dynamite 42–46
Douglas, Gordon 62, 182, 209, 211, 213, 215, 219
Douglas, Kirk 116, 152, 155, 235
Douglas, Paul 135
Duck Soup 97
Dukes, David 231, 232
Dunaway, Faye 230, 232

Eastwood, Clint 187, 224
Edwards, Blake 169
Eisenhower, Dwight D. 59
Ekberg, Anita 176
Elam, Jack 222
Ellington, Duke 202
Epstein, Jules 83
Errol, Leon 9, 11
Evans, George 43
Evans, Robert 213
Experiment in Terror 169

The Facts of Life 170
Fairbanks, Douglas, Jr. 164
Falk, Peter 182
Farrow, Mia 194, 198, 201, 210, 213, 214, 215, 235
Faye, Joey 80
Ferrer, Mel 201
Fields, W.C. 6
The First Deadly Sin 223, 227–233, 234
Flags of Our Fathers 187
Follow That Dream 182
Fonda, Jane 199
For Me and My Gal 17
Ford, Glenn 109
Ford, John 95
Ford, Wallace 10
Foulger, Byron 195
Four Daughters 62
4 for Texas 175–179, 221
Franciosa, Anthony 202
Frankenheimer, John 168, 169, 170, 171
Freeman, Kathleen 195
Frees, Paul 57
From Here To Eternity 2, 49, 51–56, 61, 63, 69, 85, 88, 93, 104, 116, 121, 128, 190, 193
Furie, Sidney J. 205

Index

Gabel, Martin 219
Gable, Clark 53, 71
Gabor, Zsa Zsa 152
Gardner, Ava 2, 43, 46, 50, 52, 53, 105, 106
Garfield, John 62, 85, 86
Garland, Judy 17, 36, 95, 108, 15
Gates, Nancy 56, 57, 60, 128, 129
Gaynor, Mitzi 111–112
Gigot 170
Gilda 109, 116
Les Girls 95
Gleason, Jackie 156, 170
Goetz, William 201
Graham, Ronny 80
Granger, Farley 69
Granger, Stewart 165
Grant, Cary 95, 96, 102, 105, 106, 115, 155, 164
Grayson, Kathryn 19, 21, 22, 24, 30, 31, 32, 34, 36
Graziano, Rocky 211
The Great Dictator 95
The Great Escape 190
The Great Train Robbery 166
Green, Johnny 97
Greene, Shecky 210
Gregory, James 169, 170
Griswold, Claire 169
Guinness, Alec 201
Guiol, Fred 164
Gunfight at the OK Corral 164
Gunga Din 163, 164, 165, 166, 167
Guns of Diablo 177
Guys and Dolls 2, 69, 70–79, 84, 87, 104, 105, 228

Hale, Alan 63
Hale, Barbara 9, 11
Haley, Jack 9, 10, 11, 14
Hans Christian Andersen 71, 109
Harper 205, 209, 228
Hartman, Grace 12
Hartman, Paul 12
Harvey, Laurence 169, 170
Hayden, Sterling 57, 60
Hayward, Mae Cadwell 95
Hayworth, Rita 17, 109, 113, 116, 117, 118, 120
Hecht, Ben 164
Hell in the Pacific 187
Henried, Paul 145
Henry, Hal 118
Henry, Pat 216
Hepburn, Audrey 124
Hepburn, Katharine 95
Here Comes the Groom 135

High Society 2, 84, 93, 94–99, 100, 102, 104, 105
Higher and Higher 7, 8–12, 14, 16, 17, 149
Hitchcock, Alfred 95
Hodges, Eddie 135, 136, 137, 138
Holden, William 86, 87
A Hole in the Head 134–140
Holm, Celeste 81, 83, 84, 95, 96
Hope, Bob 22, 97, 170, 172, 182
Howard, Cy 199
Howard, Trevor 191
Hughes, Howard 43
Hunter, Alexis 139
Hunter, Kim 80
Huston, John 172
Hutton, Brian G. 229, 231
Hyer, Martha 129, 132, 134

The Ipcress File 205
It Started with Eve 84
It's Always Fair Weather 42

Jaeckel, Richard 177
Jaffe, Sam 164
James, Harry 5, 6, 22, 225
The Jazz Train 102–103
Jeffreys, Anne 15
John, Errol 201
Johnny Concho 99–103, 105, 124
The Joker Is Wild 2, 104–113, 124, 126
Jones, Carolyn 79, 84, 135, 138
Jones, Dean 144, 147–148
Jones, James 51, 128
Jourdan, Louis 150, 152
Judgment at Nuremberg 212

Kastner, Elliot 228
Kaufman, Millard 142
Kaye, Danny 71, 109
Keel, Howard 41
Keith, Roberrt 63
Kelly, Gene 17–23, 32–42, 49, 63, 71, 73, 80, 95, 109, 114, 121, 181, 204, 225, 228
Kelly, Grace 95, 96, 98, 105
Kennedy, Arthur 129, 132, 134
Kennedy, Burt 221
Kennedy, George 221, 222
Kennedy, John F. 154, 160, 163, 167–168, 181, 184
Kennedy, Robert 167
Kerr, Deborah 52, 56, 195, 196, 197
Khrushchev, Nikita 152
The Kid from Brooklyn 71
Kings Go Forth 122–127
Kingsley, Dorothy 117, 149
Kipling, Rudyard 164, 166
Kirk, Phyllis 100, 102

Kiss Me Kate 95, 116
Kiss Tomorrow Goodbye 62
Kissing Bandit 29–32
Kjellin, Alf 202, 204
Klugman, Jack 213
Knock on Any Door 51
Koch, Howard W. 164
Komack, James 136
Kramer, Stanley 66, 67, 103, 105, 107, 212
Kubrick, Stanley 221

Ladd, Alan 105
Lady in Cement 216–220, 221
Lancaster, Burt 2, 51, 52, 53, 56
Lansbury, Angela 169, 170
Lansing Joi, 43, 138, 139, 194, 195, 197
Las Vegas Nights 7
Last Train From Gun Hill 164
Laurel and Hardy 62
Lawford, Peter 23, 24, 135, 143, 153, 154, 155, 156, 157, 163, 165, 166, 167, 168, 181
Lear, Norman 173
Lederer, Charles 149, 153, 157
Legend of the Lost 105
Leigh, Janet 169, 171, 172
Lennon-McCartney 220
Leonard, Jack 5
Letters from Iwo Jima 187
Levene, Sam 73
Lewis, Jerry 80, 84, 127, 128, 129, 168, 173, 197
Lewis, Joe E. 2, 104, 107, 108, 109, 110, 112, 216
Lilburn, James 57
Lisi, Virna 202, 203
The List of Adrian Messenger 172
Loesser, Frank 70
Lollobrigida, Gina 144, 145, 147, 176
The Longest Day 190
Lopez, Trini 198
Loren, Sophia 103, 105, 176, 235
The Love Boat 203
Love Me or Leave Me 109
Lovely to Look At 41
Lund, John 95, 96

MacArthur, Charles 164
MacLaine, Shirley 128, 130, 131, 134, 148, 150, 151, 152, 153, 158, 159, 234
The Magnificent Seven 164, 177
Magnum P.I. 234
Malone, Dorothy 63
Man with the Golden Arm 2, 84–93, 104, 105, 136, 193
Manchurian Candidate 2, 168–172, 175, 221
Mankiewicz, Joseph 71, 74, 85, 185

Mann, Abby 212
Mann, Anthony 166
Mark, Flip 197
Markson, David 221
Marriage on the Rocks 194–200
Martin, Dean 79, 80, 132, 134, 135, 143, 152, 155, 165, 175, 178, 179, 180, 183, 194, 195, 196, 197, 198, 222
Marx, Groucho 13, 14, 42–45
Marx, Harpo 22
Marx, Zeppo 13
Marx Brothers 13, 97
Mary Poppins 184
Mazurki, Mike 177
Maxwell, Marilyn 43
McGavin, Darren 89, 90
McGiver, John 170, 195
McGuire, Marcy 11, 16, 22
McHugh, Jimmy 9, 46
McLaglen, Victor 164
McMahon, Ed 229
McQueen, Steve 144, 147, 148, 157
Meet Danny Wilson 2, 46–51, 64
Melcher, Martin 65–66
Member of the Wedding 52
The Men 52
Menjou, Adolphe 14, 157
Milestone, Lewis 157, 185
Miller, Ann 13
Minnelli, Vincente 95, 127, 129, 133, 185
Mississippi 6
Mitchum, Robert 67, 68
Mogambo 53
Monroe, Marilyn 51, 69, 150, 152
The Moon Is Blue 86
Morgan, Michele 9, 11
Munshin, Jules 35, 36, 37, 38, 40, 42
Murphy, George 13
Musante, Tony 213

The Naked Runner 204–207
Needham, Hal 234
Nelson, Mervyn 103
Never So Few 141–148
Newman, Paul 205, 209
Nicholson, Jack 235
Niven, David 86, 95, 152, 165
None But the Brave 185–189, 198, 205, 208
Nothing Lasts Forever 215
Novak, Kim 90, 116, 117, 120, 152
Not as a Stranger 66–70, 107

Oceans 11 143, 150, 153–159, 164
O'Connor, Donald 80
Olivier, Laurence 73
On the Town 2, 33, 34, 36–42, 43, 57, 73, 88
On the Waterfront 71, 87, 116

Our Gang 62
Outer Space Jitters 121

Pal Joey 2, 48, 104, 113–122, 126, 149, 177, 178
Panic in the Streets 226
Parker, Eleanor 85, 89, 135, 136, 139
Parker, Tom 154
Parrish, Leslie 169, 170
Parsons, Louella 47, 80, 86, 93, 142
The Party 221
Payne, James 206
Peck, Gregory 155, 225, 235
Peck, Steven 219
Petit, Michel 197
Peyton Place 198
The Philadelphia Story 95, 96, 105
Pidgeon, Walter 165
The Pirate 95
Poitier, Sidney 160, 235
Polanski, Roman 213
Pollack, Sydney 169
Porter, Cole 95, 97, 149
Porter, G.M. 166
Preminger, Otto 85, 86, 87, 88, 89, 90, 92, 93
Presley, Elvis 94, 98, 114, 154, 155, 166, 172, 183, 220, 235
Preston, Robert 80
The Pride and the Passion 103–107, 109, 113
Prowse, Juliet 150, 152, 155, 169
Pully, B.S. 139

Rains, Claude 62
The Rat Pack 2, 24, 95, 117, 134, 143, 144, 148, 150, 153, 155, 156, 158, 159, 164, 166, 167, 168, 171, 175, 177, 179, 181, 182, 184, 193, 194, 202, 217, 235
Ray, Aldo 52
Reagan, Ronald 206
Requiem for a Heavyweight 170
Remick, Lee 213
Resnick, Muriel 199
Reveille with Beverly 7
Reynolds, Burt 159
Reynolds, Debbie 79, 80, 82, 84
Riddle, Nelson 56, 61, 74, 175
Rio Bravo 131, 135
Riordan, Christopher 194, 197–198
Ritter, Thelma 135, 136, 138
Rizzo, Jilly 218
The Road to Hong Kong 172
Robards, Jason 199
Robin and the Seven Hoods 168, 179–185
Robinson, Edward G. 134, 135, 137, 140, 152, 180, 182
Robson, Mark 192, 213

Rodgers and Hammerstein 207
Rodgers and Hart 9, 81, 115, 119
Romero, Cesar 156, 195, 196, 197
Rosemary's Baby 213
Ross, Frank 124
Rowlands, Gena 210
Rubin, Benny 139
Rubin, Mann 230
Runyon, Damon 70, 75
Russell, Jane 43, 45, 71
Russell, Rosalind 155

The Sad Sack 84
St. John, Jill 209, 218
Santopietro, Tom 50, 233
Saps at Sea 62
Sawyer, Connie 139
Sayer, Joel 164
Schlesinger, Michael 171
Schulman, Arnold 135
Schulman, Max 83
Selleck, Tom 234–235
Sellers, Peter 201
Sennett, Mack 6
Sergeants 3 165–168
Serling, Rod 202
The Seven Year Itch 169
Sherwood, Bobby 118
Show Boat 116
Silk Stockings 95
Silva, Henry 156, 157, 159, 164
Simmons, Jean 73
Simon, Neil 172, 173, 174, 175
Sinatra, Antonio Martino "Marty" 5
Sinatra, Frank, Jr. 184, 235
Sinatra, Nancy 197, 198, 207
Sinatra, Natalina "Dolly" Garaventa 5, 226
Sinatra, Tina 220–221
Skelton, Red 41
Slezak, Walter 14
Some Came Running 127–134, 142, 150, 179,
A Song Is Born 71
Stark, Ray 201
Stevens, George 164
Stewart, James 95, 97, 166
Stordahl, Axel 6, 11
Strauss, Robert 89
Sturges, John 142, 164
Suddenly 2, 56–61, 62, 64, 69, 100, 129, 171, 193
Susan Slept Here 80

Take Me Out to the Ball Game 32–37, 38, 42, 64
Taylor, Dub 139

Taylor, Elizabeth 190
Ten Thousand Bedrooms 128
The Tender Trap 79–84, 104, 105
Them! 62
Thorp, Roderick 213, 215
Three Stooges 121, 177–179
Three Stooges Go Around the World in a Daze 179
Three Stooges in Orbit 179
Three Stooges Meet Hercules 179
Tony Rome 207–211, 213, 216, 217, 218, 219, 228
Torme, Mel 9, 11
Tucker, Sohpie 111
Turner, Lana 43
Two Arabian Knights 157

Ullman, Ellwood 97

Vaccaro, Brenda 231
Vallée, Rudy 5
Vanderbilt, Gloria 101–102
Van Heusen, Jimmy 95, 192, 184
Vidor, Charles 108, 108, 112, 113, 124
Vogel, Joseph 142
von Bulow, Claus 95
Von Ryan's Express 189–194, 198, 208, 213, 221

Warner, Jack 62
Wayne, David 81, 84
Wayne, John 105, 131, 135
Welch, Raquel 218
The Westerner 164
Whatever Happened To Baby Jane 89, 176
Whitmore, James 229
Who's the Boss 235
Wilde, Cornell 69
Wilder, Billy 124
Williams Esther 21, 33, 34, 35, 36
Willis, Bruce 216
Winchester '73 166
Windom, William 213
Winters, Shelley 47, 50, 152
Wood, Natalie 123, 124, 125, 126, 127
Wynn, Keenan 136, 139

Yellow Sky 164
You Can't Take It with You 139
You'll Never Get Rich 116
Young, Gig 62
Young at Heart 2, 61–66, 182
The Young Lions 12

Zanuck, Darryl 86, 190, 193
Zinneman, Fred 52

www.ingramcontent.com/pod-product-compliance
Lightning Source LLC
Chambersburg PA
CBHW032035300426
44117CB00009B/1070